Complete Horoscope

2022

Monthly astrological forecasts for 2022

TATIANA BORSCH

Translated from Russian by Sonja Swenson-Khalchenia
Translation copyright © Coinflow Limited, Cyprus
AstraArt Books is an imprint of Coinflow limited, Cyprus
Published by Coinflow Limited, Cyprus
For queries please contact: tatianaborsch@yahoo.com

ISBN: 978-9925-579-54-9 (print)
ISBN: 978-9925-579-55-6 (ebook)

Contents

2022 – A World Still in Flux 5

2022 Overview for All Zodiac Signs 10

January 36

February....................56

March 74

April....................93

May.................... 111

June.................... 130

July.................... 148

August 166

September 185

October 205

November 225

December.................... 245

A Guide to The Moon Cycle and Lunar Days.................... 263

A Guide to Zodiac Compatibility 292

Love Description of Zodiac Signs.................... 300

2022 – A World Still in Flux

We survived the incredible stress of 2020-2021, when our world's very foundation seemed to be falling apart under us. What does 2022 have in store?

According to the stars, the coming year can be divided into two distinct periods: a very favorable time during the first half of the year, and trouble during the second half.

Politics and Economy

From January to July, things will be serene and predictable.

Jupiter and Neptune will dominate this period, and nearly all year long, they will have very strong energy in Pisces. Jupiter's contact with other planets, including Uranus and Pluto, will be exceptionally favorable during the first half of 2022, so we can count on calm, steady waters...

Together in Pisces, Jupiter and Neptune rule the areas of medicine, oil, space, and the sea. Their favorable aspects mean that this is where we can expect a lot of developments in 2022. In addition to medicine, oil, and space, Jupiter and Neptune also rule the arts, so we can expect incredible feats in film, music, and painting. Many of these pieces will have a space or maritime theme.

Neptune also rules everything related to drugs and alcohol, and 2022 may bring a trend toward legalizing drugs in many countries. This will mainly include "soft" drugs, such as marijuana. This is also a promising time for the wine industry, and Jupiter's powerful influence means that we might see increasing production, and more public attention on elite, luxury wine brands.

For now, we will still have to deal with problems related to the economy, but during the first half of the year, they will likely be somewhat mitigated and under control. One way or another the world will start to shake off the coronavirus epidemic, with help from vaccines and new, effective treatments.

Many countries, including Russia, the United States, and China, will rebuild their economies, and shift their direction and approach. Here, we can consider China as the unrefuted global leader.

During the first half of the year, we might see cryptocurrencies experience serious growth, along with the emergence of new cryptocurrencies.

Things are looking less sunny for the EU countries. Despite the fact that the interminable lockdowns will finally come to an end, economies will continue to struggle, and political clashes will continue.

However, during the first half of the year, from January until mid-August, these negative trends will be somewhat less noticeable.

Things in the United States are looking much more peaceful, though Republicans will become more powerful and influential in 2022.

During the first half of the year, the political horizon of our turbulent world is looking relatively quiet. There will be a trend toward resalable relationships toward war and peace, and there may even be major agreements between countries, which will be largely responsible for this state of affairs.

Beginning in the second half of August 2022, however, things will suddenly take a dark turn. Confrontation from Mars is the theme of the second half of the year. This will lead to negativity, crises, and war. In May 2022, Jupiter will also shift from neutral Pisces to belligerent Aries.

The international stage will once again become difficult, and many countries will fail to shoulder their agreements, with hotspots popping up all over the globe. This may become extremely challenging, as Uranus, an abrupt planet full of the unexpected, will be in the same degree of Taurus that it was in 1938, which was a fateful year for the entire world.

Remember that 1938 was the year that Germany, Poland, and Romania divided Czechoslovakia with the agreement of England and France. From an astrological point of view, this is the event that triggered World War Two. Of course, astrology is not alone here – when describing the dissolution of Czechoslovakia, Winston Churchill himself stated that "England has been offered a choice between war and shame. She has chosen shame, and will get war."

Uranus has an 84-year cycle. Its passage through Taurus has always brought large-scale war, including in 1853-1856, with the Crimean Wars, between the Russian Empire and a coalition made up of Britain, France, the Ottoman Empire, and Sardinia.

Uranus entered Taurus on May 5, 2018, and will remain there until April 26, 2026. We already know that between 2018 and 2021, military tensions have escalated around the world. Unfortunately, this is only the beginning of what may continue for a long time into the future.

Warmongering rhetoric and possibly even clashes in hotspots will be more common during the second half of the year, but this will result in the weakening of NATO countries, with China and Russia growing stronger. This may continue into 2023-2024.

During this time, many countries will experience spontaneous protests and unrest. People will begin to resist authority much more strongly, which will force authorities to make some concessions and adopt certain measures, as many countries will find themselves moving closer to revolution. Countries suffering from economic instability are likely to see changes in government, if not outright political chaos.

The horoscope for the United States indicates that in the second half of 2022, there will be turbulence as well as the revelation of certain secrets. Former President Donald Trump will take on an active role and should not be written off. His influence on US citizens will only grow, but political positions will in general become more hardline. All of that will go along with a serious struggle and clashes with democratic institutions.

Protests and unrest are to be expected in Russia, too, during this time. However, President Putin will hold onto power, though there may be some changes to various government bodies. The changes that began with changes in government in 2020 may continue. Of course, some people will suffer, but overall, this will be a good thing for society.

The economic and political situation in Ukraine may worsen in the long term. Military activity in the eastern territories of Luhansk and Donetsk will continue, and that may end poorly for Kyiv, and it will become clear that these territories will never be returned to Ukraine.

Problems that arise during the second half of 2022 will continue during the three months of 2023.

Climate

The climate will continue to change. Jupiter and Neptune will bring major floods that are worse than what we have seen in the last several years. People living in coastal areas should consider this and take the utmost precautions when preparing for spring. Volcanos will also become more active. Glaciers will continue melting, and there is nothing we can do to halt this process.

In late May, Jupiter will move into fiery Aries, and remain there until the end of October. This means that during this time, we can expect fires to break out around the world, causing major ecological and human losses.

In seismically active zones, we can expect major earthquakes.

Health

In 2022, we may see new, unique treatments for serious illnesses such as diabetes and cancer.

From May to November, people should be very careful if they suffer from heart disease or various allergies. In the fall and winter of 2022, we might see new outbreaks of respiratory infections.

During the second half of 2022, we might also see the emergence of new types of diseases. We may also learn new information about the manmade origins of coronavirus, which dominated our world in 2020 and 2021.

Personal Life

The first half of 2022 is a good time for buying real estate or opening up a business.

Single people might meet someone special, and Pisces, those born in the first ten days of Aries, as well as Virgo and Capricorn will be ahead of the rest of the planet in this regard.

Any marriages that take place between January and May are sure to be stable and happy.

Children born in 2022 might grow up to be talented musicians, highly creative, and have extrasensory abilities. In time, they will become inspiring leaders who will steer the world to a positive place.

During the fall and winter of 2022, things will be rocker in politics as well as personal relations. Many people will reconsider their links to others, and a real crisis or breakdown is likely.

If that is your case, remember that any crisis and break with the past is the key to true change, new opportunities, and a new life! This is the only way we can deal with the twists and turns Fate throws our way!

2022 Overview for All Zodiac Signs

Aries

For you, 2022 is like a big project – it is a serious, difficult transition to a new level. But that is just how life is on Earth – the second you stop moving forward, you are sure to begin sliding back.

Work. When it comes to work, you can divide 2022 into two very different periods. The first part of the year – from January to September, things will be overall favorable and positive.

Entrepreneurs and managers of every level will be busy expanding their business. You might be acquiring land and real estate, or carrying out major construction. These trends may have already begun in the past, in 2021, and they are now continuing along a logical path. You will have to work hard, but you are sure to see results!

During this first part of the year, you will enjoy the support of managers and official bodies in everything you do. This will make it possible to succeed in even the impossible – you will literally build your business out of thin air.

Employees will have a few different possibilities in front of them – will they seek something new or remain on familiar ground? This will be on your mind, but the stars recommend waiting a bit. Your moment in the sun will come later, and the next year is mainly for further growth. There is a chance of starting a family business, and if that is part of your plans, the stars are giving you the go-ahead.

Closer to the middle of the year – at the end of August and into

September, things will start to change – your ruler, Mars, will begin to move into retrograde. The clouds on your professional horizon will start to darken, and you will run into competition and enemies. In some cases, that may involve business partners in other cities or abroad, and on the others, auditing agencies, inspectors, and unexpected legal problems.

As of September, your opponents will be gearing up for war, and things will get much worse than you would expect. During the second part of the year, you will seem to jump from one source of stress to another, so get ready for battle and know who your allies are in advance.

What's more – keep an eye on your assistants and subordinates. Not all of them are sincere, competent, or reliable, so try to assemble a team you can rely on when the going gets tough.

Employees may see trouble brewing on their team in late 2022; perhaps there will be changes at your company – and as the Chinese say – "God forbid you live through times of change." Keep your head down, watch your reputation, and don't go to your managers with requests – they will neither listen nor understand.

Your unpleasant streak will end by late December, and by 2023, they will say "Don't judge the winners!" when talking about you.

Money. Your finances will be healthy during the first part of the year. During this time, in addition to your own income, you can count on favorable credit, profits from successful real estate transactions, and an inheritance. Your parents, spouse, and loved ones will help if you are not part of the working world.

During the last part of the year, however, things will be less sunny, which is only natural given all of your problems at work.

Love and family. Those who are more focused on their personal lives during the first part of 2022 will be dealing with housing issues. You are getting a new home, apartment, summer home, or in more modest cases, you are updating your current residence.

Your family relationships will be harmonious during the first part of the year, though that is likely to change drastically during the last half of the year. For various reasons, you will have disagreements with your spouse, and in September and October, you may have a serious argument. You will not go so far as to divorce, but things are definitely going to cool off between you. In many families, you can also expect serious issues with relatives.

It is hard to predict how things will go for unmarried couples though many will decide to live together and overcome challenges hand in hand, and there are sure to be many of those later in the year! If you end up separating, remember that the world is vast, there are many fish in the sea, and you will find the right person for you! You can expect to do just that in 2023.

Health. In 2022, you are feeling a bit sluggish, so don't test your own strength and remember that moderation is the key. Many Aries will have a tendency to put on weight, so don't forget to exercise, walk in nature, and follow a balanced diet.

Be careful when driving and traveling during the second half of the year.

Taurus

You are looking at an exciting, interesting, creative year, but it will also bring you conflicts. It will resemble a fairy tale, with a peaceful beginning, difficult middle, and a happy ending.

Work. Taureans who are part of the working world will be on a high from January to July. this is a good time to promote new projects, build necessary connections, and networking with highly placed individuals. You will have a lot on your plate, so roll up your sleeves and be bold as you move ahead.

Uranus is the planet of change, and this is the third year it has been in your sign, so your motto is "life is too short to sit still, you have to keep moving forward".

Eclipses, which are accentuating the Taurus-Scorpio axis all year long, also point to change.

This is a great time for those working in creative fields – they can expect greater popularity, and higher income to go with it.

During the first half of 2022, however, the stars recommend paying close attention to the terms of any cooperation and carefully study any documents, especially those that are financial in nature – during the second half of the year, you may face unforeseen circumstances, and possibly even force majeure that will have a negative impact on your contacts and business.

These various problems will reach their zenith from September to December. If you keep a sensible approach, even difficult scenarios will be resolved by the end of the year or in early 2023.

Employees should be careful with their duties, as there are likely to be situations that require both restraint and serious professionalism. The heavens will be testing your honesty and strength – remember that and you will be fully armed as you tackle every challenge Fate throws your way.

Money. The first part of the year will be rather uneventful when it comes to your finances, and things will go as you hoped and planned. During the second half of the year, however, you will face a myriad of financial crises, in all their unsightly glory. Be very careful if you work in finance or similar fields related to things of material value – there is a high likelihood of losses and unplanned expenses from June to December. Be sure to do all the math ahead of time and do not, under any circumstances, take any risks!

Those who are not part of the working world will have to face problems with their family, children, and this will dominate the lion's share of the family budget.

Love and family. This year will bring serious changes to your personal life, too. In early March, Mars will unite with your ruler, Venus, and this is a sure sign that you are about to see love come into your life. This is great for single people, but those who are already partnered up will have to be very careful.

From September to December, you will see your relationships from a new perspective, and think about what they really offer your life. At the end of the year, you will have to make a final decision, and the ball will be entirely in your court. This is most relevant for unmarried couples, but if your marriage is on the rocks, it concerns you, too.

Many Taureans will plan on a move, perhaps to a new home, or else they will carry out major construction where they are already living. These plans will come to fruition in the summer of 2022, and continue into 2023. If that is your case, expect major expenses, which the astrologer predicts for the fall and winter of 2022, which is only natural.

Couples with a stable relationship will work on their children's future and dedicate part of the family budget to their upbringing and education. Alternatively, your children might face trouble and only money will make things right.

In that case all of the problems will crop up during the second, stressful half of 2022.

Health. During the first half of the year, you are energetic, confident, and very charming. Of course, these qualities mean you will fend off any illnesses. During the second half of the year, things will be more complicated, mostly due to nerves and stress. You might face various injuries as well, so be very careful and avoid risks, do not put yourself to the test unnecessarily.

Gemini

Right now, the most important thing for you is to hold onto your current rhythm. Move ahead, change your life, your time has come! Of course, there are always problems, but you are able to overcome them all. What else can you do? There's simply no other option.

Work. For anything work-related, the first half of 2022, from January to June, is the best time of the year. Entrepreneurs will be able to strengthen their position and expand their sphere of influence, including with favorable deals and high profits.

Employees will have an incredible opportunity to move up the social ladder, and that may be at your current workplace, or perhaps at a new, more promising company. This is most likely to happen in late February, March, April, June or the second half of May, July, and August.

Cooperation with colleagues in other cities or abroad will develop as usual during the first half of the year, without any major hiccups. You might receive support from old friends and former business partners.

During the second half of the year, things will grow more complicated for employees and business owners alike.

Beginning in the second half of September, your relationship with certain partners or the powers that be will experience serious disagreements. Things may worsen, and in the second half of 2022, your cooperation will be seriously hampered.

Employees can expect conflicts with management during the second half of the year. You might be partly responsible for that, as given your recent success, you may have gotten too big for your britches and become aggressive and uncompromising, which will lead to discontent and eventually a major argument.

Alternatively, your company may undergo major changes, which will worry you and make you question the future. This will be resolved by December, when the true picture of the future will become much clearer.

Money. During the first half of 2022, you will not deal with any financial trouble. Money will be coming in regularly, and you will see significantly more of it than before. During the second half of the year, however, things will take a much more difficult turn. You will not end up in ruins, but you are likely to experience anxiety and doubts about the future.

Love and family. During the first half of the year, your romantic and family relationships will go through some changes. You are very likely to have a romantic encounter in late May or June, which will lead to some magical summer days.

This is a good thing for those who are single, but it will lead to a world of hurt for married couples. The stars are not forcing you to do anything – nothing is preventing you from breathing new life and fire into your old relationship.

During the second half of the year, belligerent Mars will move into your sign and remain there for seven months (instead of the usual seven weeks). You will be nervous, aggressive, and rigid, which will immediately be reflected in all of your relationships, whether romantic or professional.

Latent resentments with each other might suddenly explode, and in the most extreme cases, lead to a total breakdown in the relationship or even divorce.

If spouses work together or share business ties, the situation will only be worse. If this kind of disaster is not part of your plans, then remember to be as meek as doves and wise as snakes, or the future will at times be difficult.

Health. In 2022, your energy is running high and you have no reason to fear any diseases. However, you are likely to experience a lot of anxiety during the second half of the year, which may periodically knock you off of your feet. In this case, strict discipline and belief that there is a light at the end of the tunnel are key. And indeed, there will be.

Cancer

2022 is twofold for you. On one hand, you will bid adieu to your troubles from the past, while on the other, you will begin to understand that dreams are not always served up on a silver platter. Reality might be more interesting, though it is certainly more difficult.

Work. Generally speaking, 2022 can be divided into two distinct periods. The first part of the year will be from January to September, when things will be relatively calm and predictable.

Entrepreneurs and managers will be connecting their interests to their colleagues in other cities or abroad, and put all their energy into reaching their cherished goals. You might have plans to take your business somewhere far away from home or set up shop somewhere new.

Alternatively, you may find a promising new idea and throw yourself into making it a reality.

Employees will be looking for a new job, and many will find one. The spring and summer of 2022 are especially promising for this.

This is also a good period for making new connections, and if you are hoping to start something new, there is no better time to do it.

During the second half of the year, however, things will abruptly change. You will see new setbacks and problems, which may look differently depending on each case.

Perhaps you will be on track to reaching your objectives, and suddenly have to grapple with legal issues, which might cause you to doubt everything you have recently achieved. Or your colleagues from other cities or abroad will behave inappropriately. Your cooperation may be hampered by various circumstances out of your control which might even be considered force majeure.

Entrepreneurs and managers should also prepare for audits, which will unexpectedly pop up during the second half of the year, and continue until December.

Employees can expect changes at work, and trouble on their teams – perhaps there are whispers and gossip, or even enemies openly working against you. If that is your case, stick to your guns and have faith that the sun will surely rise for you again! This will happen at the end of

December, and you can expect to reach a zenith in the early spring of 2023.

Money. Your finances will experience a lot of ups and downs.

During the first half of the year, you will not see any windfalls, but you will also not face any losses. During the second half of the year, things will become more difficult. Your troubles at work will be reflected in your bank account, which will suddenly shrink. As you move forward, you can say that in 2023, your finances will be significantly better.

Love and family. You can consider 2022 a period of renewal at work and in your personal life alike. You will begin a new life cycle, and you will finally cast aside your problems from previous years.

If you recently went through a breakup or divorce, nothing is stopping you from finding the right partner. The eclipses of this year will accentuate the love sector of your sky, so romance is highly likely. The spring and summer of 2022 are a particularly good time for this.

Many will link their plans to faraway places and plan a move to another city or even abroad. Though everything will turn out as you hoped and planned during the first half of 2022, during the second half, you will have to overcome various challenges which may literally appear out of thin air.

You may also run into problems with foreign legislation and force majeure circumstances, which at first glance will seem unsurmountable – though that is not the case. The planets will eventually settle down, and everything will fall into place.

In what is already a trying time from October until the end of December, you can also expect unflattering information to be revealed. If you are keeping any secrets from your loved ones, be careful – everything eventually comes to light.

Health. This year, you are feeing energetic, but the stars urge you to be careful when driving and traveling. The second half of 2022 is particularly unfavorable to you. Those who are weakened or elderly may face health problems, so take care of yourself and take measures against any chronic disease.

Leo

For you, 2022 is a time of transitions. As a director prepares for an upcoming premier, you are building the scenery and rehearsing before performing before a general audience. This is also a time to discard everything that has outlived its usefulness.

Work. It is hard to consider 2022 a favorable year for you at work. You might face serious envy from business partners, and while during the first half of the year, things look stable and predictable, get ready for major changes during the second half.

Entrepreneurs and managers might be thinking about expanding their business, though they may be short on resources, so you will be talking to your business partners about loans and credit. No matter how things look at first, be careful – during the second half of 2022, you can expect conflict and demands.

From September to December, stress and drama are in store for you. During this time, you might have serious arguments with friends, like-minded people, or someone highly placed in society. It may be over money, mutual obligations, or other material values. In many cases, you may even end up in court.

During the summer, many Leos will be thinking about a move or cooperation with colleagues in other cities or abroad. These ideas are sure to come to fruition in 2023.

Employees will be thinking about a new job, but that may not actually happen until the end of 2022, or even the spring of 2023, so don't rush things, and take the time to think things through before taking any action.

Money. During the first half of 2022, your financial situation will be favorable. You might profit from successful real estate transactions or bank deposits. You might also receive support from partners, or what initially appears to be very favorable credit.

Those who are not part of the working world can also count on support from parents or a spouse.

During the second half of the year, things will become ruinous, however. Many Leos will have to pay back debts, credit, or even deal with financial liabilities and overdue debts. So be sure to save money during the first, more positive part of the year, and don't forget about what is in store for you as the months wear on. Forget about any risks or anything likely to incur losses in the meantime.

Love and family. Your personal life may look differently, depending on situations in the past. Many Leos will be thinking about buying a new home, and that may come true during different points of 2022.

You may spend huge amounts on your children – for their studies or living expenses. That will be expensive, as will much of 2022, which is only natural given your very costly undertakings.

This is a difficult year for many couples whose marriage is on the rocks. During the second half, there may seem to be no rhyme or reason to anything, and you can expect endless arguments, demands, and few will be able to withstand the onslaught. In the most difficult situations, you may end up separating or divorcing.

Alternatively, your spouse might fall ill or go through difficult times, and you will have to shoulder an additional burden.

Some Leos will be thinking about a move. In some cases, that may be to simply a new home, while in others, you will find yourself in another city or even abroad.

Health. Throughout 2022, you are feeling less than energetic, so take care of yourself and remember that moderation is the key.

Virgo

The most important task in 2022 is to strengthen your relationships both at work and in your personal life. Right now, remember – there is safety in numbers.

Work. In 2022, you will see a lot of ups and downs at work. At first, things will be rather favorable, and you might be busy with interesting joint projects with people you already know, as well as new partners. Beneficial, useful offers might come in from colleagues who live faraway.

At first, things will look very positive, and your partners will support you in both words and deeds.

During the second half of the year, however, things will become more difficult and conflicts will begin to emerge. You may unexpectedly realize that you and your colleagues have wildly different ideas about how your business should develop and what you want the future to look like. You clash over joint investments or everyone's contributions.

All of this will lead to disagreements and arguments, and you may even divide up your joint venture. Remember that your opponents' positions are often more sustainable than yours, and you may be the one who has to give in.

Alternatively, you might face problems with high-level authorities, and your business will suffer for it.

Employees will see changes in the workplace, and this may be positive in the long term. You can be sure of a full shakeup at work, which will affect your position and working conditions, and you may not receive severance if you are laid off. Keep that in mind and try to take preventive measures during the first, more favorable half of 2022.

The most challenging time for your relationships is from September to December.

Money. This is a difficult year for your bank account. You will have money coming and going, and closer to December, you will have to accept that your overall balance sheet is rather disappointing at best – if it is not zero.

Love and family. In many cases, you will spend more of 2022 focused on your home and family, and couples who were already on the rocks will have a particularly difficult year.

Though the winter and spring will look stable, during the second half of the year, it will become clear things are not well, and you have seen this movie before. It is hard to say who is in the right and who is in the wrong here, but that doesn't matter, anyway. What is important is that things didn't work out, and you will have to start over from scratch!

If you share a business or joint property, things will be even worse. If that is your case, don't be greedy, and don't instigate anything – have a calm conversation, which will be more constructive than a series of demands. Otherwise, your other half is likely to dig in even further, and you will end up being the one to make sacrifices.

Couples who get along may overcome obstacles, which are likely to be numerous later in the year, as they rely on wisdom and eternal love.

This is an interesting year for single people. From March to May, someone intriguing may appear in your social circle. A romance will bloom all summer, and by fall, you may reach the point in which you start seriously considering the future.

All of the turbulence of October and November will quiet down by December- this is the point when everything will be resolved.

Health. In 2022, you are feeling a bit sluggish, and you might often feel fatigue and exhaustion, which will be most noticeable during the second half of a difficult year.

Libra

2022 will be a hard year full of selfless labor. This is not a burden, per se, and is in fact a continuation of the path you have been on for some time. But keep moving forward, and don't forget to look behind you every now and then. You need to watch your back!

Work. Overall, 2022 is a positive time for you. During the first half, you will advance and achieve stable professional growth. Entrepreneurs will continue developing their business, which they began in the fall of 2021, and by the summer of 2022, they will have reached a new level, with commensurate profits.

Employees can expect incredible career opportunities, either right where they are or at a new, more promising company. You might have additional responsibilities which will improve your professional and financial situation.

Starting in September, however, what seemed like a stable situation will unexpectedly start to waver. You might expect audits, which will cause you to doubt everything you have recently achieved. Unflattering information may be released, which will seriously harm your reputation. This is the case for both employees and entrepreneurs.

Employees might even be fired over the revelations.

Alternatively, partners in other cities or abroad may behave aggressively, and their erratic behavior will cause a breakdown in your relationship as well as major business losses.

Remember this during the first, favorable half of the year, especially if you work with colleagues who are far away. The problems may become very serious, and are likely to drag on until December.

Money. During the first half of 2022, your income will be noticeably stable, especially in late February, March, the second half of June and July. During the second half of the year, in late October and November, things will also look decent.

Love and family. Your personal and romantic life might look less noteworthy than work and the litany of tasks taking up all of your time.

In late May, June, and July, you can count on meeting people and possibly a romance, which will continue until the fall. It is impossible to predict what will happen during the difficult fall months, but many families will face problems involving relatives – likely your in-laws or the family of your most recent fling.

This may lead to arguments or issues with a close relative.

The stars recommend carefully examining all potential outcomes and laying the groundwork as soon as possible so that you are not caught off guard.

Health. In 2022, many Libras will quit their bad habits and finally take their health seriously. The stars urge you to get some exercise, follow a healthy diet, and practice regular self-care.

From September to December, be careful when traveling and driving – there is a high likelihood of traffic accidents.

Scorpio

For you, 2022 will be a very creative, mercurial, and capricious year. Sometimes, it may seem that you have managed to grab luck by the tail, before it suddenly grows wings and flies away. Your task is to hold onto the bits it left behind.

Work. For those who are part of the working world, the period from January to August will be a very positive time for you. You will be promoting your projects and networking with the right people – that might come easily and quickly, without any problems or hiccups. You can forget about the stress that plagued you in 2020 and 2021, as work is on just the right track, and everything is going smoothly.

This is a great time for those in the creative professions – they are more popular, and that means greater income.

August will be the climax of your professional success, and by September, the clouds will be gathering on the horizon.

Unforeseen circumstances, including force majeure, will be the rule of the day and this will have a negative influence on your business and contacts. Many Scorpios will have to pay back loans or throw some money at an unexpected problem at work.

If you take a reasonable approach, this difficult scenario will be resolved by late December or early 2023.

During this time, employees should be careful with their duties, as you can expect situations that will require both restraint and the utmost professionalism. The heavens are testing your honesty and strength – remember that and tackle everything Fate throws your way.

Money. The first half of the year will be calm, and things will be rather predictable. During the second half, however, you can expect financial crises in all their hideous glory.

Be especially careful if you work in finance or with things of material value – you are likely to incur losses and unexpected spending from September to December.

Those who are not part of the working world can expect problems with your family and children, which will dominate the lion's share of your family budget.

Love and family. This year will bring major changes to your personal life. Jupiter, Uranus, and the eclipses will bring you adventures and cause you to reconsider your current relationships. If you are facing a romantic dilemma, it is worth considering that all secrets come to light, and you can expect that to happen to you in the second half of the year. From September to December, you will see your relationship from a new perspective, and think about what you truly value. You're at a fork in the road, which way will you go? The ball is in your court.

This is what unmarried couples, or those with a rocky marriage can expect.

Spouses who get along will once again work on their children's future and invest in raising them, as well as their education and training, which will take up a large part of the family budget. Alternatively, your children might face problems and you will have to save the day – with money.

In this part of your life, all of the unpleasantness will take place during the second, unfavorable half of 2022.

Many families will see new children or grandchildren this year, but if that happens during the second half of the year, be careful during pregnancy and only see experienced, proven doctors.

Health. During the first half of the year, you are healthy, confident, and energetic, and you will not face any illnesses. During the second half, however, you will grapple with stress and injuries, so do your utmost to avoid risk and adventurism.

Sagittarius

2022 may tear you to pieces – at work, at home, in your relationships... But remember – things might look daunting, but whenever you get to work, things start to look up. With this in mind, you will be able to get back on the horse and in fighting form in no time.

Work. During the first half of the year, entrepreneurs and managers at every level will be thinking about expanding their business. You might acquire real estate, land, or start major construction. If you already began that in 2021, you will continue those efforts in 2022.

During the first half of the year, you can expect smooth sailing at work – slowly, but surely, you are working toward your goals and by late summer, you will reap the results.

You might reconnect with former business partners and old friends who now live in another city or abroad.

However, in October, things will suddenly take a sharp turn – aggressive Mars will begin conflict with your ruler, Jupiter. This portends a difficult streak. Specifically, someone will try to take away your property, or something you consider yours. Your opponents may look differently – perhaps they are an auditing agency, or enemies and competitors who may be working against you covertly or in the open.

In sum, get ready to defend yourself and begin gathering allies in advance. Go even further and assemble a team you can count on when the going gets tough. The stars are suspicious of your current assistants – most of them may not be competent or reliable.

Employees can expect trouble on their teams – there may be changes underway at work, changes in leadership, or other types of events that led to the Chinese expression "God forbid you live through changes". Keep your head down and do not go to your managers with any needs – they will neither listen you nor provide any help.

This time of troubles will last until late December or 2023, when people will say "Don't judge the winners!" when they talk about you.

Money. Financially speaking, the first half of the year will be positive. You may have your own salary in addition to favorable terms of credit, profit from successful real estate transactions, and even an inheritance. You may count on help from your parents or loved ones.

From October to December, things will be less sunny – though you will be able to ensure that everything you earned previously does not go up in smoke.

Love and family. If you are more focused on your personal life, the stars predict a series of changes headed your way. Couples who get along might buy a new home, apartment, or summer home, and the first half of the year is a great time for this. However, be sure to look over any documents carefully when undertaking such a major, fateful task. During the second half of the year, you can expect situations that will shed doubt on the reliability of what you have built or purchased.

Couples whose relationship is on the rocks might begin divorce proceedings, and will clash over their apartment, home, summer home, or other property. Your partner will take a rigid stance, and be unyielding, aggressive, and in the worst cases, he or she will drag you into court. You will not be able to reach a compromise until late December, and your children may act as peacemakers.

You will feel Jupiter's influence on your personal life during the summer. Single people will easily find romance, but are unlikely to be ready for things to last very long. You may face a conflict of interest, demands from a new lover, or possibly, things will flame out and there will be nothing left to salvage.

Alternatively, you will be torn between an old relationship and someone new, and that is never an easy predicament to be in. Any unfaithful spouses or those trying to decide between two people should keep in mind that this fall, all of your skeletons will be dragged out of the closet.

The eclipses of 2022 will shed light on a lot of secrets. Don't forget that if you are keeping things from your partner, no matter your field or marital status.

Health. In 2022, you are feeling sluggish, so do not push your own limits and practice moderation. Many Sagittarians might tend to gain weight in 2022, so do not forget to exercise, spend time in nature, and naturally, follow a balanced diet.

Capricorn

In 2022, it will be clear to you that you have started a new chapter in your life, and many things have come to an end. You will have to make new plans, which will be different from what you had in the past. Get ready for some changes and be bold as you charge forward!

Work. Many Capricorns will be bringing their interests to colleagues in other cities or abroad this year, and putting all of their efforts into achieving their goals. You might move, open a business in another city or abroad, and put a lot of effort into networking.

You can expect to meet new business partners and reconnect with colleagues from the past.

This summer, you will deal with some tasks related to real estate, but they will not be completed until 2023.

Some Capricorns will go into business with older relatives, and at first, things will look rather promising.

The first half of the year is a good time to begin studies, start a new profession, or learn new things. Take advantage of this if you have any desire to, and continue working on self-improvement.

During the first half of 2022, things will generally be predictable, and you will be able to get a lot done.

In September, however, things will suddenly take a dark turn. You can expect a variety of problems to emerge, regardless of what happened in the past. That may involve a move, or laws may get in the way of doing business in a new place. Alternatively, you may face legal challenges related to another country's laws. You might also face challenges due to changes on the international stage, which will force you to postpone plans that had seemed very real until recently.

Entrepreneurs and managers should prepare for an inspection or audit, which is highly likely between September and December. It will not be easy, so get any documents ready in advance, and avoid breaking any laws in the meantime.

Employees will face disagreements with colleagues later in 2022, and you may see changes at your company that will be a cause for some worry and concern. That will drive you to look for a new job, or open your own business, which may come to fruition in 2023.

As you move forward, keep in mind that the problems you face in the second half of 2022 will not be resolved before December, and possibly into 2023, though things will start looking up by then.

Money. During the first half of 2022, your finances are looking neutral. You may not have a lot of money coming in, but you are also not expected to face any major expenses. The second half of the year is looking much worse, which is only natural given all of the problems you have accumulated. Have a financial cushion, which will save you from a lot of grief and allow you to continue fighting on all fronts.

Love and family. Changes are also underway in your personal life. Many have decided to move, and this year you will actually be taking your first steps in that direction. This summer you might be looking at real estate, most likely in another city or abroad.

In more modest cases, you will be looking at homes or summer homes in the countryside.

You might move due to a situation involving relatives, who will be able to help you get a new place ready.

This is a good year for love. You may begin a new romance in February or March, when Mars and Venus will both be in your sign. That may happen on a trip, or among people who have come from far away.

Summer will also be a positive time, but in September you or your partner will start to have doubts. Romantic intrigue will not look like what happened in the past, and will cause a lot of changes. If you are not ready for that, or your partner starts to waver, then just wait – the decisive moment will come in late December. During the fall, the source of your worry will come to light, and you may reach a better understanding of each other, allowing you to make the right decision.

In September, nearly all Capricorns will face a series of problems that might look differently depending on the person. That includes unexpected problems with relatives, the laws of other countries, and problems at school. Remember this and try to steel yourself for what is to come.

Get ready to face the challenges head on, and remember that the road is mastered by he who walks it.

Health. In 2022, you are healthy, adventurous, and able to draw a lot of positive attention to yourself.

During the second half of the year, be careful when traveling or driving – you face a high probability of accidents, injuries, and other unpleasant incidents on the road.

Those who are weakened or elderly should take measures against old illnesses – they are likely to resurface in the second half of the year.

Aquarius

Overall, 2022 is a positive year for you. You will have new opportunities in both work and your personal life. However, try to control your emotions and finances as you surrender to the will of Fate.

Work. During the first half of the year, most Aquarians who work will manage to climb the career ladder and seriously improve their resumes. It may not be everything you dreamt of, but in time, you are sure to appreciate its value, as well as your future prospects.

This includes cooperation with people in other cities or abroad. The first glimmers of this will appear during the summer – from late May until August. Things will become more formal in 2023.

In 2022, entrepreneurs can count on lucrative deals, while employees can count on a promotion and salary bump.

In September, however, things will begin to change, and not for the better. Those who depend on contacts with colleagues from afar might face various types of roadblocks – some things will still need to be finalized, or perhaps shifts on the global stage will become a real thorn in your side. Perhaps issues in your personal life will appear and throw a wrench in your plans. Remember, everyone's got problems, so consider your options and act accordingly.

During this time, entrepreneurs will have to invest resources into their projects, and it will end up being more costly than they had anticipated. From September to December, you will face ruin on many fronts, and the things you worked so hard for may simply go up in smoke.

Closer to the end of the year, many Aquarians will have a chance to resolve most of these issues and get things back on track with their colleagues in other cities or abroad.

Money. You will experience a lot of financial ups and downs in 2022. During the first half of the year, you will have more money, but later on, you will have to rely on what you make in late October and November. In September, October, and December, you will face a lot of expenses, either related to work, your personal life, or your family and children's needs.

Love and family. Various areas of your personal life may undergo changes this year.

You may have a summer romance, and you would like to have something beyond just sex and having fun with each other. This may happen on a trip or among people who have come from far away. This fall, however, your relationships may turn sour, for various reasons. In any case, one thing is clear – you can forget about a peaceful, tranquil life.

In December, you will be able to fix everything, so do not make any rash decisions, and just try to get through it. Things may not be so bad, after all, and next year, you will have an opportunity to continue the relationship.

Many couples will be busy dealing with matters related to real estate in 2022, and this is sure to dominate their plans.

Spouses might face problems with their children during the second half of the year. In the best-case scenario, you will have to spend money on their development, studies, or training, and in the worst cases, you will have to resolve their problems for them, and that may take up the lion's share of your family budget.

Many Aquarians will have plans related to a move, and in some cases, that will be to a place where you have previously lived or visited several times before. That will happen in the summer of 2022 at the earliest, and into 2023 at the latest.

Health. In 2022, you are feeling less than spritely, so live a healthy lifestyle and take good care of yourself.

Pisces

2022 will open the door to many new opportunities for you! Jupiter – the planet of strength and success will be lighting your path nearly all year. Decide what you want and keep your eye on the prize!

Work. Most of the year will be a positive streak for you at work. Many Pisceans will be riding a high wave at work, and over the next three years, you will be able to accomplish a lot.

Lucrative deals and new, promising projects are in store for entrepreneurs and managers, which will have a positive effect on your finances.

Great opportunities also await employees – they may get a new job, or if they recently did that already, they may receive a promotion.

Your ties to colleagues in other cities and abroad are moving along nicely, and you may travel frequently.

In short, this is your time to shine!

Remember though, there is always a fly in the ointment, and this time, that will be particularly true from September to November.

During that period, entrepreneurs will face problems with real estate, land, or other major assets. It is hard to predict each individual case, but expect some turbulence. In the best-case scenario, you may have to rebuild the base of your business, and in the worst cases, you will have to fight off various claims to what you believe is yours.

As you charge ahead, victory is on your side, and in December, everything will be clear.

Employees will see a lot of major restructuring at work during the second half of the year. Despite your concerns and worries, you will not only be spared, in the end, you will flourish.

Money. For most Pisceans, your financial situation in 2022 will be sustainable, with a clear upward trend. Even though you are likely to face challenges later on in the year, your bank account will be spared. It is worth mentioning that 2023 will also be a bumper year for you.

Love and family. You will have to make some big decisions when it comes to love and your family. Couples may decide to get married or live together.

If you are single, you can expect to meet someone new, especially between March and July. This time, things will not seem like mere intrigue, as they have in the past. Jupiter amplifies everything, and in 2022, that is becoming quite clear.

Closer to the end of the summer, couples who get along will be dealing with issues related to their home. You may be making major acquisitions, building something, or doing repairs. The fall will bring various household challenges, for example, not everything will go as you had hoped and planned. This may drive even the strongest marriages to argue frequently. If you were already on the brink of divorce, you will find yourselves closer to it than ever.

If that is your case, you will have to suddenly think about dividing your property, starting with your home.

In many cases, you may have to make a difficult choice between love and duty. Cruel Fate reminds us- rarely can we have our heart in two places, and you may have to bid someone goodbye.

Health. In 2022, you are feeling energetic and have no reason to fear falling ill.

January

New York Time		
Calendar Day	Lunar Day	Lunar Day Start Time
01/01/2022	29	6:06 AM
02/01/2022	30	7:10 AM
02/01/2022	1	1:35 PM
03/01/2022	2	8:06 AM
04/01/2022	3	8:51 AM
05/01/2022	4	9:29 AM
06/01/2022	5	10:01 AM
07/01/2022	6	10:30 AM
08/01/2022	7	10:56 AM
09/01/2022	8	11:23 AM
10/01/2022	9	11:49 AM
11/01/2022	10	12:18 PM
12/01/2022	11	12:50 PM
13/01/2022	12	1:27 PM
14/01/2022	13	2:08 PM
15/01/2022	14	2:56 PM
16/01/2022	15	3:49 PM
17/01/2022	16	4:46 PM
18/01/2022	17	5:47 PM
19/01/2022	18	6:49 PM
20/01/2022	19	7:52 PM
21/01/2022	20	8:56 PM
22/01/2022	21	10:00 PM
23/01/2022	22	11:06 PM
25/01/2022	23	12:14 AM
26/01/2022	24	1:24 AM
27/01/2022	25	2:35 AM
28/01/2022	26	3:45 AM
29/01/2022	27	4:51 AM
30/01/2022	28	5:50 AM
31/01/2022	29	6:40 AM

London Time		
Calendar Day	Lunar Day	Lunar Day Start Time
01/01/2022	29	6:42 AM
02/01/2022	30	7:49 AM
02/01/2022	1	6:35 PM
03/01/2022	2	8:42 AM
04/01/2022	3	9:21 AM
05/01/2022	4	9:51 AM
06/01/2022	5	10:15 AM
07/01/2022	6	10:36 AM
08/01/2022	7	10:54 AM
09/01/2022	8	11:12 AM
10/01/2022	9	11:30 AM
11/01/2022	10	11:51 AM
12/01/2022	11	12:15 PM
13/01/2022	12	12:44 PM
14/01/2022	13	1:20 PM
15/01/2022	14	2:05 PM
16/01/2022	15	2:58 PM
17/01/2022	16	3:58 PM
18/01/2022	17	5:05 PM
19/01/2022	18	6:15 PM
20/01/2022	19	7:26 PM
21/01/2022	20	8:38 PM
22/01/2022	21	9:52 PM
23/01/2022	22	11:06 PM
25/01/2022	23	12:23 AM
26/01/2022	24	1:42 AM
27/01/2022	25	3:02 AM
28/01/2022	26	4:19 AM
29/01/2022	27	5:30 AM
30/01/2022	28	6:28 AM
31/01/2022	29	7:13 AM

You can find the description of each lunar day in the chapter "A Guide to The Moon Cycle and Lunar Days"

Aries

Cast your doubts aside in January and take a decisive step forward. Despite some minor bobbles and what they say around you – "Fortune favors the bold!"

Work. January is a good month for you, professionally speaking. That's no surprise, as the best time is right after the holidays, from January 1-13. It is a good time to tie up loose ends and start new projects.

Your relationships with colleagues in other cities or abroad are also moving along nicely, and you are likely to travel.

Expect to see old friends, renewed relationships with former mentors, and new plans related to expanding your business. Many are seriously considering buying real estate and will make considerable progress in that direction this year.

January 14 to 31 is less auspicious. Mercury will be in retrograde, which means that this will be a good time to take a step back and examine the last year, and to discuss plans for the future. You will have to refrain from launching new projects or holding any major work-related events during this time.

You might face a variety of obstacles at work- and for many reasons, the people you need might disappear. Expect financial disagreements with friends or otherwise like-minded people.

But there is also another option – you might just push work-related troubles to the side and head to a sunny beach or the countryside.

Money. January is a good month for your bank account, especially during the first two weeks, when significantly more money will be coming in regularly.

Major expenses are likely during the second half of the month, and there may be many reasons for that. However, in any case, be careful with your team, with friends, and others in your inner circle, and watch your spending like a hawk. There is a high likelihood of errors and even scams from January 13 to 31.

Love and family. Things are relatively calm in your personal life, though some flexibility and expert maneuvers around thorny issues are useful. You are approaching an important period, when many couples will have to answer difficult questions about increasing their living space, major repairs, and you will absolutely need to see eye-to-eye.

During the second half of the month, many families will be consumed with taking care of their children, resolving their problems, and spending a large amount of the family budget in the process.

January is less-than-promising if you are hoping to see romantic relationships grow. Things will remain as they are, without any changes one way or the other.

This is not a good time to meet new people. Venus is in retrograde all month, and from January 14, Mercury will join it. That means that anyone you happen to meet will likely be unreliable or just plain unnecessary in your life.

Health. In January, you are feeling energetic and need to use this only for peaceful purposes.

Taurus

The stars recommend that you think of new opportunities and possibilities. No matter how difficult the decisions you are grappling with now, keep in mind that it is all sure to pay off.

Work. For many of your fellow Taureans, January is a great time to improve your opportunities at work. Though most of this month is dedicated to laying the groundwork, that shouldn't get you down. Everything should come together in mid-February, and you have plenty of time to think things through and get ready for changes.

It might not be now, but a bit later, you will be able to count on help from friends or highly placed individuals.

Expect to build new ties with colleagues from other cities or abroad, and there is a high likelihood of travel.

You will probably not manage to see through all of the ideas you came up with in January, but positive changes are likely, and it is definitely worth taking full advantage of this.

Employees might face changes in their company, but it's nothing to worry about. All of the changes you see now will be for the best, and in February, that will become clear.

Money. Financially speaking, January is a neutral month. Both expenses and income will be reasonable.

Love and family. Many Taureans will find renewed interest in faraway places and countries, and you are likely to spend a week or two traveling. However, it is a good idea to study the route before you go, or select a destination you have been to before.

Venus traditionally rules Taurus, and it will be in retrograde all month. On January 14, Mercury will join it. That is why new people and places will not bring you positive emotions, but old friends and regions you have been before will seem more inviting than ever.

Many will rekindle an old flame who now lives in another city or abroad, visit relatives, or remember old friends.

January is the ideal time to reconsider your current relationships, and maybe take them to the next level.

Health. In January, you are feeling rather energetic, though the stars recommend that you keep an eye on your clear tendency to worry about things.

Be sure to get your body moving! That is a sure way to stay strong and clear your head. If you can't do that, then at least try to spend some time in nature.

Gemini

It's hard for you to relax during the holidays. You have to resolve a variety of organizational matters, while also dealing with mundane family issues.

Work. All month, you can expect things to be somewhat uncertain. On one hand, that is only natural during the holidays, but Venus will also be in retrograde for almost all of January. Mercury will also be in retrograde from January 14 to February 4. That will put the brakes on things and force you to reconsider and rework your plans.

Despite it all, January is a good time to get ready for a very important, and even decisive period during the second half of February and March of this year.

Though the first half of the month will be relatively quiet, the second half will be full of difficult decisions with colleagues from other cities or abroad. Due to reasons beyond your control, negotiations with partners from afar might drag on or even hit a roadblock. But just hold on! Time resolves everything. And once January is over, things will gradually fall into place.

Employees might be thinking about looking for a new job or at least taking some steps in that direction. The stars recommend that you avoid rushing things and do it right. It's best to update your resume and get ready for some meetings during the second half of February.

Money. January is fairly neutral for you, financially. You should not expect any major expenses, though not a lot is coming in, either. During difficult times, you will be able to count on relatives, older family members, or loved ones.

Love and family. In many cases, the biggest moments in January will take place in your personal life. Perhaps you will redecorate your home, make small repairs, or see other developments involving real estate.

Things are relatively calm in your family. And though things with your better half may get tense, you will be able to find a release for the pressure. You may experience some trouble with relatives during the second half of the month, though most couples will not face any major conflicts.

Many people will be on vacation during the first ten days of the month – some will travel far and wide, while others will simply head to the countryside. In any case, you need to reset and gather your strength to conquer new heights.

Health. You are not exactly feeling your liveliest this month. Take care of yourself and don't overdo it. Be careful traveling and behind the wheel. This goes for the entire month, but especially January 4, 5, 11-13, 25, 29, and 30.

Cancer

This month, you might be feeling unsure of your relationship with many people, or even about your own future. Just hold on a little longer, and you will start taking your first steps on a new path!

Work. January will be a busy month for you, full of contacts with different people. Though the first half of the month is relatively calm, you are sure to find yourself resolving delicate, complicated financial issues during the second half.

Many Cancers may be seeking a new path in life and for their future. The stars are on your side here, though you may have to wait a bit. In March and April your star will also rise, but for now, get ready to be up to the task.

Money. Most of your financial moves this month are likely to be unsuccessful. Many will find themselves having to settle old debts, spending money on their business, or resolving problems in their personal life. In any case, be careful with any material issues, including the people involved in them.

You are likely to see some unexpected expenses this month. You might have to settle accounts with people who provided you with services in the past, but their prices will be high. If that happens to you, don't give in, negotiate, and don't hurry. You've got plenty of time.

Love and family. Your personal life is great this month. If you are single, this is a time to look at old friends with new eyes, maybe one of them is interested in you.

Old flames or former partners may resurface, regardless of why things may have ended. Your ability to start afresh is the main theme of this month, and you should take full advantage.

Other couples might find themselves dealing with various day-to-day issues, relying on their wisdom and undying love.

Many Cancers will have moving on their mind, and that might happen later in 2022.

In some cases, you may be moving into a new home, and in others, a new city or even abroad.

Health. In January, you are feeling a bit sluggish, and that is most noticeable during the last ten days of the month. Watch your health, and don't spread yourself too thin. Don't forget that your nerves are behind every kind of trouble, so don't get worked up, get a good night's sleep, and don't skip meals.

In January, you will have a chance to go somewhere far away. Take advantage of the momentum and the opportunity to relax a bit and step away from work and the usual sources of stress.

Leo

January is a time to sit back and relax? Not for you! While others are relaxing, you are busy working and picking up the pace.

Work. This is a good time for you at work. Difficult situations will be resolved in your favor, and colleagues may help you fix many problems.

Business owners can rely on their employees, and employees can count on coworkers.

Along with the upward trends this month, there are also some downsides. During the second half of the month, business owners at every level and managers will face unpredictable behavior from partners, who may start shirking their duties, which will slow everything down to a degree. On one hand, that behavior may be intentional, on another, this is just one manifestation of uncertainty and an unwillingness to be decisive.

Once again, the root of the problem is differing opinions on how business should develop, and possibly going separate ways. Despite all of the challenges, you are going to have to make a big decision, and soon. You might benefit from having a better handle on the task at hand than your opponents.

During the second half of the month, employees might face competition, but, as they say, all you need is patience and a little effort.

Most Leos will see varying degrees of success handling work-related challenges during the first half of the month.

Money. Despite your ongoing challenges at work, financially speaking, January is not bad at all. Money will be coming in regularly, and the amount will even increase a little. Expect to receive the largest sums on January 2, 3, 11, 12, 21, 22, 29, and 30. Expect bonuses, too.

Love and family. Your personal life is going through some difficult times. Your spouse might be evasive and contradictory. If you need a frank conversation about reconsidering the relationship or other, serious issues, January is not the time. February is a more positive time for this kind of discussion.

Alternatively, loved ones might be going through hard times, and you will have to provide support, in word and deed.

Things are somewhat better for those who are not yet married, though some issues may arise. For various reasons, you may begin seeing somewhat less of each other than you would like, or something will make it difficult to strike a harmonious balance in your relationship.

Many families will make plans related to acquiring real estate for themselves or their children.

Health. In January, you are not feeling your liveliest, so make time for yourself, despite your busy schedule. As a holiday gift to yourself, go somewhere where you are sure to take in positive vibes, which will do your body and soul a world of good.

Virgo

This month, you can finally relax and set work aside! Finally!

Work. January is not a particularly promising month for work, with the exception of those working in creative fields or whose line of work is somehow related to the entertainment industry. They can expect profit and success. For the rest of us – it is time to sit back, relax, and have a good time with our loved ones.

During the second ten days of the month, you can expect to suddenly face some challenges at work.

Business owners and managers will once again have to deal with recurring issues involving colleagues in other cities and abroad. This time, however, things are not so pressing. The tide may move in a favorable direction.

Alternatively, you may face legal trouble, if you have already found yourself in this position in the past.

Business owners and managers should keep a close eye on their subordinates and carefully check their work, as well as any important documents. Virgo is ruled by Mercury, and from January 14 to February 4, it will be in retrograde, which means you can expect misunderstandings at work, in your relationships and mistakes on documents.

Money. Financially, this month brings a lot of ups and downs. You can expect major expenses during the first ten days of the month, most likely related to vacations, travel, and meeting your family's needs.

During the second half of the month, things are looking up, and you can expect the largest sums to come in on January 13, 14, 23-25.

Love and family. During the first half of the month, your personal life is running at full steam, but you will also run into a lot of contradictions.

Venus is in the love sector of the sky, which means lovers can look forward to a lot of enjoyable moments together, especially if their relationship began prior to December 19, 2021. From December 19 to January 29, Venus will be in retrograde, and new people who appeared in your life prior to this period are unlikely to stick around for long.

However, partnerships that began before that time can weather the changes and see their feelings for one another blossom.

Those with a family will spend a lot of time with their children and find a way to keep them happy.

Many Virgos will spend some time on the road, and this is likely to work out very well if you go with people you know, to places you have already visited.

The last ten days of the month will be less romantic, so enjoy the first two weeks to their fullest.

Health. During the first twenty days of January, you are healthy, energetic, and very attractive. You might start to slow down a little during the last ten days of the month, and the elderly or those with chronic conditions should be especially careful. Take care of yourself and be sure to lead a healthy lifestyle.

One more piece of advice – all month long, you should be cautious when traveling or driving. There is a high likelihood of accidents.

Libra

The first month of the year is a time for you to sit back and take stock of the past year. You are beginning a new stage, and it's best to get ready in a calm, family environment.

Work. During the first half of the month, work is quiet. From the outside, it might look as though nothing is happening, but it's just the calm before the storm. You might not notice, but work is taking you on a path toward career growth.

Nothing will happen before the second half of February, or even March, but right now, in January, there is nothing stopping you from pondering and discussing the advantages and disadvantages with your loved ones and inner circle.

If you give yourself some time away, then the stars will ensure that things continue moving without you.

Your ties to colleagues in other cities or abroad will move along with varying success. Some things will work out, and others will not. Just like anything.

Business owners might be immersed in organizational tasks, and likely to be dealing with various concerns related to real estate.

Money. January is likely to be modest, financially. Both expenses and income are predictable, moderate, and reasonable this month. You can expect to receive money on January 16, 17, 25, and 26. In addition to your own money, expect help from a family member.

Love and family. For most Libras, January, particularly the first two weeks, is a long-awaited opportunity to spend time with your family and loved ones, and no matter where you to prefer to spend the holiday season – at the beach, on the couch, or in the countryside, you are sure to find love and care with those you love.

The second half of January will involve spending time taking care of your children, and once again, they are going to require a large share of the family budget.

Many Libras will deal with issues related to real estate. You might have to do some minor repairs, or major constructions, or something similar.

Couples will face stormy waters during the second half of the month. During this time, you can expect disagreements, a lot of back-and-forth, and uncertainty about yourself as well as your better half.

You may find yourself having to go back in time to revive still-simmering relationships that are ready to erupt with new vigor. In theory, you are trying to put an end to this love story – after all, it brings you nothing but trouble, and in general, nothing is going right. But that is unlikely to actually happen…

Health. It seems you have been between a rock and a hard place for a while now, and you're tired of it. Remember, exhaustion leads to illness. The prescription is easy – just rest, and then rest again! January is the perfect time for it!

Scorpio

Everything is going your way in January. Pack your bags and get ready to take on the world!

Work. You are on a positive streak at work. During the first half of the month, you will step up your contact with colleagues far away and you might take a successful trip. Even if it is for leisure, nothing is stopping you from mixing business and pleasure – you are able to resolve many issues remotely. Whether under the palm trees or in a cozy country house, it is sure to be more comfortable than the office. Perhaps you will even find yourself in a destination that would be a nice place to work.

During the second half of the month, most Scorpios will be grappling with a variety of issues related to real estate. You might be expanding your business, or dealing with other organizational and administrative tasks.

Unfinished business with various partners will be challenging for you this month. Conflicts are to be expected, though in time, the misunderstandings will gradually fade away.

Money. Most of the month will be dedicated to money, and for a good reason! January is a great time for most Scorpios, and you can expect to have more money than usual.

Expect to receive large sums on January 8, 9, 18-20, 27-29.

You will not have many expenses, and they will all be related to the holidays, travel, and your children and loved ones.

Love and family. Your personal life is up and down. Everything depends on the past situation, and on your future plans. In any case, however, you will be prudent and know when to tiptoe around, as misunderstandings are likely during the second half of the month, even among the closest families.

You are likely to be looking at some kind of real estate, and you and your spouse will have differing opinions on this important matter. In the most difficult cases, you might find yourself considering divorce or separation. In easier cases, you might disagree on repairs or how to best make use of your joint assets. You might have some time to decide, and only resolve this matter at the end of the year. However, things are much easier than they were in 2021, and your problems may eventually resolve themselves.

Children bring joy and happiness, and many Scorpios are considering expanding their families.

During the first ten days of the month, you will see a lot of your relatives, and you might even take a trip together. You might even reconnect with family members who live in another city or abroad.

Health. You are feeling energetic this month and have no reason to fear health problems.

Sagittarius

The first month of 2022 will be an auspicious time for you. But if you haven't made your first million yet, there's never been a better time to start!

Work. It's hard for you to relax as you settle into January. First of all, you will have to deal with a variety of administrative issues, as the work doesn't wait.

Many Sagittarians are dealing with concerns related to real estate. Entrepreneurs are thinking of expanding their business, and have their eye on new facilities with this in mind. These concerns may be in the background all year long.

Things are going well for those who are employees, too. If you got a recent job offer, now, you are thinking about how to strengthen your position.

Those who are not satisfied with their current jobs may be thinking about opening their own business, and taking some steps in that direction.

Your relationship with colleagues in other cities or abroad is moving along and you are seeing success, which will be most noticeable during the second half of the month. There is nothing new here, you have seen these issues before, and now you know how to respond. To be fair, these challenges will gradually resolve themselves, so remember, "He who tries wins" has never been more appropriate.

Money. Your finances are really looking up this month. Money will be coming in regularly, and there will be noticeably more of it, too. Expect to receive the largest sums on January 2, 3, 11, 12, 21, 22, 29, and 30. Expect it to come from both official and unofficial sources.

Love and family. A lot of decisive events are taking place in your personal life. Many will make drastic changes in their day-to-day lives, whether that means moving to a new apartment, building a home, cottage, or something else – maybe you will start major repairs on your current home.

During the second half of the month, your relationship with a relative will become difficult, most likely due to old arguments and unresolved issues from the past.

Couples will not be particularly happy in January, but they also will not suffer. If your relationship is smooth and stable, it will remain that way. If that is not the case, things might get worse. In either case, keep an eye on your loved ones and hold your tongue – your criticism might have the opposite of the intended effect in January.

Single people should keep in mind that anyone new you meet in January is unlikely to be reliable. They may disappear, leaving behind nothing but unpleasant memories.

Health. You are feeling a bit sluggish this month, so take care of yourself and remember that moderation is the key. Be careful on any trips or while driving – this is especially the case during the second half of the month.

The stars suggest avoiding any travel to faraway places, unless you absolutely have to. If you do travel anyway, choose a place you have been to before.

Capricorn

This is the time to take your first steps on a new path, and it will be more difficult than you anticipated. The recipe for success is simple – worry only about yourself, keep your eyes on the prize, and trust your own intuition.

Work. Over the last few years, you have accumulated a lot of potential, and you are probably thinking of what your next steps should be, and where you should focus your energy and skills. January is an opportunity for you to stop, take a look around, and decide on a plan for the future – however, this is not the time to begin actively taking any concrete steps.

All month, Venus will be in retrograde, and after the 14th, Mercury will join it. That will create a sensation of confusion and ambiguity. Wait until February, when you will be able to resolve current issues, and don't rush things – time is on your side!

The more difficult times in January will involve financial issues, and that uncertainty will cause you to worry and feel frantic. You may be consumed with old arguments over money, but the good news is that soon, everything will be resolved. In any case, you will have the last word, which is the most important thing, even if it is not right now!

Many Capricorns have plans to develop their business in another city or even abroad, and that will take shape during various periods of 2022. In some cases, that means you will take a trip, but that depends on each individual situation, your current plans, and your intentions.

Money. Financially speaking, January is full of ups and downs. Of course, you still have an income, but your expenses are high, sometimes due to business, and other times, your personal life and loved ones are the culprits.

Love and family. In many cases, the major events in January will be personal in nature. All month, Venus will be in your sign, which means that your emotions will intensify. Venus is also in retrograde, and Mercury will join it during the second half of the month.

All of that will lead to tension and misunderstandings with your loved ones.

Remember that though the influence of two planets in retrograde – Venus and Mercury – will lead to changes in your relationships, this is not the time to meet new people.

January is a great time to reconnect with old acquaintances, whether friendly or romantic. You might reconsider old relationships or go back to something you previously lost. If you really want to, go for it. You still have a chance.

During the second half of the month, families will see a continuation of problems involving children, though this is nothing new. It might be the same issues you dealt with in 2021. You may end up spending a large portion of the family budget on your children.

Many Capricorns are thinking about moving, and during various periods of 2022 those plans will come to fruition.

Health. This month you are feeling energetic and have no need to worry about any illness.

Aquarius

Luck is on your side – right now, you have incredible potential, and you can channel it as you see fit. Surprise yourself and others!

Work. Most Aquarians are grappling with organizational matters this month. You may have to deal with a property dispute, most likely over real estate, but this is not the first time something like this has arisen. A large part of the challenge will take place during the second half of January, and things will not be resolved until the second half of February. You have the potential to win – most likely in the distant future – slow and steady wins the race. Keep your head down and put your nose to the grindstone.

There might also be new opportunities for you on the horizon this year. You might see the first glimmers in January, but things will be much clearer in March and April.

Money. Your financial situation is stable, with a clear upward trend. In addition to your usual income, this month you can count on support from partners, credit, and even profit from various real estate transactions.

Those who are not part of the business world can count on assistance from parents, your spouse, or a loved one.

Love and family. In many cases, the major events this month will involve your personal life. During the first ten days of January, you might finally get a chance to relax and forget about work for a while. It doesn't matter where – at home, on the couch, on a hammock on a sunny beach, or the countryside – the important thing is getting a chance to relax and get away from it all.

During the last twenty days, you will feel agitated, and you might have to deal with some issues related to your place of residence. That might be repairs, acquiring something new, or redecorating.

In other cases, you may be dealing with a lengthy divorce, difficult negotiations involving joint property or a joint residence.

For couples, January looks neutral. There is nothing new, and that is neither good nor bad.

Health. This month, you are not particularly energetic, so try to give yourself time to relax, especially since January provides you with so many opportunities to do just that.

Take care of elderly members of your family, as they are likely to face various types of problems.

Pisces

You are in high demand in January, and in touch with people who are able to radically change your life – for the better, of course!

Work. In January, you are surrounded by old friends and people in high places. That may inspire new business ideas and give you a chance to advance your career. However, this will only come from old connections who have stood the test of time, and not much will come out of new, unexpected acquaintances.

During the first ten days of the month, you might go on a trip, and even if it is planned for pleasure, there is nothing stopping you from making new business contacts along the way.

During the second ten days of January, you are feeling restless and conflicted, mainly due to some misunderstandings that began a while ago. In some cases, this will be due to gossip from competitors and those who do not wish you well, and in others, expect old legal problems to resurface.

Some of these troubles may be covert, and you will not be able to figure out who is responsible. But these are the same people who have created obstacles for you in the past.

Your relationship with colleagues in other cities or abroad is moving along with success. During the second half of the month, you might see agreements hit a road bump or disappear altogether, but know that in the near future, you will be able to smooth things over, thanks to your own efforts and support from the Heavens.

Money. Financially speaking, January will bring a lot of highs and lows. You will see money going both in and out, likely more of the latter. Travel, gifts, and holiday celebrations will drain your wallet, but don't get down on yourself – first of all, you get what you pay for, and secondly, you'll be back on your feet in no time. By spring, things will be booming.

Love and family. January is a good time to set priorities in your personal life. During the first half of the month, you might take a trip to a city you loved or a country you have been to before. Most likely, you will see friends and have a wonderful time. However, the relationship you thought you needed might turn out to be what you expected or dreamed of. Regardless of what happens, the stars recommend not making any rash decisions this month, because things will not turn out the way you want, and only leave you feeling more confused. It is not worth trying to delve into the nitty-gritty of your relationship or start making complaints, even if something is bothering you.

During the second half of January, many Pisceans will struggle with gossip, intrigue, and people both secretly and not-so-secretly working against you. If you fall into this trap, don't get worked up over things. Soon, you will be able to deal with all of this, and live your best life.

Many families will face problems with relatives, either from old arguments resurfacing, or having to help family members who have fallen on hard times.

Health. Most of January, you are feeling energetic enough, and you have no reason to fear falling ill. But be careful while traveling or driving, especially during the second half of the month.

February

New York Time		
Calendar Day	Lunar Day	Lunar Day Start Time
01/02/2022	1	12:49 AM
01/02/2022	2	7:22 AM
02/02/2022	3	7:57 AM
03/02/2022	4	8:28 AM
04/02/2022	5	8:56 AM
05/02/2022	6	9:23 AM
06/02/2022	7	9:50 AM
07/02/2022	8	10:19 AM
08/02/2022	9	10:50 AM
09/02/2022	10	11:25 AM
10/02/2022	11	12:04 PM
11/02/2022	12	12:50 PM
12/02/2022	13	1:40 PM
13/02/2022	14	2:36 PM
14/02/2022	15	3:36 PM
15/02/2022	16	4:38 PM
16/02/2022	17	5:42 PM
17/02/2022	18	6:47 PM
18/02/2022	19	7:52 PM
19/02/2022	20	8:58 PM
20/02/2022	21	10:06 PM
21/02/2022	22	11:15 PM
23/02/2022	23	12:25 AM
24/02/2022	24	1:34 AM
25/02/2022	25	2:40 AM
26/02/2022	26	3:40 AM
27/02/2022	27	4:31 AM
28/02/2022	28	5:15 AM

London Time		
Calendar Day	Lunar Day	Lunar Day Start Time
01/02/2022	1	5:49 AM
01/02/2022	2	7:48 AM
02/02/2022	3	8:15 AM
03/02/2022	4	8:38 AM
04/02/2022	5	8:57 AM
05/02/2022	6	9:16 AM
06/02/2022	7	9:35 AM
07/02/2022	8	9:55 AM
08/02/2022	9	10:18 AM
09/02/2022	10	10:45 AM
10/02/2022	11	11:18 AM
11/02/2022	12	11:59 AM
12/02/2022	13	12:49 PM
13/02/2022	14	1:47 PM
14/02/2022	15	2:52 PM
15/02/2022	16	4:01 PM
16/02/2022	17	5:13 PM
17/02/2022	18	6:26 PM
18/02/2022	19	7:40 PM
19/02/2022	20	8:56 PM
20/02/2022	21	10:12 PM
21/02/2022	22	11:31 PM
23/02/2022	23	12:50 AM
24/02/2022	24	2:07 AM
25/02/2022	25	3:18 AM
26/02/2022	26	4:19 AM
27/02/2022	27	5:08 AM
28/02/2022	28	5:45 AM

You can find the description of each lunar day in the chapter "A Guide to The Moon Cycle and Lunar Days"

Aries

Throughout February, you will be responsible and serious, both at work and at home. There is no doubt that is a good thing at work, but the stars recommend that you take a softer, more indulgent approach in your personal life.

Work. When it comes to work, everything is coming up roses in February. You can show off your negotiation skills and resolve many difficult issues involving the authorities.

Employees at every level can turn to their bosses, as well as the "powers that be" and know that they will be heard out and understood. Be bolder! Some reasonable level of risk is a good thing, right now. Things are looking brightest after February 4. Mercury will be back on a straight path, and bring clear progress, which you will see borne out in your own dealings.

Entrepreneurs will continue to face difficulties related to expanding their business and attract a lot of funds to this end. Thanks to this, any real estate transactions will quickly move forward.

Money. February will be a great month for your finances. Money will be coming in regularly, and it will be significantly more than usual. This will encourage you to have a bold view of the future and actively work to move things forward. Expect to receive the largest sums of money on February 7-9, 16-18, 26, and 27.

Love and family. This month will have you busier than ever at work, and you may not have enough time for your personal life. The exception is those whose own interests are somehow related to work. They can count on a torrid love affair, which will only improve things at work. This is the case for lovers and spouses who share professional interests.

Single people can expect to meet someone interesting, but the common thread might be work or shared professional interests.

Spouses with a solid marriage may find themselves resolving challenging issues together, possibly related to building a new home, as right now, you have the money for this kind of thing.

Many people will be thinking about growing their family, and toward the end of the month, women have a high probability of pregnancy.

What's more, February is a time for fun gatherings with friends, and a time for liveliness, a bit of extravagance, and quick wit- a time to change things up and come out of our shell. Sometimes, that is a good thing!

Health. Throughout February, you will be in top physical and intellectual form, and have no reason to fear any diseases.

Taurus

Sometimes, life is hard, and sometimes, it's a bowl of cherries – like right now!

Work. For anything work-related, you can expect things to become most interesting and promising after the 5th of the month. This is when Mercury begins moving on a straight line, which is sure to be reflected in business and your contacts. You are headed for a rather positive streak – your problems from earlier months are moving closer to a friendly resolution, and you may benefit from strong support from your friends or someone in high places.

Your relationships with colleagues in other cities or abroad are moving along nicely, and you might even take a successful trip. You might also have an opportunity to shine in promising negotiations.

The second half of the month is the ideal time for any decisive career changes, and any employees who want to make a change to their professional status or find a new job should take note. The opportunities will be there.

Money. Your finances are stable this month. Money will be coming in regularly, and there are no financial troubles on the horizon this month. You have expenses, but they are predictable and within reason.

Love and family. Your personal life is looking up in February. Mars will conjunct Venus in the sector of the sky associated with faraway places, which means that single people and those who have been disappointed by love in the past can count on a fateful meeting while traveling or among people who live far away. You might rekindle things with an ex who now lives in another city or abroad. This time, you will be able to define things that once uncertain. A marriage proposal or living together is highly likely.

The stars recommend that partners whose feelings are waning to go on a long trip together. This is the best way to bring the love and romance back to your relationship.

Health. This month, you are feeling energetic and have no reason to fear any illnesses.

Gemini

This month promises to bring changes – to your day-to-day life, your personal life, and at work. Remember, change is a good thing!

Work. You've been stagnating for a while, but you're ready for a serious leap forward.

Freelancers and managers at every level might make some real progress in developing and expanding their business, and may even carry out some large-scale transactions related to real estate.

Employees can count on a new job offer or major promotion at their current place of employment. This may lead to changes in your lifestyle, a move, or new residence.

The most positive time for any professional matters will be after February 5. You are ruled by Mercury, and after the fifth of the month, it will begin moving on a straight line, meaning that the areas where you have been dedicating both time and energy will begin to cheerfully and quickly charge ahead. Your success will become much more noticeable as we head into March.

But be aware – relationships with colleagues from other cities or abroad will continue to be a thorn in your side, albeit less than before.

Money. February is good to your wallet. In addition to your usual earnings, you can count on lucrative credit, support from business partners, and even unexpected profits, which are highly likely during the second half of the month.

Those who are not part of the business world can count on support from parents, their spouse, or a loved one.

Love and family. This month's major events will revolve around your personal life. Many Geminis have been working on a move – in some cases, that may involve a new residence in the same city, and in others, you might find yourself in a new city or even abroad. This may involve finally following through with plans that have been in the works for some time.

Relationships within your family are harmonious, and partners who get along will be resolving complicated, everyday issues with the help of love and wisdom.

Single people can count on a fateful meeting, which is likely to take place during the second half of the month.

During the second half of the month, your relationship with your in-laws might become difficult due to various circumstances, but this time, you will be able to overcome it, especially if you don't let yourself get bogged down in the details and refrain from digging up old wounds.

Any trips planned for February are sure to be a success, though the stars remind you to pay close attention to any documents, and double-check your luggage before leaving home.

Health. You are feeling lively this month and have no reason to fear any illnesses.

Cancer

In February, it is worth taking the time to make sure you take the right path, which will turn out to be life changing. The ideas you have been nurturing for so long are about to take shape! Happy travels!

Work. February's developments will force you to reexamine your life from a new angle, and turn the page after a period of prolonged challenges, which you can now be certain has come to an end.

Entrepreneurs and managers at every level will be involved in developing new projects, and employees will be starting a job search. Closer to the end of February, or possibly in March, all of your efforts will pay off. Many will be thinking about moving, expanding their business to another city or abroad, and February will be a time for making major strides in that direction.

In all areas, the strong and positive influence of business partners, friends, and acquaintances in high places will be palpable. In addition to people you have been working with for some time, mid-month, there are some new people on your horizon. No matter how the first impressions may be, the stars recommend that you keep in mind – not all that glitters is gold.

Money. Money is looking tight this month. Many will find themselves having to settle old debts and obligations. This may be the last obstacle in your way.

Love and family. February is a time of serious changes in your personal life, and in many cases, these changes may be life-altering. Single people and those who have been disappointed by love in the past may meet someone intriguing during the second half of the month. Only time will tell how serious this relationship will be, but there is a chance of something long-term!

All Cancers can expect success and to be at the center of attention this month. If you are planning on expanding your social circle or reconciling with an ex, there is no better time! Thanks to the unique placement of the planets, you are resolving many issues, but things feel effortless.

Those planning on moving to a new city or abroad might face many of the logistical issues that a major event like this entails.

Health. You are not particularly energetic this month, so take care of yourself, and don't test your limits with excess.

Leo

Don't stop when you're halfway to your goal. Even if things seem impossible, you are sure to find a way out of any quagmire! Remember, he who looks will find!

Work. February is a very important month for you. This month, you will spare no efforts in convincing partners and adversaries alike that you are on the right track. You will have to prove yourself in both word and deed, but you will excel at the task and lay down your own rules of the game.

Managers can count on subordinates, and employees can rely on their colleagues. Together, you will achieve a real breakthrough at work.

Challenges will rear their heads when it comes to your relationship with partners or an adversary, and you can expect some disagreements over certain issues. However, this time, your arguments will prevail, and things will be resolved closer to the end of the month.

Money. February is a good time for you, financially. Money will be coming in regularly, and in addition to your usual income, there is hope for financial support from partners. You may receive credit on beneficial terms.

Those who are not part of the business world can count on help from parents, loved ones, or their spouse. You might profit from successful real estate transactions.

Love and family. A lot is going on in your personal life. Many families continue to grapple with problems that began in the past. In some cases, that means relationships have grown chilly, and in others, your partner is dealing with a lot of difficulties. In the first case, if it comes to a separation, you may find yourself discussing how to divide up real estate. If that happens to you, this is not the time to fly by the seat of your pants. This time, things are serious.

Families with friendly relationships will be able to resolve many issues related to real estate, both for themselves and their children.

For partners, this month is full of ups and downs, especially for those who are able to see both sides of things. You may have to make a very difficult, if not impossible choice. However, the stars promise to greenlight a romance in which you are brought together by both feelings and business.

Health. In February, you are feeling a little sluggish, so take care of yourself and keep an eye on things.

Virgo

This month, you will be walking a tightrope trying to balance work and family. Let your partner choose their own path, but monitor every step! Your motto this month, both at work and in love, is "trust but verify!".

Work. Your crowning achievement this month may be strengthening your relationship with former partners and new colleagues. There is no doubt that any contacts you make after February 5 will pay off in the future. From January 14 to February 4, your ruler, Mercury, will be in retrograde, which means that everything you have been working on may come to a halt. But once that impulsive planet returns to the straight and narrow, you, and it, will be on a smooth path to active development.

Your relationships with colleagues in other cities and abroad are moving along with positive changes. There are still some things that need to be discussed and some kinks to iron out, but this is a working, natural process. What's more, you can expect some achievements, which will be most noticeable in the second half of the month.

If you do any traveling, pay very close attention to any documents, especially during the middle and end of February. They are the key to your success, and right now, your future.

Money. February is neutral for you, financially speaking. You will not see any windfalls, but your expenses also are modest and reasonable. Most of them are related to children, travel, and your loved ones.

Love and family. When it comes to romance, February is a unique time. The love planets- Mars and Venus- will be joined together in the love sector of the sky, but that's not all! They are being strongly supported by Jupiter – the harbinger of stable success!

Single people and those who have been let down in the past can expect an interesting encounter, which may lead to a whirlwind romance. Jupiter promises to keep things going, and by the end of the year, you may be living together or even married. So, don't miss out on any fun parties, make sure you look good at all times, and you won't be waiting long to meet the man or woman of your dreams!

Those with stable families will be pleased by their children's success, and you might even see a family trip bring you all closer together.

Spouses whose relationship leaves something to be desired might count on the positive influence of their children, who will become a bridge between their warring parents.

Health. This month, anyone weak or elderly should be especially careful. Their health is not in tip-top shape, and they should strive for an especially healthy lifestyle and consult with a doctor at the first sign something may be wrong. Do not try to treat yourself.

Young and healthy Virgos should remember to take some time to relax on a regular basis and get a good night's sleep.

Libra

You are moving forward in leaps and bounds, but the competition is breathing down your neck, trying to steal your place in the sun. Don't let your guard down, keep moving, and do whatever you think you have to.

Work. In February, you will be preoccupied with organizational and other logistical duties. You might be expanding your business, or be working on various real estate transactions. This time, everything you planned will go off smoothly, without a hitch, which will become much clearer toward the middle of the month.

Expanding your business might require new skills, and new, more skilled assistants. Responsible entrepreneurs and demanding bosses will be looking to recruit someone, and closer to the end of the month, they will find their diamond in the rough. You will find the right people, and this will reflect positively on your business.

Employees might be given additional responsibilities, and the stars see this as something very promising. In some cases, you may even be promoted or receive a raise.

Money. Your finances are looking stable this month. In addition to your usual income, you can count on something extra, possibly from a real estate transaction. You can expect credit on beneficial terms, or financial support from a business partner.

Those who are not part of the business world can expect support from parents, a loved one, or their spouse.

Love and family. In many cases, most of your attention will be focused at home and on your family. You are facing difficult issues related to real estate. You might be continuing major construction, restoration, or purchasing a house, apartment, or summer house. That might be for your own family's needs, or for one of your children.

You can expect a lot of hassle and expense, but things will work out in your favor. You will be able to handle the task at hand.

Couples might channel their desire for home improvement, which will only bring them closer together. Romance is very sexy and all, but your day-to-day concerns aren't going away.

Health. You are beginning a long period in which you will need to take your health very seriously. Your diet, a healthy lifestyle, and getting enough sleep are the key to taking care of your body and mind. You need to find an inner balance right now in order to achieve stability, both at work and in your relationships.

Scorpio

A thirst for knowledge and striving to reach new heights are with you all month long. This month, you have a lot to learn, but what, exactly, is up to you!

Work. The main theme this month is making new connections and expanding your circle. You might actively work on developing your relationship with colleagues from other cities or abroad, or even go on a successful trip.

Whether reconnecting with old acquaintances or meeting new people, you can expect a fresh stream of work that forces you to keep your chin up and charge ahead.

Problems from the past related to real estate are still a reality, but this time, they aren't quite so acute, and you will be able to resolve them, for once and for all. Of course, you will have to sort things out, but as they say, *"he who tries, wins,"* and you are sure to do just that!

If you work in a creative field, you can expect to be particularly successful this month – actors, artists, writers, musicians – your popularity will grow, and you might even have a successful tour.

Money. Your finances are looking neutral this month. You will not see any major profits, but you will not suffer any losses, either. Both expenses and earnings will be predictable and reasonable this month.

Love and family. Get ready for some pleasant surprises in your personal life. Single people and those who have been disappointed by previous relationships can expect a fateful meeting, probably while you are traveling or among people who have come from somewhere far away. This is no ordinary fling, either. It is real, deep feelings and passion. Time will tell how it will pan out, but there is a real chance this will develop into something long term.

This is a good thing for anyone who is single and fancy free. But those who are already taken will face a painful choice, as new love will turn everything on its head, causing a lot of trouble, right from the start. Think about this long and hard before you decide to plunge in, headfirst.

People with a stable family life will be pleased with their children, who are seeing success and on a very favorable streak. Adult children might provide you with some serious moral or financial support.

Many families will reconnect with older relatives, and might travel to see family members who live in another city or abroad.

Those who are dealing with real estate disputes will move closer to a solution they can live with.

Health. You are feeling rather energetic in February and have no reason to fear falling ill.

Sagittarius

In February, you will be incredibly active. So much that you will even surprise those close to you, who are already aware that you are a ball of energy with a nonstop stream of ideas. Luck is on your side, so buckle up!

Work. Everything is coming up roses for you at work and when it comes to anything professional this month. Entrepreneurs and managers can count on some new and beneficial deals, as well as some additional profits from work you completed earlier.

Employees can expect new job offers that might be a big step up from your current position. The ball is in your court, and that's always a good thing!

Your relationship with colleagues in other cities or abroad is moving along nicely, though some problems from prior months are no longer so pressing, and any remaining issues can be dealt with later.

Any transactions involving real estate that you began in the recent past are moving forward in your favor.

Money. This month is one of the best of the year for your bank account. Money will be coming in regularly, and there will be noticeably more of it. In addition to your usual earnings, you can count on profits from unofficial sources.

Employees might get a bonus or money from a second job. Expect the largest amounts on February 4, 7, 8, 17, 18, 22, 26, and 27.

Love and family. Some big changes are on the horizon when it comes to your personal life. You may begin or continue major repairs or construction. There is also a possibility of obtaining a new apartment, home, or summer home, maybe in another city or abroad.

Your family is getting along, and partners with a friendly relationship are tackling some challenging domestic issues, and this month there will be a lot of them. Your relationship with some relatives has suffered in the recent past. Things will remain as they are, as they say, "no peace, no war".

It is hard to say what is in store for those in a romantic relationship, as February is so focused on work and your home itself. The exception is those who are, as fate has it, tied to someone born under the sign of Capricorn. If that is your case, expect your relationship to develop very rapidly, which will be rather useful at work, too.

Health. You are feeling full of energy in February and unlikely to experience any illness.

Capricorn

If you want to avoid burnout, you need to set firm boundaries between work and your personal life, with a special focus on the latter. Right now, "business before pleasure" should not be your focus.

Work. The main event of this month will be strengthening and developing your ties with partners abroad or in other cities. You might travel, and you will find yourself combining business with pleasure – you will get the job done and spend some time relaxing, as well.

Regardless of your field, this month, you will see that you are making a name for yourself and becoming well-respected among your colleagues. You have earned your stripes, and now it is time to reap the fruits of your hard work.

People working in creative fields can expect particular success, perhaps an exciting tour, and recognition from both fans and their colleagues.

Those planning on expanding their business to another city or abroad will make a lot of progress in that area this month.

Money. Your wallet is seeing a lot of ups and downs this month. Money will be coming in regularly, but you will also see costs go up. The astrologist predicts that a lot of this will be related to your personal life, and demands from your family, children, and loved ones.

Love and family. You might not be known for being a romantic hero, but when it comes to love, in February, you have a chance to be at the head of the pack. Mars and Venus will come together in your sign on February 16, which means you can expect some intense feelings.

Single people and those who have been let down by love in the past might meet someone interesting in February, and even get married in the near future. You will face a difficult choice between old and new affections, and settle on new love. In many cases, the main events in your love life might happen while you are traveling or among people who have come from far away.

In February, many Capricorns will find themselves doing a lot of the heavy lifting when it comes to their loved ones, as this is the only way to keep moving forward in the right direction.

Spouses with a strong bond will be pleased with their children's success, and can expect a lot of positive changes. But remember, in order to support your progeny, you are going to have to make an investment in their education and development, which will take up a lot of the family budget.

Health. Throughout February, you are bounding with energy and have no reason to fear any illnesses. What's more, all month long, you will be so charming and attractive that you are able to win over anyone Fate brings your way.

Aquarius

All month long, you will heroically overcome the obstacles that have been rearing their heads lately. But this time, the circumstances are just right, and you will be able to overcome it all!

Work. Your main task this month will be something very important related to some sort of property, possibly land or real estate. It seems that this time, there is a real desire to resolve a longstanding problem, but there are a few loose ends you need to discuss, first.

Alternatively, you may be trying to expand your business or deal with major construction. This will give you the upper hand, whether you are a manager or entrepreneur. If this is your case, you will have to grapple with a series of organizational tasks, but thanks to your discipline and hardworking nature, you will manage just fine.

Employees can get ready to see some success during the second half of the month or even in March. There is a promotion on the horizon, or possibly some additional responsibilities in your current position. Naturally, all of this goes hand in hand with a raise.

Money. Your financial situation will be stable, with significant improvements this month. In addition to your usual earnings, many Aquarians can also count on large profits from favorable real estate transactions. You might also receive a loan on very favorable terms, or financial support from a business partner. Those who are not part of the business world can count on support from parents or a loved one.

Love and family. Many Aquarians are fully immersed in their personal life this February. There are a lot of domestic tasks on your agenda – fixing up your home, repairs, buying or selling real estate. In some cases, you might receive an inheritance.

Families are feeling stable this month. Some slight friction is likely at the beginning and end of the month, possibly related to how busy you are with your house.

Even divorced couples might find themselves getting along well enough to deal with some material issues.

Health. This month, you are feeling energetic and have no reason to fear falling ill, especially if you do not overeat and take time to walk around in nature. This is especially relevant if you tend toward weight gain.

Pisces

Don't fall into the winter doldrums just yet! Some very positive changes are just on the horizon!

Work. There is a saying – "A friend in court is better than a penny in purse". Right now, that is very relevant to your life. Thanks to support from your friends, and maybe someone who is highly placed, you are able to move mountains and significantly improve your position at work.

The problems that have cropped up in the past seem to be fully resolved, now. Rome wasn't built in a day, but things are definitely on an upward trend.

Some minor misunderstandings are likely at the beginning and end of the month, but they are unlikely to cast a shadow over the generally positive course of events. Right now, you have a lot of like-minded people on your side, and they are able to provide you with great support when negotiating with obstinate colleagues in other cities or abroad, or when grappling with any legal problems.

Your relationships with colleagues in other cities or abroad are coming along nicely, and generally successfully. Any trips you have planned in mid-February will be a success, and resolve a lot of issues.

Employees can also expect some positive changes at work – like a promotion, new job, or additional responsibilities. You might just be laying the groundwork for these changes, but they are sure to come to fruition in March. In some cases, though, that might happen in mid- or late February.

Money. Your financial situation is stable. Money will be coming in regularly, and your expenses are reasonable and predictable. Everything is as it should be, and money is no exception.

Love and family. February is a good month for your personal life, too. You might begin a new romantic relationship, which is likely to turn into something serious. Alternatively, while with an old friend, you might realize there is something more between you. Does he or she might live in another city or abroad, or will you will have your realization while traveling? In any case, get ready for what promises to be a long-term, passionate romance.

If you're already partnered up, then this month promises to bring you to a new level of intimacy, harmony, and trust.

In many families, you are reconnecting with relatives, maybe someone who has come from far away. Though you might have had some friction with this person in the past, this is the time to forgive and forget.

Any trips planned for the middle of the month promise to be a great success.

Health. The influence of the stars points toward your spirit being stronger than your body this month. In order to overcome that imbalance, try to spend more time relaxing and be sure to get enough sleep.

March

New York Time		
Calendar Day	Lunar Day	Lunar Day Start Time
01/03/2022	29	5:53 AM
02/03/2022	30	6:25 AM
02/03/2022	1	12:38 PM
03/03/2022	2	6:54 AM
04/03/2022	3	7:22 AM
05/03/2022	4	7:49 AM
06/03/2022	5	8:18 AM
07/03/2022	6	8:48 AM
08/03/2022	7	9:22 AM
09/03/2022	8	10:00 AM
10/03/2022	9	10:43 AM
11/03/2022	10	11:31 AM
12/03/2022	11	12:25 PM
13/03/2022	12	1:23 PM
14/03/2022	13	2:24 PM
15/03/2022	14	3:27 PM
16/03/2022	15	4:32 PM
17/03/2022	16	5:38 PM
18/03/2022	17	6:45 PM
19/03/2022	18	7:54 PM
20/03/2022	19	9:05 PM
21/03/2022	20	10:16 PM
22/03/2022	21	11:26 PM
24/03/2022	22	12:34 AM
25/03/2022	23	1:35 AM
26/03/2022	24	2:28 AM
27/03/2022	25	3:13 AM
28/03/2022	26	3:52 AM
29/03/2022	27	4:25 AM
30/03/2022	28	4:54 AM
31/03/2022	29	5:22 AM

London Time		
Calendar Day	Lunar Day	Lunar Day Start Time
01/03/2022	29	6:15 AM
02/03/2022	30	6:39 AM
02/03/2022	1	5:38 PM
03/03/2022	2	7:00 AM
04/03/2022	3	7:19 AM
05/03/2022	4	7:38 AM
06/03/2022	5	7:57 AM
07/03/2022	6	8:19 AM
08/03/2022	7	8:45 AM
09/03/2022	8	9:16 AM
10/03/2022	9	9:54 AM
11/03/2022	10	10:40 AM
12/03/2022	11	11:34 AM
13/03/2022	12	12:36 PM
14/03/2022	13	1:44 PM
15/03/2022	14	2:55 PM
16/03/2022	15	4:08 PM
17/03/2022	16	5:23 PM
18/03/2022	17	6:39 PM
19/03/2022	18	7:57 PM
20/03/2022	19	9:17 PM
21/03/2022	20	10:37 PM
22/03/2022	21	11:57 PM
24/03/2022	22	1:10 AM
25/03/2022	23	2:14 AM
26/03/2022	24	3:06 AM
27/03/2022	25	4:46 AM
28/03/2022	26	5:17 AM
29/03/2022	27	5:42 AM
30/03/2022	28	6:04 AM
31/03/2022	29	6:23 AM

You can find the description of each lunar day in the chapter "A Guide to The Moon Cycle and Lunar Days"

Aries

March is a time for you to stop and take stock of everything around you. Your achievements certainly impress, but what's ahead is just as important. Buckle up!

Work. March is a time for delving into a lot of administrative tasks, as well as a litany of day-to-day matters, and both entrepreneurs and various levels of management will find themselves doing just that. You are expanding your business and involved in various real estate transactions. There is the possibility of achieving a real breakthrough that will solve many of your problems.

But life is never easy. You can expect some difficulties this month in your relationship with someone highly placed, among friends, or otherwise like-minded people. It will involve financial responsibilities and you will have to come back and discuss some of these issues again at a later date.

You have seen this situation before, and it might crop up again from time to time in the future. When explaining yourself, take care to be restrained and cautious, as a lot of problems can be traced back to impulsiveness, hotheadedness, and a failure to think before you act.

Employees can expect to be immersed in family issues. Many may take a short vacation and spend it as they see fit.

Money. Your finances are seeing a lot of ups and downs this month. Entrepreneurs will invest a lot of money into expanding their business, and those who are not part of the working world will do the same for their home, family, and children. In any case, keep a close eye on your budget and avoid any unnecessary expenses. Be especially cautious if you work in the financial world – bankers, brokers, or accountants. Avoid any risks this month; you will be on the losing end of things.

However, you will not find yourself completely penniless – you may receive money from unofficial sources, or support from your loved ones.

Love and family. For many Aries, March is a time for family. Once again, you are looking at a new dwelling or major repairs where you currently reside. This time, you may find an appropriate, and even elegant solution to complicated everyday, household tasks.

Married couples are moving in the same direction, but there are still areas where they diverge – finances! One is ready to spend more, while the other is more cautious. In this case, things will end up falling into place and being resolved for you.

Those in romantic relationships will have to accept that a loved one's intentions and appearance do not always live up to your expectations. But if you don't make mountains out of molehills, you will be able to avoid a lot of problems. Remember that in love, the less you demand, the more you will get. Act accordingly.

Health. In March, you are not as energetic as in the past, and you might experience frequent mood swings and occasionally worsening health. In order to get back on your feet, take a week off and get away from both work and home. It's not worth constantly thinking that everything will come to a halt without you!

Taurus

March is full of ups and downs for you. The stars' positive influence will alternate with the negative, and you will have to be flexible as you maneuver to take advantage of the good while dodging the bad.

Work. Your professional life has a lot of surprises in store for you this month, most of them good. Entrepreneurs will receive attractive offers, and employees can expect to grow at work. In any case, you can expect to feel supported by your friends or some highly placed individuals, which will pave the way for a lot of accomplishments.

Alternatively, your company may be undergoing some changes – perhaps there is new leadership, a new structure, or production target, which will lead to some worrying and fretting. Just keep in mind that any changes right now will only benefit you. You are in a strong position, and able to avoid a lot of problems altogether.

The only advice the stars can give right now is to be very cautious when communicating with any managers or high-level bodies. You've been a bit brusque with people lately, and this will only bring you unwanted and time-wasting confrontation.

Money. Your finances are stable, but that is it. You won't see any major profits this month, but you also won't suffer any losses. Expect to receive the largest sums of money on March 9, 10, 18, 19, 27, and 28.

Love and family. You can expect to be invited to a lot of parties and gatherings with friends this month, and your charisma and charm work their magic on anyone Fate places in your path. Active Mars and your ruler, Venus, unite, and at least some sort of romance seems inevitable.

You've recently met someone who doesn't seem like any ordinary affair, and he or she may change your entire life. This leads to a lot of questions – for example, is this The One? Will this romance interfere with the way you live your life? Don't try to control love yourself – first of all, you can't, and second of all, if you trust your feelings, they will not fail you.

If you already have a long-term partner or spouse, remember that your future is in your hands, and your hands alone.

Stable couples who get along might work together to overcome some problems this month, likely related to work and professional activities.

Health. In March, you are healthy, energetic, and ready to climb mountains. You might feel a bit of a slowdown during the last few days of the month, but that is easy to get through if you get enough sleep and don't try to overdo things.

Gemini

Expect success and all eyes on you this month. If you are reaching for the stars, don't hesitate to grab the bull by the horns, the time is now!

Work. March is one of the best times of the year for you when it comes to work. Both entrepreneurs and managers can count on new projects and lucrative offers to work together.

Employees can count on a promotion at their current workplace, or an offer at a new, more promising company.

But nothing is ever perfect. Your relationship with colleagues from other cities or abroad may turn out to be the fly in the ointment. This is not a new problem either, you have most likely been here before.

In some cases, that might be yet another border closure due to another insidious virus, and in others, the unpredictable and inappropriate behavior of faraway colleagues. Regardless, you are capable of, if not fixing, at least softening any problems that may come up. Near the beginning of the month, your efforts should pay off, so hold strong and remind yourself often that the journey of a thousand miles starts with a single step.

Money . Your financial situation is stable, with a strong trend toward improving. This month, you can expect money from both official and unofficial sources. Those who are not part of the business world can count on help from their parents and loved ones.

Love and family. This month, your personal and family life may take a backseat to work. However, Mars and Venus are connected in the sector of the sky responsible for long journeys and short trips, which means that despite the various issues they are facing, couples might go on a trip together, and single people can expect to meet a future flame, either while traveling or among people who have come from afar.

If you are planning any travel, the stars recommend that you take care with your preparations and consider any potential options, not least of which, the less pleasurable ones.

Health. In March, your energy potential is rather high, and you have no reason to fear any illnesses. Despite this, the stars once again warn you to be especially careful when traveling and behind the wheel!

Cancer

Searching for your place in the world might lead you to important discoveries in your career and at work. March is a very important turning point for you, between the past and future.

Work. Most of this month will be very favorable to you. This is a good time to make important decisions and get a good start on new projects. This goes for both entrepreneurs and managers at any level.

Your ties with colleagues in other cities or abroad will take on new significance, and you may begin actively working together, seek new partners, or even open your own business in another city or abroad.

Employees can also expect to begin a new chapter in their professional lives. If you are seeking a new job, you can be assured of success in March or April. In any case, you will be able to count on help from friends or highly placed individuals. You may meet new people who are very useful to your business.

Things may become more difficult for you close to the end of the month, as you will be dealing with your financial relationships with both partners and adversaries. You may be facing various complaints, and in some cases, you may see old legal issues rear their heads again.

If that applies to you, you will be in the clear as long as you have a good attorney, along with support from people who wield power and influence. With their help, you can significantly improve your situation, but things are unlikely to resolve themselves on their own. Each step you take will bring you closer to victory over the problems that are getting in your way of living life to its fullest and moving your business ahead.

Money. Your financial situation is experiencing a lot of ups and downs this month. You won't find your wallet empty, but you are facing a lot of expenses. Many Cancers will need to pay off credits and old debts, and that will be a difficult task. But there is hope that you will prevail, and next month things look much more stable.

Love and family. Your personal life will also undergo some changes in March. You may be moving to another city or abroad, or there is a real possibility of opportunities related to this. What's more, you are beginning a long period favorable to studying, spiritual growth, and mastering new skills. For example, you may experience a desire to study something far away from your hometown, or seek out a job in another city or abroad.

A recent romantic entanglement is playing out tumultuously, with a lot of emotions and not going particularly smoothly. If you experience any difficulties, remember that you are living in the real world, not a utopia, and there is no way out of this without making some compromises.

Your relationship with friends has become difficult this month for various reasons. There are many questions, but this is nothing new to you – these issues have come up before, but this time, they may take a new, unexpected turn.

Health. In March, your energy potential is right where it should be, and any illnesses will simply pass you by.

Leo

This month, you may have to sacrifice some principles in order to get ahead in the coming weeks. But it's all worth it!

Work. In March, both entrepreneurs and managers of every level will be grappling with a series of loose ends that will seriously put the brakes on your business development, unless you tie them up. In all likelihood, this involves financial investments in projects that the stars promise to "green light". Finding funding will take up most of the month, but you will manage to find it and things will move forward.

In other, more problematic cases, long-term partners may start eyeing your business, and you will have to throw all your efforts and resources into defending it. Either situation stems from the past, so you are able to select the option that is closer and more realistic.

Employees will be facing some stiff competition – envious colleagues take no rest, and are actively trying to cause trouble for you. This month, you may have to reconsider many things and draw a line after a long period, which according to the stars, has come to an end. You have outgrown your current job and it is time to find greener pastures.

Money. Your finances might look differently in March. Those with their own business might find additional resources to fund their projects. For example, that might be in the form of credit, financial help from friends, or support from a spouse or loved one.

If you are dealing with a conflict involving your superiors or business partners, you will manage to negotiate acceptable terms for ending your partnership, and receive financial compensation – this time, it will be something appropriate.

Love and family. Events in your personal life are also up and down, depending on previous situations and what you have decided to do in the future.

Partners whose relationship is on the rocks might once again find themselves fighting, and it is possible that this fight will be the straw that breaks the camel's back. You will have to deal with dividing up property, first and foremost your place of residence. In the case of spouses who share a business together, things will only get worse.

Alternatively, your spouse or a loved one may fall ill or experience hard times, and that will have an effect on the entire family, which is feeling unmoored and anxious this month.

Happy couples might resolve various problems together related to buying, exchanging, or selling their home. You may also be purchasing a home for your adult children. In many families, the instability is explained by this troublesome and anxiety-inducing process.

Health. This month, you are feeling somewhat sluggish, and old health issues may crop up again, or you may unexpectedly face new ones. Take care of yourself and prevent infections, colds, and keep an eye on what you eat. It might be a good time to begin a diet, especially since Lent begins in March, this year. Take the time to get a massage, go to the beauty salon, or visit a spa. The stars recommend any form of self-care!

Virgo

You will be focused on your relationships in March – whether professional or personal. It all depends on your plans, intentions, and priorities.

Work. New acquaintances, meetings, and negotiations form the backdrop of this month for you. What's more, you will be taking on a lot of work in order to translate your words into reality.

Your relationship with colleagues from other cities is moving ahead successfully – on one hand, there may be clear progress, but on the other, there may be some issues requiring corrections and revisions. But thanks to your hard work, and the assistance of helpful colleagues, you will be able to resolve many of them.

Alternatively, the situation might become very real and objective, regardless of what you do, just as already happened in the recent past. It might be a virus, pandemic, or some other kind of hostile attack!

Moreover, the stars recommend that any entrepreneurs keep a close eye on their subordinates, and employees on their colleagues. There may be all kinds of intrigue, and poor faith, multiplied by blind ambition and unprofessionalism.

Money. There is nothing particularly of note when it comes to finances this month – there are no major achievements here, but you can avoid miscalculations. Expect the largest sums of money on March 1, 9, 10, 18-20, 27, and 28.

Love and family. March is a favorable and somewhat unusual time for your personal life. Those who have been partnered up for some time might reach a new level of trust, understanding, intimacy, and harmony.

If you are single, then the stars recommend paying close attention to your social circle, particularly new people – someone interesting might turn out to be the one who changes your entire life.

If you are looking for love and renewing your personal life, there is no better time than the present! Trips, parties, and outings are welcome – you are sure to be the belle of the ball. And if partners in the past have left you feeling disappointed, there is nothing stopping you from finding a worthy replacement.

Health. This month, health problems are likely among those who are elderly or weakened. They should take special care to lead a healthy lifestyle, and protect their bodies from any colds or infections.

Young and healthy people need to take care when traveling and driving. There is a fairly high likelihood of accidents in March.

Libra

This month your hard work and dedication is a thing to envy. You will succeed wherever you go, be everywhere, and excel at whatever task you take on. Just how do you do it? ☺

Work. You'll have a lot of work on your plate this month, and most of it will be administrative in nature. Entrepreneurs and managers will be checking on their subordinates, and maybe changing up their staffing. You may see new employees arrive, and they will provide much needed and highly valued assistance.

Employees may be given additional responsibilities and a nice bonus to go with. There may even be a promotion and raise on the horizon.

Overall, you're on an active, productive streak, and the stars recommend you remember that the more original and out-of-the-box your ideas are, the more successful they will be.

Money. In March, money is at the very forefront, and you can expect to see a lot of success here. You will have regular income and a lot more than usual. In addition to your usual salary, you can also count on additional profits, either from a bonus, raise, or support from your business partners, or loved ones.

You might even receive some nice dividends from banking transactions or a beneficial loan.

Expect to receive the largest sums on March 2, 3, 11, 12, 21, 22, 29-31.

Love and family. For much of March, you will be focused on work, and you might not have much time left over for your personal life. But just as before, many Libras will find themselves paying more attention and money to their children. You are facing regular expenses related to your children, and the stars recommend that you analyze the situation carefully – do your children really need such largesse? If they do, then there is nothing else to say, but if there is any doubt, think things over again before getting your wallet out.

Things are looking complicated for couples – you might argue, and it might become something constant. This is not just any lovers' quarrel. One of you may tire of the constant tensions and start to wonder - "What am I really getting out of this?"

Health. In March, you are not particularly energetic, and should be especially careful if you are elderly or suffer from chronic disease. If this is you, the stars recommend being very attentive to your own body and not overdoing it.

Young and healthy Libras might feel tired of constant pressure at work, and the stars recommend that you find the time to relax and be sure to get enough sleep. These are easy ways to calm your nerves and any irritability.

March is the ideal time for any wellness activities, such as massage, some light cosmetic procedures, or simply spending time in nature.

Scorpio

In March, you are bounding with energy, just be sure to use it only for peaceful purposes! Be open to new opportunities and you are sure to move forward, despite any minor setbacks and whispering around you.

Work. The major trend this month is continuing to develop your relationships. You can expect to meet new people, and move things forward with some of them.

At the same time, your relationships with former business partners might become somewhat complicated, though this has been going on for some time, so the situation is neither unpredictable nor new for you. Perhaps this is over some property dispute, most likely involving real estate, and you can expect to have to resolve several issues in a slightly different environment. Be patient, as things may not be resolved overnight, but in the end, there will be a situation that everyone can be satisfied with.

What's more, March is a rather creative month, and is an especially good time for artists, musicians, writers, and poets. But even if you don't work in the arts, many Scorpios will find themselves cooking up interesting ideas and thinking outside the box when it comes to problem solving.

Money. March is a relatively neutral month for your finances. Your income is moderate, but your expenses are modest, and mostly related to your home and family.

Love and family. Many Scorpios will find that their personal life is where they are most active this month.

Those with families will spend a lot of time with their children, who will continue to go through positive changes. Young children may begin doing better in school and behaving themselves, while older children will succeed at work or in their personal lives.

Couples going through a rough patch might still be able to deal with shared property, especially housing.

Single people and those who have been let down by love might find themselves a partner – this will be something passionate, stormy, but also very fleeting. Remember that if you are still tied to someone more reliable.

Some families will welcome new children or grandchildren, and in some cases, Scorpios will think about expanding their brood.

Health. This month, you are feeling healthy, energetic, and incredibly attractive. Everyone Fate places in your path is noticing, too.

Sagittarius

It's time to forget about work, let your hair down, and relax a little. If you really feel like working, focus your efforts on your home and family affairs. All of that is important, right now.

Work. If you are one of those incorrigible workaholics who just can't switch it off, March is a time for you to get all your papers in order, organize your office, or maybe even work on expanding your business. That is the most likely scenario for any entrepreneurs or managers who are feeling restless these days. You may be acquiring new real estate or busy with major repairs.

The challenge this month might be in your relationship with colleagues from other cities or abroad. You might see unexpected difficulties, changes to existing agreements, or simply circumstances over which you have no control.

You might see some roadblocks with planned trips or misunderstandings along the way. If you have plans to go on a business trip, examine every possible outcome to make sure you don't end up stuck somewhere. You may face various limitations similar to what we experienced during the pandemic.

Money. Your financial situation is stable and is showing a significant upward trend. In addition to your usual salary, this month you can also count on additional income. That may stem from real estate transactions or some favorable credit. You may also get help from your parents, a loved one, or a spouse.

Love and family. Many people this month are fully immersed in their personal lives. Anyone planning any renovations might experience a real breakthrough in such a difficult, cumbersome task. You might even be busy building a new home, acquiring an apartment, summer home, or land. In some cases, you may simply be making plans related to your home, and in others, you may actually be right in the thick of it.

Many families will have to grapple with challenges involving your relationship with relatives. Old problems may rear their ugly heads again, and you will have to put some elbow grease into solving them.

In March, many will feel the desire to get away from it all for a little, and you will find time for it. But if you are planning a trip, keep in mind it may not actually happen for reasons beyond your control.

Health. This month, you are feeling healthy, but the stars recommend you take extra care when driving and be more careful while traveling.

In March, many Sagittarians will tend to put on some weight, so the stars recommend avoiding any excess calories and follow some folk wisdom here – "breakfast like a king, lunch like a queen, and dinner like a pauper."

Capricorn

All month long, your trump card will be your ability to react and quickly come up with creative solutions. Your motto this month is "keep your eye on the prize."

Work. You are in for an action-packed month. You can show off your enviable energy and confidence in anything you do.

Your relationships with colleagues in other cities and abroad are moving along very nicely, and you might take a trip or meet new partners who are just what you need to develop your business. Those planning on expanding their work to new cities or abroad will be able to make important steps in that direction this month.

Luck is on your side this month, regardless of your status or field. You are becoming a more trusted source, and as your popularity grows, so will your self-confidence.

What's more, March is the beginning of a long period favorable for studying, spiritual growth, and mastering new skills. In short, the world is your oyster, and only you can decide where to go and how.

Money. Your financial well-being is always very important to you, especially now. Promoting your business and problems in your personal life both cost money, and these are just things you have to pay for.

When it comes to financial affairs, try to avoid any risk – losses are inevitable.

Plan your budget ahead of time, and as much as possible, rein in any expenses that might be unnecessary. You are sure to succeed – after all, you are well-known as a strategist.

Love and family. Your personal life is going through some protracted changes that began in the past. A new romance is sure to develop, though it requires many sacrifices. You might take a trip together, although that does entail some costs.

Many Capricorns tend to be thrifty, if not outright stingy. But this shouldn't stand in your way – go for love, and believe in the stars. They will show you the surest, most reliable path.

People with stable families will spend a large amount of money on their children, but there's nothing new there.

Those dreaming of a move this month might finally decide on their plans and make decisive steps toward carrying them out.

Health. This month, you are feeling rather energetic, and can expect any illnesses to pass you by.

Aquarius

You are looking at an active, exciting month ahead. Your motto in March is "less talking, more doing!" If you keep that in mind, you can move mountains!

Work. Despite a series of challenges, which are very likely in the beginning of the month, you are making notable progress at work.

Employees are able to strengthen their position at work, which will certainly be reflected in their finances, which will see significant improvements.

Entrepreneurs who are striving for development and expanding their business are able to resolve a series of thorny matters related to real estate, either in whole or in part.

If you experience any ups and downs along the way, you will be able to resolve them if you harness any opportunity, both financial and legal. You still have people with power and influence on your side, as well as old friends.

Money. Your financial situation looks very stable in March. Money will be coming in regularly, and the amount will significantly increase. In addition to your usual income, you can also count on additional sources this month. For example, someone will pay you back a loan, or you might receive a bonus or payment for some extra work.

You are likely to receive some credit or additional profits from various real estate transactions. Expect to receive the largest amounts on March

2, 3, 6-8, 21, 22, 27, and 28.

Love and family. Your personal life has become extremely complicated. You have a very high risk of conflict this month, and the greatest source of tension is none other than you. You are inherently abrupt, emotional, and unpredictable in March, and that might provoke a strong reaction from your loved ones. In the most difficult cases, you might see a truly revolutionary scene play out when things finally come to a head.

A variety of arguments related to real estate are also on the horizon, and they are a continuation of problems that began in the past. Some issues will be resolved this month, but the stars believe not everything will be fixed, and you will be grappling with this again later on.

Just remember that your risk diminishes with each step you take, and eventually, you will be able to reach a favorable end to this journey. Remember that you can't win if you don't try, and don't let yourself forget that!

Spouses suffering from trust issues and anyone else who feels like they are sitting on the fence need to make a choice, given that being able to hold onto old ties as well as new love is highly unlikely.

Health. This month, you are feeling energetic, though the stars recommend that you use this only for peaceful purposes. Your mood swings and emotional outbursts this month will have a negative effect on all areas of your life.

Pisces

You are charging ahead, but there are many behind you, breathing down your neck, hoping to watch you trip and fall. Put the pedal to the metal and don't slow down, now – Jupiter is on your side, and everything will turn out great!

Work. Your main achievement is figuring out what is most important to you and quickly developing your relationships with colleagues in other cities or abroad. Thanks to your knowledge and efforts, your situation will have significantly improved, but you still have a long road ahead.

There are some forces out there that, for various reasons might throw a wrench into your plans, and not always in an open or honest manner. Some old intrigue might refuse to go away, or old conflicts may rear their heads again. But this time, you are much stronger, and your adversaries' machinations are likely to be in vain.

The silver lining this month might be new partners who will facilitate renewing and developing your business.

Any travel planned for March might be successful, especially if you avoid March 18-22. That is a very difficult time for all relationships, when you are likely to face a variety of challenges, especially while on the road.

Regardless of your field, the stars strongly advise all Pisceans to follow the criminal code to a T this month – violating any laws or even instructions might lead to the most unexpected consequences!

Money. Your financial situation is stable and might improve toward the end of the month. The good news is that this is a favorable trend expected to continue through April. This month, you can expect to receive the largest sums on March 23 and 24.

Love and family. March will bring many pleasant surprises to Pisces with romance on their minds. A recent entanglement is moving along nicely, and you are likely to meet new people.

At the same time, this month anyone leading a double life should be aware that everything will come out, sooner or later. Consider that not everyone wishes you well, and behave more considerately. Someone working in the shadows might shed light on things you would rather keep a secret. That goes not only for romantic partners, but also friendships and relatives.

Those with longstanding issues involving a close relative will have to deal with that person once again. But you should be aware that there are no new surprises here.

Health. This month, you are healthy, energetic, charming, and leave a lasting impression on anyone Fate sends your way.

However, the stars strongly recommend being careful while traveling or driving. That is particularly relevant all month long, but especially from March 18 to 22.

April

New York Time		
Calendar Day	Lunar Day	Lunar Day Start Time
01/04/2022	1	1:27 AM
01/04/2022	2	5:49 AM
02/04/2022	3	6:17 AM
03/04/2022	4	6:47 AM
04/04/2022	5	7:19 AM
05/04/2022	6	7:55 AM
06/04/2022	7	8:37 AM
07/04/2022	8	9:23 AM
08/04/2022	9	10:14 AM
09/04/2022	10	11:10 AM
10/04/2022	11	12:09 PM
11/04/2022	12	1:11 PM
12/04/2022	13	2:14 PM
13/04/2022	14	3:19 PM
14/04/2022	15	4:26 PM
15/04/2022	16	5:35 PM
16/04/2022	17	6:46 PM
17/04/2022	18	7:59 PM
18/04/2022	19	9:12 PM
19/04/2022	20	10:23 PM
20/04/2022	21	11:29 PM
22/04/2022	22	12:25 AM
23/04/2022	23	1:13 AM
24/04/2022	24	1:53 AM
25/04/2022	25	2:28 AM
26/04/2022	26	2:58 AM
27/04/2022	27	3:25 AM
28/04/2022	28	3:52 AM
29/04/2022	29	4:19 AM
30/04/2022	30	4:47 AM
30/04/2022	1	4:30 PM

London Time		
Calendar Day	Lunar Day	Lunar Day Start Time
01/04/2022	30	6:41 AM
01/04/2022	1	7:27 AM
02/04/2022	2	7:00 AM
03/04/2022	3	7:21 AM
04/04/2022	4	7:45 AM
05/04/2022	5	8:14 AM
06/04/2022	6	8:49 AM
07/04/2022	7	9:32 AM
08/04/2022	8	10:23 AM
09/04/2022	9	11:22 AM
10/04/2022	10	12:26 PM
11/04/2022	11	1:35 PM
12/04/2022	12	2:46 PM
13/04/2022	13	4:00 PM
14/04/2022	14	5:15 PM
15/04/2022	15	6:33 PM
16/04/2022	16	7:54 PM
17/04/2022	17	9:16 PM
18/04/2022	18	10:39 PM
19/04/2022	19	11:58 PM
21/04/2022	20	1:07 AM
22/04/2022	21	2:04 AM
23/04/2022	22	2:48 AM
24/04/2022	23	3:21 AM
25/04/2022	24	3:48 AM
26/04/2022	25	4:10 AM
27/04/2022	26	4:29 AM
28/04/2022	27	4:47 AM
29/04/2022	28	5:05 AM
30/04/2022	29	5:25 AM
30/04/2022	1	9:30 PM

You can find the description of each lunar day in the chapter "A Guide to The Moon Cycle and Lunar Days"

Aries

This month, you are going to have to stick to your guns as much as you will have to expand some boundaries. And everything will turn out for the best!

Work. April is one of the best months of the year for you, when the planetary conjunctions bring a plethora of opportunities your way. That includes reconnecting with old acquaintances and meeting new people who will prove very useful for developing your business. Both new partners and old colleagues will be able to discuss projects with you, and most importantly – find money, which you need in order to keep things moving ahead. This is the case for both businesspeople and managers at any level.

Employees can count on support from their managers – right now you are able to approach them with any suggestion or request, and they are likely to give you what you want. In short, it's time to roll up your sleeves and get to work, after all, success doesn't wait.

Money. April is a good time for your finances. Any agreements you reach this month will have a notable effect in both April and May. Nearly all Aries can count on significantly higher income, from both official and unofficial sources.

That may include funds stemming from various real estate transactions, credit, or support from loved ones. This month, your good fortune means that anywhere you put your energy, no matter what it is, will bring success.

Love and family. In your personal life, you are managing to do a lot of things to improve your day-to-day living. Construction, repairs, and other household projects are turning out well, and you won't have to wait for help from every corner.

Couples might look back at the past and reconsider their relationship. If you have recently quarreled, this month, you might be able to overcome things and find the understanding you need to reconcile.

If you are feeling guilty, apologize, and your partner will likely respond in kind.

Your children may be causing you some problems, and this month you have a great opportunity to smooth things over with them. It is time for everyone to kiss and make up!

Health. In April, you are experiencing a powerful surge of energy, and despite the mountain of work you are facing, you are feeling great. Naturally, you have no reason to fear any illnesses.

Taurus

Right now, you are holding incredible potential, and the stars urge you to think big. No matter what you start, you will be successful, so dare yourself – the sky is the limit!

Work. This month, you are able to really count on those around you. You can count on massive support from your friends, as well as some highly placed people, and most importantly of all – the stars! You can be assured that luck is on your side, and circumstances are working for you.

April is the ideal time to resolve any difficult issues in an official capacity, where someone from your circle is able to act as an intermediary.

You are beginning a very lucky period, and employees should get ready for some changes for the better. Closer to the end of the month, or perhaps in May, you might be promoted, and in early April you might be laying the groundwork to promote your own interests. You recently experienced some misunderstandings with your superiors, but that will stay in the past and resolve in your favor.

Money. Your finances are likely to be neutral this month. Your income is steady and in line with your expenses, but nothing unexpected will come up. On the other hand, you might see some happy surprises, which in some cases may look like material benefits in the very near future, and in others, unexpected help, whether moral or financial.

Love and family. This month, your personal life is in full swing! A recent encounter will quickly develop into a stormy romance, and those who have not yet found a partner might count on changing up their social circles and meeting interesting people.

Most likely, this will be someone from your group of friends, so be sure to not miss any fun parties and make sure you look your very best!

Those with a steady partner can also count on meeting new people this month. Uranus, which is in your sign, might make you completely rethink your feelings. In that case, be attentive and think long and hard about how strong your attachment to new encounters really is, and about your true feelings for your current partner. Remember that not all that glitters is gold, and tread carefully.

Health. In April, your energy is all over the place; you will have periods of vigor and strength, followed by exhaustion and a desire to rest and relax. Do not ignore your body's needs and find the time to take a break, especially when the opportunity arises. A few days away from the usual hustle and bustle will give your body strength and clear your mind.

Gemini

You are beginning an active and extremely positive period in your life. The stars recommend grabbing the bull by the horns and turning your words into deeds. The ball is in your court!

Work. April is a great time for almost all Geminis, regardless of your field. Ideas you have been marinating for a while are finally coming to life.

Entrepreneurs and managers are off to a good start with their projects; they will also come up with great ideas and start working on them.

Employees might be promoted this month, and if that already happened recently, they will strengthen their position. You might also receive new, unexpected offers from large and promising organizations.

Your connections to colleagues from other cities or abroad are looking quieter this month, though the main, underlying problem has not yet been resolved, and you will have to face it again sometime.

You are likely to meet new people this month, who will also help you strengthen your position at work. You might also count on friends, highly placed people and various official organizations. In short – your time has finally come, and you deserve it!

Money. Your finances are also improving, which is no surprise, given all your gains at work and in business.

Money will be coming in regularly, and you will see significantly more of it, too Expect the greatest sums on April 8, 9, 17, 19, and 25-27.

Your expenses in April will be predictable, reasonable, and even enjoyable.

Love and family. Your personal life might be on the back burner this month, since you will be so preoccupied with work.

However, given your very spirited disposition, like a servant to two masters, you can be everywhere at once.

Single people might find a new flame among their circle of friends or at a new job. Only time will tell how long it will last, but there is a chance that things will continue.

Those with families will be please those at home with their success at work. That will compensate, at least in part, for the perpetual busyness and lack of time for family this month.

Health. This month, you are fresh-faced, energetic, charming, and sexually attractive. Naturally, you have no reason to fear any ailments at all!

Cancer

Forget about any troubles, keeping your guard up, or any preconceived notions you may have – the more open you are right now, the more successful this period will be. There is a new life out there, and it is knocking at your door!

Work. Long-awaited improvements are on your horizon at work. April is a good time to start new projects, change jobs, and even directions.

Your ties to colleagues in other cities or abroad are developing very successfully, and you might go on a trip that is sure to bring good luck. Those hoping to open business somewhere faraway are closer than ever to making their dreams come true.

Your difficult relationship with a business partner, a friend, or like-minded person will get somewhat better. Nothing is likely to be perfect, but in April, you are able to make a lot of progress in this direction, and it is worth taking advantage of this opportunity. You might once again be dealing with pending financial disputes or longstanding obligations, whether moral or material.

This month is almost an ideal time to begin any studies, seek out information, and define your future objectives. So, figure out what you need, and don't waste your time on anything else!

Money. Your finances are somewhat better, but not so much that money is no longer a concern for you. Though day to day, your material affairs are becoming clearer, and that will lead to resolving things. You can expect to receive the largest sums on April 1, 2, 10-12, 19-21, 28, and 29.

Love and family. Single people and those who have been let down by love in the past might pack their bags and head to other cities or abroad in April. You are likely to see a love story play out this month, and it is likely to be while you are traveling or among people who have come from afar.

If you are planning on learning anything new this month from people

Fate has placed on your path, you might meet someone unusual and very intriguing.

Couples who are married or have been together for a while might go on a trip together, and that is always the best thing for your relationships. If you face any dilemma – total relaxation or work hard – just finish your project and then head off to your favorite spot.

Health. In April, you are feeling a lot better about yourself, and any illnesses from last month will quickly fade away.

Leo

You are probably not starting April with a clean slate, you have plans, ideas, and most importantly – the will to see them through. And as they say, all you need is a little patience and hard work!

Work. In April, you may find yourself heavily dependent on partners or people with whom you have various business ties and shared circumstances. However, you have been here before, and each time, you are able to work your way out of the problem. This time is no different – you are able to reach an agreement with your partners, even if it is not always easy.

In some cases, this involves an injection of cash into shared business, and you will have to present your arguments and back them up with the facts, as no one is going to give you any financial help if you don't. In other, more severe cases, you are dividing up your business and dealing with lengthy negotiations about shared financial and moral agreements. Despite this, in April, work will be somewhat easier, and near the middle of the month, you can count on a favorable result for both sides.

Your relationship with colleagues in other cities or abroad is moving along with varying degrees of success, and you might take a trip, which is best if planned for the end of the month.

Money. Financial matters are getting off the ground, but we aren't talking about your money. You might get some favorable credit, various types of loans, or support from a business partner, or maybe even profits from various real estate transactions.

Those who are not part of the working world can count on help from their spouse, parents, or a loved one. Many families will take on credit.

Love and family. You will see several processes that began in the past continuing in your personal life. This is still with regards to construction, repairs, or acquiring a new residence either for yourself or your children.

Divorcing partners will be able to sit down at the negotiating table this month, and this time things will go much more smoothly, possibly even productively.

And there is more in store for you this month – It is surprisingly good for anyone who is dreaming of expanding their family. There is a very high chance of pregnancy, right now, which anyone hoping for a bundle of joy should keep in mind.

Health. In April, your energy is lagging, and you might experience mood swings and periods of feeling low. In order to get back on your feet, take a few days off and spend it however your heart desires. A trip somewhere faraway might be just what you need to relax and see things around you more clearly.

Virgo

All month long, you are quick, disciplined, and hardworking. This, along with your meticulous nature, is sure to pay off in droves. Hold on!

Work. Your main task this week is to convince partners to help finance your very promising ideas. The stars advise that this is absolutely necessary in order to develop your business. If you don't have any reliable colleagues just yet, then you should focus on looking for them. April is almost an ideal time for that. You can expect new acquaintances, meetings, negotiations, where you are able to catch the eye of the people you need.

Be bold as you strive for your goals, some reasonable risk is welcome, right now. Remember that a lot is riding on your persuasive abilities, so write down some powerful arguments and back them up with as many facts as you can. The stars are certainly on your side.

Closer to the end of the month, you will have more contact with colleagues in other cities or abroad, and you might go on a successful trip. Your ideas might interest a faraway partner.

Money. Despite the clear success you are having with making contacts and new connections, you might face some financial difficulties. This should not upset you too much – things will settle into place in time. Everything you are doing this month is sure to bring results, if not now, in the near future. You won't find yourself penniless in April, though you might have less cash than you would have expected.

Love and family. There are a lot of changes in your personal life. In couples that get along, you are reaching mutual understanding and agreement with each other. Your loved ones will experience success, which will bring you great joy.

Those who have recently divorced or lost a loved one can count on a favorable solution this month to a material problem, as well as a new encounter.

You have waited for stability in your relationship for a long time, and now you have it, whether you are married, have a long-term partner, or in the middle of a romance.

Closer to the end of the month, or possibly in May, you are likely to go on a trip, and it will be very successful.

Health. In April, you are not particularly energetic, and that is especially noticeable around the New Moon – April 1 and 2, as well as the Full

Moon, on April 15-17. During these periods, try to avoid overdoing things and keep an eye on yourself.

Libra

April is a great time for slow, analytical, painstaking tasks, as well as business or personal meetings. Make some real plans in order to take advantage of this.

Work. Entrepreneurs and managers will be busy getting everything in order for their teams. You will need to check the work of some longtime employees, as well as new arrivals – this will be the bulk of your workdays this month.

Entrepreneurs and managers will also have to find a way to get rid of those who are holding you back unnecessarily, and closely consider who is hardworking and professional. Naturally, you have been considering that for a while now, though the time has come to take another step forward in order to improve your team's work and breathe new life into it.

Employees have a great opportunity to improve their position, and if that recently happened, then April is a great time to strengthen that gain. This is the perfect month for meetings, new people, and discussing financial issues. The latter is important for anyone seeking to expand his or her business.

Money. April is a good time for your bank account. Money is coming in regularly, and you can expect to receive the largest sums on April 8, 9, 17, 18, and 25-27.

In addition to your normal income, you can expect some successful credit and loan negotiations, as well as help from a sponsor. Those who are not part of the business world can count on help from loved ones, a spouse, or parents.

Love and family. When it comes to family and your love life, try not to go against the flow, and carefully consider your loved ones' interests – in this case, your relationship is beginning a new phase of understanding, trust, and love.

Single people might meet someone interesting at work, on your team, or among new employees. In April, the stars are giving the green light to any office romances.

Couples who are getting along might see activities related to new real estate or rehabbing their current dwelling.

Health. In April, you are a bit sluggish, so take care of yourself and strive to live a healthy lifestyle. This is a good time to get a massage, visit a spa, or otherwise engage in some self-care.

You can consider your lifestyle and say no to any bad habits if you have any, and keep an eye out for any diseases. After all, you can't be too careful!

Scorpio

In April, you are grappling with a mountain of tasks, and they might not all be related to one another. In order to manage it all, come up with a clear, well thought-out plan of action, and the stars will be on your side!

Work. You might be sick of your work routine, but in April, you can't avoid it. You will not see any serious changes, everything will continue as it has, but you will need to pay close attention to all of the tasks at hand. Your ability to work on a team, appropriate relations with your management, responsibility, and discipline are the key, and if you use it, you will be able to take care of everything on your plate.

In addition to your normal responsibilities at work, managers and entrepreneurs will have to resolve some issues related to real estate though this time, things seem more settled than they were.

New people, meetings, interviews, and negotiations are all very likely in April, and will be very beneficial to freelancers and employees alike.

Your speaking skills are high right now, and you are able to convince anyone of anything.

Money. Your financial situation is stable, with a clear upward trend. In addition to your usual income, Fate is bringing some pleasant surprises your way. This might be unexpected gifts or even a winning lottery ticket. Try your luck – you have high chances of winning out!

Love and family. Despite how busy you are at work, your personal life is still full of activity. Those with families will spend a lot of time with their children, who are continuing a positive streak. Many Scorpios will also spend more time at parties, birthdays, and gatherings than usual, and have a chance to show off their talents in full force. If you have plans for stardom, they should come true now!

If you recently began a romance, you can count on it continuing. But if you aren't partnered up yet, look around – you might find someone who would like to get to know you better. Fate works in mysterious ways, you might accidentally meet someone who turns your entire life around.

Any events related to real estate are expected to continue favorably, and this time, things look to be calm and peaceful.

Health. In April, you are feeling energetic and have no reason to fear any ailments.

Sagittarius

Throughout April, your trump card is your incredible reaction and ability to make out-of-the-box decisions. These skills have always been up your sleeve, and now they're finally getting noticed!

Work. For anything work-related, this month is looking up. Both managers and entrepreneurs can count on new, beneficial offers for everyone, along with a good outlook for the future. Your relationship with your team has significantly improved, whether you are an entrepreneur or employee. Any issues in the recent past are looking very different in April – they are less acute and closer to resolution. You might also get some new colleagues who will turn out to be hardworking, professional, and responsible.

Those who are dealing with a series of thorny issues involving partners from other cities or abroad are able to resolve them, at least in part. Given the difficult past and less-than-stable future, that is a very good thing. In short, April is a good time that you should take full advantage of.

Money. This month, your finances are looking great. You might profit handsomely from recent work and the future is looking hopeful, too.

Those who are busy with various types of real estate transactions might also count on some nice profits. This might include acquiring property on favorable terms or a successful sale. Even troublesome and expensive repairs will go smoothly this month, and be less of a financial burden than you think.

Love and family. Your personal life is also interesting this month. As in the past, your main task with your family might be acquiring a new home, construction, or major repairs. This time, however, you can expect some big changes, and in some cases, completing the major steps.

In a lucky coincidence, your finances are currently sufficient to provide support for a loved one – this will allow you to do a good deed and bring yourself closer to your aims.

Your relationship with your children is much warmer, and this month you might spend a lot more time with them than usual.

April is full of happy events – you might be a desired guest at parties, where you are able to be your very best. You are likely to meet new people, which is a good thing if you are single or your relationship has already run its course.

Your relationship with relatives has been a bit rocky in the recent past, and in April things will become more predictable. Even if you have not resolved everything, it's better than nothing. And remember, there is no such thing as bad peace or a good war.

Health. In April, you are feeling energetic and have no reason to fear any illness. April is also a great time to overhaul your wardrobe, change up your image, or undergo any cosmetic procedures.

Capricorn

You are heading toward the goal you set for yourself, and the path is wide open. There are some obstacles in your way, some of them are in the past, and the others ahead will be easy to overcome.

Work. Your main theme this month is still developing contacts with your colleagues in other cities and abroad. In April, you might have some successful negotiations on cooperation, or discuss important financial and organizational issues. Some Capricorns will be busy selecting premises for expanding their business, and if that is the case, they may be assessing both opportunities and the objective features of the location in question.

In other cases, you can count on support from family, which is especially pertinent if you are running a family business.

Employees might consider various options working at a company with a lot of ties to other cities or countries. The stars also welcome anything involving studying something somewhere faraway.

Money. Your financial situation is gradually improving. Your large expenses in previous months are no longer such an issue. However, Saturn is the planet of boundaries, discipline, and moderation, and it is still in the sector of the sky responsible for finances, which calls for being particularly responsible when it comes to money. Carefully look over your budget and cut out any unnecessary expenses. But given your frugal nature, that advice may be superfluous ☺.

Love and family. The main events this year take place in your personal life, and here is where things really get going. Many Capricorns will be busy with various types of real estate transactions, and in some cases that is related to a move to another city or abroad, while in others, it is simply a new home.

Most likely, any similar events in April will be preliminary in nature and take some time to really turn into concrete plans.

Your relationship with your children is now more predictable, and the more pressing issues are now in the past. Ahead, you can look forward to peacefully solving any lingering problems from previous months.

Divorcing couples are able to speak relatively peacefully about material issues, particularly real estate. If that is possible, try to deal with the most acute matters in April, as right now you are able to find a mutually acceptable compromise.

The influence of relatives on all family issues might turn out to be a positive thing.

For couples, April will be calm and predictable, and this month you may discuss matters related to further development of your relationship or even living together.

Health. In April, you are feeling energetic, and you are working hard, striving to bring your innovative ideas to life, both at home and at work.

Aquarius

All month long, you are active, curious, and enterprising. That is reflected in every area of your life, whether at home or at work.

Work. Overall, April is a promising time for establishing contacts with your management, as well as resolving any legal problems that may have cropped up in the recent past.

For the umpteenth time, you will have to discuss difficult issues related to real estate, land, or any other large property, but you will resolve them favorably. In some cases, you may receive financial compensation, while in others, you may sell based on mutual agreement. You are entering what look like very reasonable arrangements, so compromise is both desirable and likely.

Your ties to colleagues from other cities or abroad are moving along nicely, and you might go on a successful trip. Entrepreneurs can expect to reach a beneficial agreement with pleasing financial results.

Money. When it comes to your financial relationships, April is one of the best months of the year. In addition to your usual income, you might see additional profits from various real estate transactions. That may be related to professional activities, or perhaps events in your personal life.

You can expect to receive the largest sums on April 8, 9, 17, 18, and 22-27.

Love and family. Your personal life is predictable and fairly calm. This month, you will need to tackle a lot of household tasks, which have been scheduled since the beginning of winter, if not earlier. These are jobs related to furnishings in your home, summer home, or apartment. You might find yourself increasingly immersed in these tasks closer to the end of April, and continuing into May.

Your relationships with relatives will become very important, and you may meet with family members who live in another city or abroad.

Mars and Venus will be in your sign during the first ten days of the month, along with Saturn. That all means that you are likely to rekindle things with an old flame, reconnect with an old friend, or even meet up with a lover in another city or abroad.

Fate will give you several opportunities to find love, so take advantage of them, if you don't have anyone special in your life right now.

Health. This month, you are feeling a lot more energetic, though Saturn's passing through your sign means that you should maintain a healthy lifestyle and try not to overdo either food or drink.

Those suffering from chronic heart disease should be very careful this month.

Pisces

You are able to approach any task this month with inspiration and ingenuity. That gives you a shot at success in anything you do, whether business or personal. You have a lot on your plate, and remember, you never know what you can do, until you try.

Work. In April, issues that had kept you up at night in the past are being resolved in your favor. In some cases, this may involve longstanding legal issues that took up a lot of your time. In others, you are smoothing over relations with stubborn colleagues in other cities or abroad. You will not manage to avoid arguing altogether, but closer to the end of the month, your partners who live in other cities or abroad will reach a compromise. You will do everything in your power, and you are sure to get yours.

You may go on a successful trip or plan one.

The second half of April is the best time for anything work-related. During this period, you will see positive changes in the most difficult areas of your work, and you will see that there is no problem that can't be solved.

Money. When it comes to money, April is looking promising. Money will come in regularly, and you will see a lot more than usual. You might even say that this is the harbinger of success, which you can expect in the very near future. You will receive the largest sums on April 1, 2, 10-12, 19, 20, 28, and 29.

Love and family. Everything is going swimmingly in your personal life. You were recently experiencing some tension with relatives, but this time, everything is closer to being smoothed over. You might have to make the first step toward meeting with your family member, an effort that will be both welcome and appreciated.

Single people might have a fateful meeting while traveling or among people who have come from afar, and you may go on a trip together. But if you have recently already done that, and the romance has already begun, this is the time to think about taking your relationship to the next level. You might have a serious discussion while on the road, and that is most likely during the last ten days of April or in early May.

Health. Jupiter and Neptune are both comfortably settled in your sign, and that means that you have incredible energy potential, how you use it depends on you and you alone! Any ailments are likely to just pass you by!

May

New York Time			London Time		
Calendar Day	Lunar Day	Lunar Day Start Time	Calendar Day	Lunar Day	Lunar Day Start Time
01/05/2022	2	6:18 AM	01/05/2022	2	5:48 AM
02/05/2022	3	6:53 AM	02/05/2022	3	6:14 AM
03/05/2022	4	7:32 AM	03/05/2022	4	6:47 AM
04/05/2022	5	8:16 AM	04/05/2022	5	7:27 AM
05/05/2022	6	9:06 AM	05/05/2022	6	8:14 AM
06/05/2022	7	10:00 AM	06/05/2022	7	9:10 AM
07/05/2022	8	10:57 AM	07/05/2022	8	10:12 AM
08/05/2022	9	11:57 AM	08/05/2022	9	11:18 AM
09/05/2022	10	12:59 PM	09/05/2022	10	12:27 PM
10/05/2022	11	2:02 PM	10/05/2022	11	1:38 PM
11/05/2022	12	3:06 PM	11/05/2022	12	2:51 PM
12/05/2022	13	4:13 PM	12/05/2022	13	4:07 PM
13/05/2022	14	5:22 PM	13/05/2022	14	5:25 PM
14/05/2022	15	6:34 PM	14/05/2022	15	6:47 PM
15/05/2022	16	7:49 PM	15/05/2022	16	8:11 PM
16/05/2022	17	9:03 PM	16/05/2022	17	9:34 PM
17/05/2022	18	10:14 PM	17/05/2022	18	10:50 PM
18/05/2022	19	11:16 PM	18/05/2022	19	11:55 PM
20/05/2022	20	12:10 AM	20/05/2022	20	12:46 AM
21/05/2022	21	12:53 AM	21/05/2022	21	1:24 AM
22/05/2022	22	1:30 AM	22/05/2022	22	1:53 AM
23/05/2022	23	2:01 AM	23/05/2022	23	2:16 AM
24/05/2022	24	2:30 AM	24/05/2022	24	2:36 AM
25/05/2022	25	2:56 AM	25/05/2022	25	2:54 AM
26/05/2022	26	3:23 AM	26/05/2022	26	3:12 AM
27/05/2022	27	3:50 AM	27/05/2022	27	3:31 AM
28/05/2022	28	4:20 AM	28/05/2022	28	3:52 AM
29/05/2022	29	4:53 AM	29/05/2022	29	4:17 AM
30/05/2022	30	5:30 AM	30/05/2022	30	4:47 AM
30/05/2022	1	7:32 AM	30/05/2022	1	12:32 PM
31/05/2022	2	6:13 AM	31/05/2022	2	5:24 AM

You can find the description of each lunar day in the chapter "A Guide to The Moon Cycle and Lunar Days"

Aries

In May, if anyone asks the question "Who's in charge here?" you'll be able to answer with confidence - "I am," whether at work or at home.

Work. The theme this month is financial and other administrative affairs, and you have not one, but two eclipses calling on you to handle them – a solar eclipse on April 30, and a lunar eclipse on May 16.

Entrepreneurs and managers are still largely focused on expanding their business and increasing production. That will require resources, but you are sure to find them.

Employees can count on understanding from management on anything related to finances – that includes a raise, bonus, or other material rewards. This isn't often the case, so seize the day and don't waste any time!

The ideal time for any work-related developments, including important meetings and implementing any agreements, is the first ten days of the month.

From May 10 to June 3, Mercury, which is related to contacts, will be in retrograde, and that means that you can expect a lot of holdups. You may have to circle back to certain issues multiple times, as things change, and reconsider your plans' financial makeup. Remember that it's not worth trying to get ahead during this time, so use it to come back and carefully examine everything you have already done. Usually, during this time, it's impossible to catch people when you need them, and for various reasons (like people taking time off from work), you are distracted from everyday, administrative concerns.

Money. When it comes to financial relationships, this month, things are looking pretty good, and you can expect to receive a large amount during the first ten days of the month. Things will turn out fairly well, and Uranus will be in the financial sector of your sky in the days that follow. This time, it is ready to help. Expect to receive the largest amounts on May 1, 5, 6, 10, 11, 19, 20, and 27-29.

Love and family. Most of the month, Venus is in your sign, and most importantly, on May 10, Jupiter will join it! That means that the two most helpful planets in the sky are protecting your sign. The choice is entirely yours – If you need a safe haven, you will get it, and if you are feeling the call of adventure, then you won't have to wait for it!

However, you should be careful with new people who show up in your life from May 10 to June 3. Time will show that in the end, they will be of no use to you. This advice goes for work, as well as your personal life.

If you are planning on a trip, choose a place you have been to a few times before.

Health. In May, you are feeling energetic and have no reason to fear any illnesses. May is a great time for any conservative cosmetic procedures, such as massage, a trip to the spa, or long walks in nature.

Taurus

Fate is ready to open up new opportunities for you, and this time, they directly affect your personal life.

Work. Jupiter, which has brought you many opportunities to build up your career, is passing to another sign. That means that you will have to return to some issues that you had put off some time ago. You've been moving ahead, but that is now going to pause, and you will find yourself grappling with what you had already done, and laying the groundwork for the next phase of development.

Entrepreneurs and managers will be busy with a variety of tasks related to expanding your business, and maybe make plans to acquire real estate. For now, these are just plans, but in 2023, they will come to fruition.

The first ten days of May are the best time for any professional matters. From May 10 to June 3, Mercury will be in retrograde, which means that you will be consumed with analyzing and reconsidering everything you had completed earlier.

Employees might strengthen their position during the first ten days of the month, but might run into some friction with management stemming from the recent past, though things will resolve favorably.

Money. This is a good month for your wallet. You won't be raking in huge profits, but you will likely see some nice surprises. This is your month – so you can expect both gifts and some bonuses. You are not facing any major expenses, and those you do have will be predictable and reasonable.

Love and family. This is a time of change in your personal life. It most likely involves household matters. Many Taureans will be making plans for a new home, whether by acquiring a new residence, or totally overhauling the current one. You will be making your first steps in this direction in May, and the rest is for the future!

Couples might decide to live together, and in the near future, they may make steps toward marriage. If, during the last 20 days of the month, you are annoyed with each other and full of doubts, then don't rush anything. Discuss things, and time will tell which door you should open.

Those who recently divorced will be ready to launch a new life. In this case, the most important thing is to not cycle back toward the past, but instead, to leave the emotional baggage of old worries and problems in the past!

Health. You should take care of your health, as this month you are not particularly energetic. This is especially the case for anyone who is weakened or elderly. Young and healthy people can care for themselves by living a healthy lifestyle and getting enough sleep. You might start gaining weight, so overeat, and take care to avoid drinking too much, too!

Gemini

"Everything changes but change itself" sums up your life, right now. Stagnation was the theme from 2018-2020, but things have finally begun to shift, and you are finding that you like it.

Work. During the first ten days of the month, you are thriving at work. You have new projects opening doors to a better future, which is the case whether you are an entrepreneur or employee. You have put forth your best efforts to overcome any obstacle, and you are finally getting your turn.

Those who have experienced longstanding legal problems can finally celebrate success. And even if that is just one step in a long legal battle, time will reveal its importance.

Your relationship with colleagues in other cities or abroad has improved, and you might take a trip.

For anything work-related, the best time of the month is the first ten days of May. After May 10, Mercury will be in retrograde, and that will give you time to take a step back from work and focus on yourself, your home life, and your family. More restless Geminis might take the opportunity to get everything in order at work and carefully lay plans for the future.

The last 20 days of May are a great time to think about recent changes, and studiously examine them in order to take a little break before work and your career take over your life.

Money. May is stable when it comes to your finances. In addition to your usual income, you can probably count on additional earnings from various sources. That may be an unexpected bonus, or help from loved ones. You might also receive dividends from banking transactions.

Expect the largest sums on May 4-6, 1, 16, 23, and 24.

Love and family. Your personal life is no less relevant than your work life, this month. It is time to get your house in order, as well as your summer house if you have one, and think about finding a new residence. You might have some opportunities a little later on, in about 8-12 months, if not earlier.

You might meet some new people in your social circle, but they are unlikely to stick around for long. Remember that any new acquaintances you meet between May 10 and June 3 are not going to be particularly reliable. Most likely, they will quickly vanish, leaving behind nothing but an unpleasant memory. That is the case both at work and in your personal life.

At the same time, you are likely to reconnect with old acquaintances, old friends, and former flames. If that is the case, this time, your relationship may reach a new level of trust and understanding.

Health. In May, you might be feeling less than confident and cheerful. That trend will begin with the solar eclipse and new moon on April 30, and continue until the full moon and lunar eclipse on May 14-16.

During this time, take care of yourself, and be careful when traveling and driving!

Cancer

Mighty Jupiter is moving into Aries, which will mean putting a big, fat X on all of your past troubles, and thinking about the future. You can be sure that Jupiter is looking out for you and will make sure everything falls into place.

Work. Your career is moving upward and onward, which all Cancers are feeling right now. You can say goodbye to any debts, problems from the past, and devote yourself to work that interests you.

Employees will get a great opportunity to start somewhere new, and if that already happened, you will strengthen your position.

Your relationships with colleagues in other cities or abroad are still relevant, it is very possible that this is the source of all of the positive changes. Your friends or someone highly placed might play a major role in your life this month, and their support will turn out to be key.

In all professional matters, the best time for you is the end of April and the first ten days of May. From May 10 to June 3, things will be less promising, as Mercury, the planet that rules connections and contacts will be in retrograde. There is nothing scary about this, but keep in mind that any progress will experience some slowdowns and you might have to come back and rethink some work-related issues.

Money. Your finances are looking pretty good in May, and most importantly, this is going to continue in the future. You can expect to receive the largest amounts on May 7-9, 17, 19, 25, and 26. You will not have many expenses, and those you do face will be both planned and reasonable. Those with old debts can expect to pay them off this month.

Love and family. Everything is stable in your personal life. A recent romance is moving along nicely, and you might go on a trip together, which will be a success. Some minor misunderstandings are a real possibility during the second half of May, but remember – it's only a lover's spat!

From May 10 to June 3, you will reconnect with some people you have not seen in a long time. They might be old friends, or perhaps a former flame.

It is not worth trying to count on any new people you meet from May 10 to June 3, as they may disappear altogether from your life, leaving no pleasant memories behind.

This is the case both at work and in your personal life.

Health. In May, you are active and energetic, and might forget about your health, which is the best indication of good health.

Leo

It is time to make yet another step down a new path, and it will be harder than you expected. The door to the future is opening up, but you might freeze at the threshold before moving forward. The stars recommend being bold and remembering that you are Leo, king of the jungle!

Work. In May, you might once again find yourself ahead of the game when it comes to anything involving money and your career. Those striving to find their place in the Sun will break down any barrier, though, as always, there may be many of them.

Therefore, entrepreneurs and managers may have to find resources to promote their business. Negotiations will take the entire month of May, and at the end of the day, things will turn out positively for you.

Alternatively, you may have to make difficult decisions concerning material issues when it comes to dividing up your business. But this time, things will play out smoothly, without any drama or conflict.

Many will have a great opportunity to attract new business partners from other cities or abroad, and the first steps in that direction might take place this month.

Employees might be discussing a bonus or raise with their managers, or even expanding their responsibilities at work.

For anything work-related, the best time is late April and the first ten days of May. From May 10 to June 3, Mercury, which is responsible for connections and contacts, will be in retrograde. There is nothing scary about this, but you can expect any advancements to slow down, and you may have to come back and reexamine some work-related issues.

Money. May is a good time for your finances. You have been busy all month, and now, it's paying off!

You might expect some injections of cash from business partners, bonuses, credit, or other material benefits. Those who are not part of the business world might expect help from loved ones who have recently gotten a raise or bonus.

Love and family. May will definitely be a time for you to focus on work, and your personal life might be on the back burner, right now, though you may also be busy with various real estate transactions, construction, or home renovations, which will be one more breakthrough in this area.

Couples going through a rough patch or those divorcing will be able to favorably resolve various material issues, for example, how to divide up their home.

The stars promise to give a green light to any relationship between couples who are getting along. Any trips planned for May will be very successful.

Health. In May, you are healthy, energetic, and ready to scale mountains, and it's all because you are on the right track.

Virgo

May brings with it many promises. Most of all, there are new paths, a different alignment, and a new way of looking at things. Right now, you might be fully aware of many things, and are coming close to resolving longstanding problems.

Work. May is a great time for establishing and strengthening your relationship with friends, colleagues, and business partners. You are now in a period in which group projects will bring you the most success, which means that respect for your partners will serve you well. What's more, this is the only way to develop your business and move ahead. Your motto this month is "safety in numbers".

Your connection with those abroad or faraway is developing positively, and you might go on a trip that will turn out to be positive, overall.

For anything work-related, the best time for you is the first ten days of the month. From May 10 to June 3, your ruler, Mercury, will be in retrograde, which will significantly hamper your plans and business.

You will have to clarify agreements with any colleagues from faraway, and there may even be changes to those agreements. There is nothing critical happening here, but there will be some questions to consider. You are also likely to encounter some length red tape.

Those with longstanding legal problems will need some additional consultations and to reconsider their previous positions, in order to make things happen in June.

Money. May brings a lot of ups and downs for your wallet. You might experience length negotiations with partners with regard to an influx of money into your shared business. Only the luckiest will receive the resources they need this month, and everyone else will have to wait until mid-June.

Those who are not part of the working world will be able to count on support from loved ones this month.

Love and family. Your personal life right now depends on what happened in the past, as well as your plans for the future.

Spouses who are getting along might go on a trip, which will be successful, if not joyful. The same goes for couples in a good relationship. Your spouse or a loved one will find success and be able to shoulder a lot.

But if you recently went through a rough patch, this month, you might have yet another conflict. Each of you will stick to your own position, and it will probably be over money, property, real estate, or your children's future.

In this case, the stars recommend that you don't try to resolve any issues from a position of force, but that you understand that the best fight is one that didn't happen.

In harmonious families, you will have plans related to real estate, and in some cases, you are likely to acquire a residence far away from your hometown. Right now, you are just making plans, but a lot of what you come up with now will come to fruition in the near future.

Health. In May, you are feeling fairly energetic and have no reason to fear any illnesses.

Libra

This month is a good time to take a deep breath and focus on the little details or various administrative tasks, both at home and at work.

Work. May is not a very promising time when it comes to major projects at work. It is worth focusing on administrative tasks, where you are facing a lot of difficulties.

Entrepreneurs and managers will have to monitor their employees, who are decisive and hardworking, right now. The main issue is that these qualities do have their limits, and making sure they are not working against what you had originally planned.

Jupiter is changing position, which means that very soon, you will be surrounded by new people. If you meet them between May 10 and June 3, though, be very careful- they will likely not be particularly useful, and may even turn out to be a source of trouble. However, your relationship with previous partners and friends might reach a new level of trust and understanding.

During this time, Mercury will be in retrograde, and based on thousands of years of astrological observations, this is a bad time for new acquaintances or signing any important documents. It might be a good time for you to slow down and keep going with something you started earlier, or simply take some vacation time.

Employees should remember that discipline, responsibility, and teamwork will go a long way. It might also be a good time for you to take a few days to work on the house or spend time with your children and family.

Money. May is not a bad time for your wallet. You might be receiving money from work you have done, as well as various unofficial sources.

Those who are not part of the business world can count on support from loved ones who are doing very well for themselves at work

You can count on the largest sums of money on May 1, 5, 6, 15-16, 23, 24, 28, and 29.

Love and family. Things in your personal life are going swimmingly. You might even strike a healthy balance between work and family life, this month. You have worked hard and done a lot, and it is finally time to think about those close to you. You might strengthen that harmonious relationship by taking a trip together.

Jupiter's shifting this month will mean wonderful news for single people. Very soon, your circle of friends will expand, and you will find someone who will turn out to be a major support for you in the long term.

But remember – that is not the case from May 10 to June 2. Mercury will be in retrograde, and any new people you meet during this period might turn out to bring nothing but disappointment. Remember, not all that glitters is gold, and be mindful.

Health. In May, you will occasionally feel down and unsure of yourself. When that happens, try taking a trip to your summer home, spending time in nature, or, if you can, get a massage on a tropical beach.

Scorpio

You are looking at a jam-packed and memorable month. Everything is moving, you have changes at work and at home. The stars predict that this time, everything that happens will be for the best.

Work. May might be a time of transition for you at work. You have new offers on the horizon, and some of them might already appear this month or shortly after.

For employees, that might be a new job, and for entrepreneurs, new and interesting offers. For now, it's all just plans, but they will turn into something more in the future. Things are promising, and it is worth keeping an eye on them.

Do not get frustrated if negotiations seem to drag on forever between May 10 and June 3. Mercury, which rules connections and contacts will be in retrograde during this time, and thousands of years of astrological traditions have shown that this is a time for discussions, making adjustments, and adapting projects. You can leave any major decision-making for later, when you have thought things through better and are absolutely sure you are being mature and reasonable.

Money. When it comes to money, May is not particularly notable. Nothing unusual will happen, and only the very luckiest Scorpios can count on a bonus or some additional income. The future is looking up, however, so don't lose hope, and the stars won't let you down!

Love and family. You can be sure that this month will be a lucky time when it comes to love. A series of eclipses will mean that couples will start thinking about marriage or living together. Most likely, this is something you will discuss in May, and some major decisions will come shortly after.

Couples with a good relationship will still be busy with their children, but find a lot of joy in it.

Things are a little less pleasant for Scorpios who find themselves caught between two worlds right now. If that is the case, you are going to have to make some difficult decisions, as the way things stand, you will not be able to keep things going much longer.

If Fate has placed you in a situation like this, listen to your inner voice, as it will not let you down! The stars predict you will choose your long-term partner or spouse. Of course, there are always exceptions to the rule, and the ball is in your court! The choice is yours!

Health. This month, you are feeling energetic and have no reason to fear falling ill. But in the future, your health and taking care of yourself will be a major part of your life, so the stars recommend thinking about that now.

Sagittarius

In May, you are so active that even your loved ones who are used to you are surprised. You are in constant motion, and making strides. But after all, you're a Sagittarius!

Work. May is a month of activity and hard work. You have some new tasks at hand, and you might end up so absorbed in it all that even if you take vacation time in May, you will spend the whole time either working or thinking about work!

Because of the way you are tackling business, unfinished tasks that seemed impossible to finish will either fade into the background or somehow end up settled.

Your relationship with colleagues from other cities or abroad will look calmer this month. You may occasionally see problems from the past reappearing, but you know what to do by now, so you are able to handle things.

The best time for anything work-related is the first ten days of May. This is the best time to plan any major events or meetings. From May 10 to June 3, Mercury will be in retrograde, which will lead to some setbacks at work, the people you need being absent, and red tape.

This is a time to sit back and really focus on what you need to do while making any necessary adjustments. Be patient – later, you will be able to keep moving forward with things. If you are sure that you can handle it and you have enough time, maybe take some time off to relax.

Money. May is a great time for your finances. You will be receiving regular income, and significantly more of it, too. In addition to your usual salary, you can count on additional profits from various real estate transactions. You can also expect support from parents or loved ones.

Love and family. Your personal life is also abuzz with activity, this month. Most likely, you are busy building a home, remodeling your apartment, and all of this toil and trouble is finally coming to a blissful end.

Your children are a source of joy, and they are starting a new, much happier and favorable period, which you will start to notice very soon.

Single people are starting a new, exciting period, as well. You can expect new love, which will leave you feeling very content. The luckiest Sagittarians will see this happen in May, while others will have to wait until the summer of 2022.

Health. In May, you are not feeling particularly energetic, so try to find the time to relax, and if you can't, at least get enough sleep, and spend some time in nature on the weekends.

Capricorn

You're going to need to take a breather in May. The ongoing frenzy at work and at home might be causing you a lot of stress. Things will be easier if you take a moment to look around at all the changes in your life and let go of the idea that everything will come to a halt without you.

Work. This is not the greatest time for you at work, with the exception of those working in the arts – actors, artists, singers, or musicians, who are enjoying a wave of attention from audiences, as well as creative inspiration.

Everyone else might consider taking some vacation time and heading to a warm, sunny beach, as the opportunity will arise. It is only the most incorrigible workaholics who will continue to be busy with work, both networking and tackling administrative tasks.

Many Capricorns will make plans related to acquiring or renting real estate. For not, it's all still in the planning stage, but in the very near future, you will see it come to life. In several cases, that will happen in another city or abroad.

You will have many opportunities in May to prove yourself, the way everyone knows you are capable of doing. But remember that from May 10 to June 3, Mercury will be in retrograde, and this is not a good time for signing major contracts or any decision-making. The best thing you can do is think things through and carefully study your plans. If that isn't what you need right now, then just sit back and relax.

Money. When it comes to finances, May is not the best time for you. You will be spending constantly, and in many cases, that is related to your family, and possibly romance. At the very least, you are enjoying the money you are spending, and notably enjoying life.

Love and family. You are seeing a lot of changes in your personal life. Couples who get along are once again thinking about acquiring real estate, and in some cases, that might take place in another city or abroad.

Divorcing spouses will be able to favorably divide their property and plan on moving.

Those who are unable to reach a decision might finally do so, though it will probably not be an easy one. Sometimes, there is a huge gap between your desires and your duty, and you will have to cross it

Many people will travel in May, and the trip will be a success.

Health. All month, you are active, energetic, and incredibly charming, which will be noticed by anyone Fate places on your path. May is a good time for shopping, relaxing, and other adventures. You aren't really thinking much about your health right now, which is always an indication that all is well.

Aquarius

May is a time for you to sit back and take a look around. You can forget about work for a moment, and focus on your home and family. After all, we don't live to work, we work to live!

Work. The most stubborn workaholics who are convinced that everything will come to a standstill without them, might be busy with various everyday administrative tasks in May. You might be finalizing some real estate issues that have been troubling you or resolving some difficult financial matters. This is the case for managers and entrepreneurs at every level.

Even if they remain at work, employees will find their minds constantly wandering to their personal life and family, so the stars recommend taking a few days off and doing what you really want to be doing, right now.

From May 10 to June 3, Mercury will be in retrograde, which means this is a bad time to be signing any important documents, starting a new business, or even meeting new people. Any major deals might be held up for various reasons, for example, the people you need will suddenly be unavailable.

Money. Your bank account is looking healthy, this month. You will be getting income regularly, and not only from your employment. Many Aquarians will receive a handsome profit from real estate transactions, support from your parents, or loved ones.

An inheritance is looking very likely.

Expect to receive the largest amounts on May 1, 5, 6, 15, 16, 23, 24, and 27-29.

Love and family. Many Aquarians are going to be immersed in their home and family life, this month. You might see some real estate transactions – some will be getting a home, apartment, or summer home in order, others will be selling or acquiring a new residence.

Many will also make plans related to a move to another city or even abroad, but for now, things are in the planning stages, and will become a reality sometime during 2022 or 2023.

The best time for meeting new romantic partners is the first ten days of the month. During this time, single people might meet someone special while traveling or among friends who have come from faraway. From May 10 to June 3, you might run into old friends, former flames, and just people you haven't seen in a long time.

Your relationship with relatives will get much better, and you might even meet up with those who have been living in another city or abroad.

Health. This month, you are feeling fairly energetic and have no reason to fear falling ill. You might start gaining weight, so watch your diet and make sure to exercise regularly. Take some long walks in nature.

Pisces

This month, you can expect to keep charging further ahead. You're moving forward!

Work. In May, many Pisceans will have to choose which is more important to them – work or their personal lives. That will not be an easy decision, as success guaranteed no matter what direction you go.

You are looking at some great days for work in May, and you can count on actively developing your relationships with those in other cities or abroad, as well as a successful business trip. Those experiencing longstanding problems in this part of their lives will be able to change things around and make them as favorable as possible.

The best time for any work-related events is the first ten days of May. During the rest of the month, Mercury will be in retrograde, which means that you will have to repeatedly come back to various issues, and be very careful and attentive as you study them. Despite the setbacks, things will be looking good, thanks to your hard work, dedication, and diplomacy.

Money. Your finances are stable, with a clear upward trend that many will see that start to notice in May, while for others it will be a bit later. Powerful Jupiter is in the financial sector of your sky, and all year that means that materially speaking, you will reach a new level and stay there for the long term.

Love and family. Your personal life is looking just as good as work, this month. Couples and spouses will go on a trip together, and it is going to be a great success. Recent romances will start to develop, and any misunderstandings from previous months will gradually fade away. Of course, that is going to require some effort on your part, but you are certainly up to the task.

The best time to meet new people is the first ten days of May, while May 10 to June 3 is a better time for reconnecting with those from your past. You might run into an old flame you haven't seen in a while, or perhaps an old friend.

Your relationship with relatives will become much more active, and you might see family members who now live in other cities or abroad.

Health. All month, you are feeling energetic and have no reason to fear falling ill.

June

New York Time		
Calendar Day	Lunar Day	Lunar Day Start Time
01/06/2022	3	7:00 AM
02/06/2022	4	7:53 AM
03/06/2022	5	8:49 AM
04/06/2022	6	9:48 AM
05/06/2022	7	10:48 AM
06/06/2022	8	11:49 AM
07/06/2022	9	12:51 PM
08/06/2022	10	1:55 PM
09/06/2022	11	3:01 PM
10/06/2022	12	4:10 PM
11/06/2022	13	5:22 PM
12/06/2022	14	6:37 PM
13/06/2022	15	7:50 PM
14/06/2022	16	8:58 PM
15/06/2022	17	9:58 PM
16/06/2022	18	10:47 PM
17/06/2022	19	11:28 PM
19/06/2022	20	12:03 AM
20/06/2022	21	12:33 AM
21/06/2022	22	1:00 AM
22/06/2022	23	1:27 AM
23/06/2022	24	1:54 AM
24/06/2022	25	2:23 AM
25/06/2022	26	2:54 AM
26/06/2022	27	3:30 AM
27/06/2022	28	4:11 AM
28/06/2022	29	4:57 AM
28/06/2022	1	10:53 PM
29/06/2022	2	5:48 AM
30/06/2022	3	6:43 AM

London Time		
Calendar Day	Lunar Day	Lunar Day Start Time
01/06/2022	3	6:09 AM
02/06/2022	4	7:02 AM
03/06/2022	5	8:02 AM
04/06/2022	6	9:06 AM
05/06/2022	7	10:14 AM
06/06/2022	8	11:23 AM
07/06/2022	9	12:33 PM
08/06/2022	10	1:45 PM
09/06/2022	11	3:00 PM
10/06/2022	12	4:18 PM
11/06/2022	13	5:39 PM
12/06/2022	14	7:03 PM
13/06/2022	15	8:24 PM
14/06/2022	16	9:36 PM
15/06/2022	17	10:35 PM
16/06/2022	18	11:20 PM
17/06/2022	19	11:54 PM
19/06/2022	20	12:20 AM
20/06/2022	21	12:42 AM
21/06/2022	22	1:01 AM
22/06/2022	23	1:19 AM
23/06/2022	24	1:38 AM
24/06/2022	25	1:58 AM
25/06/2022	26	2:21 AM
26/06/2022	27	2:49 AM
27/06/2022	28	3:24 AM
28/06/2022	29	4:06 AM
29/06/2022	1	3:53 AM
29/06/2022	2	4:56 AM
30/06/2022	3	5:54 AM

You can find the description of each lunar day in the chapter "A Guide to The Moon Cycle and Lunar Days"

Aries

Life is taking a series of turns, but don't worry, once this kaleidoscope of events is over, you'll be out in front of it again!

Work. June is a time of changes. And remember, changes bring new opportunities with them!

Jupiter is a powerful driver of success, and it is now in your sign, which means that the goals you have been striving toward are now a reality.

Those who are busy expanding their business might finally conclude the most important administrative tasks that a project like this entails. Going forward, you are entering a comfortable and very successful period during which everything you have dedicated so much effort and so many resources is coming to fruition and will become profitable in time.

Employees will have a good opportunity to change their job for something better, and this month, some old friends or someone highly placed might lend a helping hand in that endeavor.

The luckiest Aries will see the positive changes this month, while others will have to wait just a bit longer. The most important thing, though, is that things are looking up, and expected to continue this way in the future.

You are reconnecting with colleagues in other cities and might go on a successful trip. Many things are unclear, right now, and you can once again expect some complications by the fall of 2022. So, keep a close eye on the situation, and look for the weak links. The stars predict that they are the same ones you dealt with in the recent past.

The best time for anything work-related is the second ten days of June. Plan anything important for this period.

Money. Your finances are looking stable, and money will be coming in regularly, in significantly larger amounts. You can't escape expenses, but the majority of them will be reasonable and perhaps even enjoyable. Expect the largest sums on June 2, 3, 7, 8, 15, 16, and 23-25.

Love and family. Everything in your personal life is going obscenely well for you. You are not experiencing any turbulence in your family, and your relationship with close relatives is great. You might go on a trip and see old friends or make new ones.

Single people might really feel the powerful influence of Jupiter in June, when their lives seem to change, effortlessly. You might meet someone this month who will become very dear to you. You might also meet them on a trip or among people who have come from faraway.

One piece of advice – don't rush things, and don't pressure those close to you – let your relationship develop at its own pace, and trust in the stars – they are guiding you right to where you need to go.

Health. This month, you are energetic, healthy, and witty, as well as very attractive, and everyone around you is taking note.

Taurus

Jupiter is shifting, and that is really causing changes in your life. The time has come to sit back, look around, and strengthen your foothold in all the milestones you have achieved.

Work. Over the last several years, you have worked hard, and an important period in your professional life is coming to an end. You are turning the page, and the next chapter will be no less important or labor-intensive. Just like a solder digging trenches before a major battle, you're strengthening your grip. You are about to leap forward, probably in the next year and a half or so, and right now, you are laying the necessary groundwork to turn that into a reality.

Entrepreneurs and managers will be expanding their business and carrying out various real estate transactions. For now, things might still be in the planning phase, but in the next year, they will likely come to life.

It seems that employees have done everything they can where they are right now, and they need to ponder the road they have taken and hold on for what's next. You might end up with more time for yourself, loved ones, and it is worth enjoying it now, as 2023 will be a time for you to charge ahead, once again. If you are thinking about changing jobs, your search is likely to drag on a bit. There is still a chance to stay right where you are.

Money. Your finances in June are stable, but that is all. You will not see any major financial achievements this month, but you also won't have any big glosses. You might see some minor improvements closer to the end of June, and that is a positive trend that will continue through July. Expect the largest sums to come in on June 9, 10, 17, 18, 26, and 27.

Love and family. You are also seeing a lot of changes in your personal life. Many Taureans will be thinking about a new place to live, acquiring new real estate or major renovations where they live now. The idea of a new place is on most Taureans' minds, but there are many reasons why that might be the case! Couples who get along will be thinking about an addition, or maybe considering a convenient location in their neighborhood. Others will want to buy an apartment for their children.

Couples who are divorcing might finally resolve something – who needs what, and from whom. This time, you might have plans related to separation. In general, though, this is a fairly quiet month.

Health. In June, you are feeling fairly energetic and have no reason to fear any illnesses. You may experience some rough waters ahead, when you are likely to feel mood swings and periodic low self-esteem. You should be especially attentive if you are elderly or weakened, as during the second half of 2022, you might experience a new flare-up of old illnesses, or unexpected new ones.

Gemini

Your ruler, Mercury, which changes rage into mercy, and is now moving in a straight line. Together with it, you are able to change your life – naturally, for the better!

Work. You will continue to see gains at work. You will have people around you who you can count on. Old friends, someone who is highly placed and wishes you well, and new acquaintances will lend a hand and their influence this month, which might turn out very well for you.

Employees can be sure to strengthen their position in a new job. If you haven't found a new job yet, your search will continue.

The best time for any professional matters is after June 10. During this time, you might go on a trip, or reconnect with a former business partner living in another city or abroad. Missed connections you made in the recent past will also resurface and turn out to be useful.

Money. Despite the series of professional victories this month, money is going to be a bit of an unexpected problem. Everything will go as planned, but the stars predict that you might have more expenses than usual – though they will be reasonable and enjoyable alike. You might have to spend on your children, loved ones, or maybe a fun night out. You might also end up spending on "hospitality expenses" or resolving day-to-day issues.

Love and family. Everything is as it should be in your family right now. You might be doing some minor home repairs, buying furniture or other materials necessary to make your day-to-day life a bit more beautiful. Your relationship with your spouse is harmonious – you are happy and supporting together, turning to your wisdom and undying love. Long-term couples are experiencing something similar.

Single people might start a casual romance, without even attempting to look for Mr. or Mrs. Right. They will come on their own – from your circle of friends, colleagues, and acquaintances.

Health. In June, you are healthy, energetic, and ready for progress at home and at work.

Cancer

Jupiter is moving high in your sector of the sky, and that changes everything – for the better. The coming years will be best of the last decade, so get ready to see your long-awaited success become a reality.

Work. This month, you are enthusiastic when it comes to your projects, and have no doubt that they will turn out as you have hoped. You don't have much left to do, just some preparations and administrative tasks, in order to really get your ambitious plans off the ground.

A relationship you have with some people has, for various reasons, become a bit of a problem, but is now looking better. You might gradually be taking care of old debts, both moral and material. Some of the issues will be overcome this month, while others will take longer, but everything that has been bothering you recently will soon be taken care of forever.

Employees might be negotiating a new job in a different, more promising organization, or getting a promotion where they currently work. These negotiations are sure to be a success, if not this month, then in the near future.

Money. Your financial situation is looking good, this month. You are having money coming in regularly, and there is significantly more of it. Expect to receive the largest amounts on June 4, 5, 13-15, 21, and 22.

Love and family. Though June is a busy time for your social calendar and at work, your personal life is not falling by the wayside, either. Any time is a good time to start a new romance, so don't be a wallflower and try to always look your best.

Many believe that real love needs to be wild, passionate, and sweep away anything in its path. However, right now, you need something else, something less crazy. You need someone to take care of you, warm your heart, and provide you with gentleness.

You can expect some key developments in your love life in mid-summer, but while things are quiet, just have trust in Fate.

Spouses in a stable marriage will see some things improving in their family situation, both morally and materially.

Health. This month, you will probably feel a lot of ups and downs. You can expect cheerfulness to alternate with periods of lethargy and apathy. When that happens, the stars recommend that you spend some time in nature and make sure to get enough sleep.

Leo

The best path is forward, especially for you. In the next three years, you can expect nothing but onward and upward!

Work. You will continue seeing success at work. In June, many problems will appear to be resolved – the road is wide open for you! Entrepreneurs and managers will be busy with some lucrative work that will lead to a tangible, financial payoff. Employees might negotiate a new job that will be much better than the last one.

Your problems with managers or partners were a feature of 2021 and the first few months of 2022, but soon, that will all be behind you. By the fall of this year, you may have to come back to a few of these issues once again, so resolve everything you can right now. Things will turn out much better for you, in the end.

Many Leos will have an opportunity to cooperate with colleagues in other cities or abroad. For now, things are just in the initial stages, but you can expect further development next year. If you have any similar plans, remember that any seeds planted this month are sure to sprout in the future.

Overall, June is just one small part of a much larger process Fate has created for you. Follow in Fate's direction, and believe in your own success!

Money. Financially speaking, June will be favorable for you. You will have money coming in regularly, and significantly more of it. You can expect the largest sums on June 6, 7, 15-17, and 23-25. You will not have any major expenses, anything you do spend is both predictable and reasonable.

Love and family. This month, your work and finances may take precedence over your personal life. If you really can't stand a month without love at all, then remember that June is the best time for reconnecting with old ties. Divorced people or others who aren't getting along with their spouses will be able to find a common language on at least some of the thorny issues they are dealing with. Might you reconcile? Not yet. Though that doesn't mean you should just sit back and do nothing. Try to take the first step, maybe the results will surprise you. That goes for those who need to resolve various material issues, problems concerning your children, and those who for various reasons are trying to get their relationship back on track.

In families where your other half is going through tough times, you will have an opportunity to improve things.

Single people might start an office romance or a relationship with someone from their circle of friends.

Health. You are healthy and energetic in June, as well as sociable and very charming. It's up to you how you use all these features.

Virgo

June is an interesting month that is full of changes. It seems that you are on an enthusiastic, promising path, and there is no end or edge to it.

Work. This month, entrepreneurs and managers will be negotiating with a partner about making a financial investment in their business. This is a difficult process, and this time, it might go smoothly enough because the hard part is already finished, and you have come so far already.

You might be actively meeting with partners from other cities or abroad, and a successful trip is also a possibility.

Employees will be able to strengthen their position both materially and professionally at their current job, and think about a new offer for their talents. For now, this is just an idea or a wish, but the future will show that your ideas will come to life. It is unlikely to take place in 2022, but nothing is preventing you from making plans and considering what sort of prospects are out there. That will mean remaining where you are, while getting ready for the future, which you can already start to make out through the endless, yet ultimately fair test of time.

Money. Financially, you are going strong. There is an upward trend this month, and in some cases, that is related to financial support from business partners, while in others, you will receive credit on very favorable terms.

Those who are not part of the business world can count on support from a loved one who is experiencing growth.

Love and family. Your personal life is changing. Many Virgos have plans related to obtaining a new residence, and in some cases, that major event might be in another city or even abroad. In the humblest of cases, that might be a small cottage outside of town or a large home. Things might still be in the planning phase, though they will come to life in 2022.

Couples and spouses might spend time traveling together, which will strengthen their relationship.

Recent romances are picking up steam and getting to the point where you want to start thinking about the future.

Many families are thinking about having more children, and the second half of 2022 is probably the most favorable time for this.

This is also a good time for studying, considering plans for the future, and defining your positions both at work and at home.

Health. In June, you are energetic, but looking ahead, many Virgos, especially those who are elderly or weakened, should be attentive to their bodies and take measures to protect themselves from old, chronic diseases.

Libra

Jupiter is shifting in the sky, and once again that is leading to changes in your life. This has both pluses and minuses, and it's out of your hands – that's life!

Work. This month, you are seeing new opportunities open their doors. The astrologist predicts that many of them will be related to your business partners who will support you both morally and materially. You can rest assured that their role in your business will be a positive thing. Despite the obvious good will of your colleagues, as well as their responsibility, there might sometimes be feelings of dependence, which in these situations, is only natural, though it is not always the most pleasant thing.

If that is the case, remember, safety in numbers, and whenever possible, sit down and carefully discuss the terms of future cooperation.

Your ties with colleagues from other cities or abroad are moving along nicely, and you might take a successful trip in June.

Money. Your financial position is stable, though you are getting most of your income from business partners, and possibly some interest-free credit. Those who are not part of the business world can count on help from a loved one who is currently on a lucky streak at work.

Love and family. Many Libras will be focused on events at home, involving their family or romantic relationships.

Spouses who are getting along will take on important household tasks together and resolve them. Fortunately, the costs will be covered by a loved one who is on an unusually positive streak and ready to share their success with the whole family.

Single people and those who have been let down by relationships in the past will meet new people in their social circles, you might start an interesting romance, and it might end in marriage.

Those who are in a relationship might make things permanent.

Any trips you take in June are likely to be unusually successful and strengthen your relationship, whether you are married or not.

Health. In June, you are healthy, energetic, charming, and witty. Everyone Fate places on your path is noticing, too. You will forget about your health for a bit, which is usually a good sign that all is well.

Scorpio

June is a pretty good month for you. You will be good to others, and they will respond in kind.

Work. Beneficial Jupiter is now in the professional sector of your sky, and that can lead to a lot of changes for you at work.

Entrepreneurs and managers will launch new projects and take on new employees. Employees will be thinking about a new job and start taking steps in that direction. The luckiest Scorpios will see success this month, already, while others will have to wait a bit longer. Jupiter never does anything halfway, and leaves its mark everywhere. Even if you have been unemployed for a while, don't have much experience, and aren't exactly confident, take the first step, and Jupiter will take care of the rest.

All month, you will run into kind people, and you will show yourself to be an excellent companion and negotiator.

The best time for any professional matters is June 4 to 16, and this is probably when most work events will take place, too.

Money. Your finances are modest this month, but also stable. You probably won't see any major income, but you have a lot of promise, and you won't be disappointed later on. Expect the largest sums on June 4, 5, 13, 14, and 21-23.

Love and family. June is a favorable time for your personal life, too. You can expect success and accolades this month. Though you might be consumed with work, no one is an island, especially you! Your longstanding relationships will take on a new level of intimacy, understanding, and trust, while single people should be more attentive when considering new acquaintances. An office romance is likely, especially if you just started a new job or are beginning one this month.

Health. Take care of yourself, both this month and later on. Your mood might swing from cheerful to lethargic. That is especially the case if you are elderly or weakened, so the stars recommend taking measures to protect yourself from chronic diseases and don't test yourself.

Young and healthy Scorpios can get away with leading a healthy lifestyle, remembering to get exercise, and sleeping enough. You are beginning a period in which many will be thinking about changing up their habits, a new image, or a new wardrobe. As a result, you can expect a lot of positive changes, of course.

Sagittarius

Your life is changing and becoming more interesting, easier, and fun. You have worked a lot, and now, just like Cinderella, it's your chance to go to the ball.

Work. June is a great time for you at work. Entrepreneurs and managers will finish up some projects that have been keeping you busy, and might think about a new start. This may involve reconsidering your staff and hire some new colleagues. They will be reliable and helpful in many areas.

Employees might begin negotiating a raise, this will turn out well for you. Alternatively, you might receive a job offer in a new, more promising company.

Your connections with others will be another positive side of June. You will have new partners and an inspiring relationship with your current colleagues, which will be easy, natural, and naturally good-willed. You will prove yourself a skilled negotiator and capable of convincing anyone of anything.

You will also begin connecting more with colleagues from other cities or abroad, and might go on a successful trip.

Money. When it comes to money, June is a lucky time for you. You will see great opportunities to improve your financial situation, and this is the case for all Sagittarians, regardless of your field. You might get a raise, bonus, or profits from projects you completed earlier, or partial payment for new ideas. Expect the largest sums on June 6-8, 13, 14, 24, and 25.

Love and family. June is a good time for your personal life, too. If you have a family, the most important events this month will involve your children, who are healthy and behaving well if they are small, and finally on the right path toward prosperity and development if they are already grown up.

Most Sagittarians can expect success and attention all month long. You will be surrounded by a lot of people, and attend a lot of events, parties, and other celebrations. So, if you are aiming for stardom, now is the time!

If you are feeling in the mood for romance, you can count on new acquaintances, and an exciting romance with an unpredictable end. This is great for single people, but it will complicate your life if you already have a long-term partner. The ball is in your court, and the stars will offer you their advice, but how things end is up to you. You might go on a trip which will be very successful and expand your social circle.

Health. In June, you are energetic, witty, and incredibly sexually attractive. You might feel a little less confident at the end of the month, during the new moon on June 29 and 30. During these days, you might feel tired from work, meetings, and dealing with others. In July, you can finally relax and actually enjoy the calm.

Capricorn

In June you might find yourself facing a dilemma – which is more important? Your personal life or work? The heavens response is both. After all, you are successful, wherever you are!

Work. This month, you'll have a lot on your plate at work, and most of it will involve administrative tasks. Entrepreneurs and managers of every level will be (once again!) thinking about expanding their business, and that is going to require considering paying reasonable rent or acquiring real estate. In certain cases, that might take place in another city or abroad. In June, you might start taking the first steps in this direction, though for now, things are in the planning and ideas phase. Whatever you have in the works now will pay off in the future.

Changes in your workplace also be affecting employees. Generally speaking, nothing bad is going to happen, but you might end up with more work than usual.

In some cases, you will decide you want to open your own business, and you will have a lot of activities related to that. If that is you, the stars promise to give you the green light and recommend doing things now, as you won't find a better time!

Money. Your finances are modest, but stable. Money will be coming in regularly, but you might face a lot of expenses, too. In some cases, this will be work-related and due to expanding your business, while in others, your personal life is the culprit.

Love and family. Your personal life might be just as busy as work, this month. In families, you will continue to see problems related to real estate, and in some cases, related to your children. This is not the first time you have thought about how to equip your children for life, but this time, things are really happening.

Alternatively, you might be acquiring a residence, and this might be related to a move to another city or abroad. Less optimistically, you might be carrying out a lot of real estate transactions, possibly due to a divorce, dividing up your property, particularly your place of residence. After the torment of the last two years – 2020 and 2021, this will end peacefully, after all. For now, things are still in the planning stages, but they are likely to come to fruition in 2023.

A love story that might have been stagnating for some time is gaining momentum. Once you reach this important stage in your relationship, you might start thinking about the future, and possibly living together. Though there is still time to consider it, there can be no question that things are moving in this direction.

Health. In June, your abundance of worries will mean that you often feel tired and lethargic. In order to avoid that, remember to follow a daily routine and get exercise every morning. Sometimes, the smallest things can be more effective than medication or a trip to the doctor's office. This is one of those times.

Aquarius

In June, the door to the future is opening, but very soon, you will see what is behind it. You have a real chance at changing your life, and nothing is stopping you from grabbing the brass ring.

Work. The challenges that you dealt with in the past are finally resolved. Entrepreneurs and managers resolve thorny issues involving real estate, land, or other major property.

Employees will be able to carry out their longstanding plans, especially if they are related to travel to different places and countries. Your ties with colleagues from faraway are developing, and this is the main trend this month.

You will reconnect with former partners, and are likely to meet some new colleagues, as well. You can expect a successful trip, as well as plans related to a move, such as working in another city or abroad.

Money. Your finances are stable right now. In addition to your usual income, many Aquarians will also receive additional profits from various real estate transactions. You might also get help from parents, a spouse, or an elderly family member.

Love and family. When it comes to personal matters, you can expect to run into people from your ancient past. An old flame might suddenly show up, but the relationship is unlikely to last for long. Right now, you are looking ahead, and aren't very interested in the past.

In addition to former relationships in mid-June you are also likely to meet someone new. Generally speaking, you won't be bored, as single people with a thirst for adventure are assured a tumultuous personal life, this month.

People with a stable family life will be busy with children, as well as day-to-day issues that piled up over the spring.

Your relationship with relatives has been difficult recently, and things are looking up. Many Aquarians will spend the year making up with a hostile relative.

Both married and unmarried couples might go on a trip in June, and it will be a great success. Some Aquarians will make plans related to moving in 2023, and things will be looking favorable.

This is a good month for studying, especially if you plan to do it in another city or abroad.

Health. This month, your energy levels are high, and you have no reason to fear any diseases. On the contrary, you are feeling so cheerful you will energize anyone you come across.

Pisces

"Happiness isn't about Money., but a lot of Money.". That sums up an interesting period that will begin this month and continue for at least three years. After a long break, the stars are finally opening the path toward material success!

Work. Some favorable changes that began in the recent past are continuing, and you are benefiting from them. Entrepreneurs and managers are thinking about expanding their business, and this month, you will be making the first steps in that direction. You might acquire or rent a space for that, which will also entail a lot of administrative tasks.

You might find yourself opening a business in another city or abroad. Your relationship with colleagues from out of town or abroad will grow, and many Pisceans can expect to take a trip this month. You have a great opportunity to expand your circle and will be meeting new people, while also reconnecting with former colleagues.

Employees might get a raise where they work, and if that is not possible, they will begin seeking a new place for their talents. This is highly likely! Keep in mind that you are beginning a new period in which material ambitions are likely to be met, and act accordingly.

Money. Many Pisceans will be entirely focused on money, and for a good reason! In June, your financial situation will likely improve. You may receive a raise, or possibly profits from completed projects, a bonus, or support from loved ones.

You have low expenses this month and all of them will be compensated by your handsome profits.

Love and family. There are also changes in your personal life. A passionate romance might come to a natural conclusion – either marriage or living together.

With regard to that, couples will be thinking about a new home together – either buying one or renting. Alternatively, you might move to another city or abroad, where your love awaits.

Those with a family might find themselves moving to a new home, possibly even in another city. If this is all just an idea in June, then you are likely to make it happen later this year.

Any thorny relationships with relatives are close to being resolved, and most likely, you can deal with the most difficult issues now.

Health. In June, you are feeling a bit sluggish, so take care of yourself and remember, moderation is the key. You might have a tendency to gain weight, so try to get some exercise and follow a balanced diet. These recommendations go for any Piscean, especially those who in some way or another are prone to diabetes.

July

New York Time		
Calendar Day	Lunar Day	Lunar Day Start Time
01/07/2022	4	7:41 AM
02/07/2022	5	8:41 AM
03/07/2022	6	9:41 AM
04/07/2022	7	10:42 AM
05/07/2022	8	11:44 AM
06/07/2022	9	12:47 PM
07/07/2022	10	1:53 PM
08/07/2022	11	3:01 PM
09/07/2022	12	4:13 PM
10/07/2022	13	5:25 PM
11/07/2022	14	6:35 PM
12/07/2022	15	7:40 PM
13/07/2022	16	8:35 PM
14/07/2022	17	9:21 PM
15/07/2022	18	9:59 PM
16/07/2022	19	10:32 PM
17/07/2022	20	11:02 PM
18/07/2022	21	11:29 PM
19/07/2022	22	11:57 PM
21/07/2022	23	12:25 AM
22/07/2022	24	12:56 AM
23/07/2022	25	1:31 AM
24/07/2022	26	2:10 AM
25/07/2022	27	2:54 AM
26/07/2022	28	3:43 AM
27/07/2022	29	4:37 AM
28/07/2022	30	5:35 AM
28/07/2022	1	1:55 PM
29/07/2022	2	6:34 AM
30/07/2022	3	7:35 AM
31/07/2022	4	8:36 AM

London Time		
Calendar Day	Lunar Day	Lunar Day Start Time
01/07/2022	4	6:57 AM
02/07/2022	5	8:04 AM
03/07/2022	6	9:12 AM
04/07/2022	7	10:22 AM
05/07/2022	8	11:32 AM
06/07/2022	9	12:44 PM
07/07/2022	10	1:58 PM
08/07/2022	11	3:15 PM
09/07/2022	12	4:35 PM
10/07/2022	13	5:56 PM
11/07/2022	14	7:12 PM
12/07/2022	15	8:18 PM
13/07/2022	16	9:10 PM
14/07/2022	17	9:50 PM
15/07/2022	18	10:20 PM
16/07/2022	19	10:45 PM
17/07/2022	20	11:05 PM
18/07/2022	21	11:25 PM
19/07/2022	22	11:43 PM
21/07/2022	23	12:03 AM
22/07/2022	24	12:26 AM
23/07/2022	25	12:52 AM
24/07/2022	26	1:25 AM
25/07/2022	27	2:04 AM
26/07/2022	28	2:52 AM
27/07/2022	29	3:47 AM
28/07/2022	30	4:49 AM
28/07/2022	1	6:55 PM
29/07/2022	2	5:55 AM
30/07/2022	3	7:04 AM
31/07/2022	4	8:13 AM

You can find the description of each lunar day in the chapter “A Guide to The Moon Cycle and Lunar Days”

Aries

In July, you will have to make a choice - which is more important to you? Your personal and family life, or, as usual, work? The planets might point toward the former, but, as usual, the ball is in your court.

Work. You might be so used to focusing on work that you can't imagine living differently. That is the case, right now – most Aries will find themselves torn between work and family.

Tireless entrepreneurs will be successfully finishing up major projects related to expanding their business, including other issues related to real estate and financial problems. Right now, everything is running extremely smoothly and predictably.

Your connections with colleagues in other cities or abroad are moving along nicely, and everything in this area is developing surprisingly well. Right now, benevolent and powerful Jupiter is with you, and it will support you, inspire you, and send any problems away, no matter how complicated they are. However, your partners abroad may not be as reliable as they seem right now, so keep that in mind and be cautious.

Money. Your finances are very important for you, as the ideas and projects that are keeping you busy right now require investments, and that will turn out to be more than you had initially planned. But if you need anything, you have friends, loved ones, and elderly family members there to support you. You can expect to receive the largest sums of money on July 4, 5, 13, 14, 21, and 22.

Love and family. Everything in your personal life is looking good. Many families are finishing up home improvements, and the hard part is likely behind you. You may have some minor quarrels with your spouse in July, probably related to household chores.

The stars recommend that the most stubborn Aries learn to be more flexible and compliant. Accept that you are not always right, and learn how to listen to your loved ones' wishes. This also goes for couples, especially if you are deciding whether to live together.

Any trips planned in July will be incredibly successful. Venus, the planet of love, is in the sector of the sky responsible for travel, as well as for social networks. This means that single people can count on meeting someone among people who have come from far away, or possibly on a dating site.

Health. This month, your energy potential is a bit low, but you don't have to worry about any illnesses. Sometimes you will feel like taking it easy, sleeping in, and relaxing among loved ones. Listen to your body, and don't fall into the trap of thinking things will fall apart without you. You deserve a break!

Taurus

July might bring a lot of ups and downs. Some things will improve, while others will seem to falter. Nonetheless, the positive influence is much greater than the negative, which is always a plus!

Work. Mars is in your sign, and supported by Uranus, which means that you are bounding with energy and ambition. You are most focused on a relationship with someone from another city or colleagues abroad, which will also become your greatest problem, this month. Entrepreneurs and managers might run into obstacles, which will require a lot of effort on their part, in order to get things back on track. Generally, this will pan out for you, so keep things in check and remember, you can't win if you don't try!

Employees will not see any major changes underway, but it may be worth strengthening your position and also keep an eye on your colleagues – there might be gossip and intrigue. Your relationship with your managers will improve, so there are no serious problems on the horizon.

Money. Your finances look great, this month, and you will see money coming in regularly, at higher volumes than usual. In addition to your usual income, you might have some unofficial earnings. The stars do not recommend breaking any financial laws, but during the second half of 2022, you might suddenly be subject to unexpected audits, so keep that in mind.

Expect the greatest sums on July 6, 7, 14, 15, 23, and 24.

Love and family. Things might look up and down in your personal life, this month. Revolutionary Uranus, which is firmly in your zodiac sign, demands change. Under its influence, harmonious couples might really shake up their family lives. Closer to the end of the month, you might continue to think about a new house, apartment, or building a summer house. By August, many Taureans will already have begun changing their lives, while the others will follow somewhat later.

Those who have recently decided to divorce or separate will think about a new place to live in other, less pleasant circumstances.

Couples' relationships are reaching the point when they will start to think about living together. That idea might come to life in the future, but is currently on your mind.

It is very likely that any travel in July is not going to go as you hoped and expected so it is worth making iron-clad plans.

Your relationship with relatives is going to get somewhat more complicated. In some cases, that may be due to ongoing misunderstandings, or possibly a blowout. Alternatively, a relative may be facing problems and you will have to help out, both morally and financially.

Health. In July, you are energetic, though the stars recommend being careful when traveling or behind the wheel.

Gemini

It seems you've found the path to the top. A whole range of opportunities awaits, and it's worth getting to know better!

Work. You're going to be spending the gorgeous summer days devoted to work, but this will pay off in the end. Recent projects that you began in the recent past will continue running smoothly. New people are on your horizon, and they may provide you with all kinds of support. You are constantly meeting new people, and you need to separate the wheat from the chaff – that is, understand what new acquaintances want from you, and what you expect to get from them in return.

Your relationship with colleagues in other cities or abroad is continuing to move along nicely, and you may reconnect with some old acquaintances. You might take a trip that will lead to good, practical results.

Employees are gradually strengthening their position at a new job, and here you will be able to discuss your salary with managers, along with some other privileges. At the end of the month, you may have promising negotiations with representatives from companies in other cities or abroad.

Money. Your financial situation is expected to have a lot of ups and downs in July. It's not that you won't have any income, but that some of your expenses are going to be high. You might be spending money on various things related to your loved ones' needs. You might also see a lot of "hospitality expenses," especially if you are an entrepreneur. At the same time, your income will go up again, so closer to the end of the month, you will be back to a healthy balance, again. Expect the largest amounts on July 8, 9, 16, 17, 26, and 27.

Love and family. Venus will be in your sign for almost all of July, which means that you will not face any turbulence in your personal life. Those who are already in a romantic relationship will be able to make things more permanent. If you are still single, you can expect to meet someone promising in July.

Spouses and couples alike might take a trip together near the end of the month, and it will be a smashing success. In early and mid-July, many Geminis might in some way or another improve their homes or daily routines.

Health. In July, you are feeling energetic and have no reason to fear falling ill. If you want to improve your health, though, take some time to relax, visit a spa or health resort- the best time for this is the second half of the month.

Cancer

July has the potential to be a great month for you. The stars are making great promises, and all they ask is that you carefully think things through and remain consistent. That's not so hard!

Work. July is a great time to start new projects and make new connections. Jupiter is in the professional sector of your sky, amplifying everything. Finally, you can expect the support you have wanted for so long at work! You can count on that for the next few years, so don't miss your moment in the sun. Get your professional and financial affairs in order whether you are an entrepreneur or employee, no matter what your field is.

Entrepreneurs might find themselves completing profitable transactions that look very promising for the future, while employees will be able to climb the ladder at work.

Those who have been unemployed for some time might find a job with a company that might take them to another level, both financially and socially. The stars' only advice is that you be careful with management and those in positions of power. It isn't worth being overly demanding right now, but a little flexibility and diplomacy never hurt anyone.

Your relationship with colleagues in other cities or abroad is coming along with varying success. Some things in this area are looking positive, while others will have to be discussed and changed. But if you are willing to grab the bull by the horns, you will be able to control the entire working process, and close to the end of the month, things will be much better.

Money. July is a fairly favorable month to you, financially speaking. Money will be coming in regularly and there will be somewhat more of it. This will allow you to take a bold look at the future and start making various plans.

Those with various debts might soon be able to settle them favorably, your finances improve. This month, you can expect the largest sums to come in on July 29 and 30. What's more, you can also expect something on July 1, 2, 11, 12, and 18-20.

Love and family. Things are not looking so good in your home life, however. That is especially the case for couples who have experienced various problems in the past. Their relationship might once again reach the breaking point, this time, over money, property, or various material problems. These may be residual issues, but that doesn't mean they aren't still there.

On the contrary, new romances are moving along well, and if you experience any friction, which is very likely in July, remember – it's just a lovers' spat.

You are choosing to be very active this month, which means that a lot of people are noticing you and wish you well. If there is any room in your plans for romantic intrigue, nothing is stopping you – the ball is always in your court!

Health. This month, you are healthy, energetic, and ready to climb mountains, though it's possible that you won't have to, and the mountains will come to you at just the right time.

Leo

For you, July is usually a time for idleness and resting and taking some time off with those you love the most. But this month is unusual, and you're being called to the front of the line.

Work. In July, you will have to plan things out, down to the last detail. The positive influence of the stars this month is strangely intertwined with the negative, which means you will have to be flexible as you maneuver, in order to take advantage of the good while avoiding the bad.

The good news in July is that the things in which you have been investing so much effort and so many resources will continue to take flight. You also have friends, assistants, and like-minded people. They will help you get through a difficult relationship with a rival who is out for blood, and resolve everything favorably.

Your relationship with colleagues in other cities or abroad is developing with varying success. Several obstacles, which are likely out of anyone's control, will throw a wrench in your plans. You can expect to see the light at the end of the tunnel at the end of July or even in August.

Entrepreneurs and managers should prepare for audits, which are very likely this month.

Employees should be careful with their colleagues and avoid any intrigue. Diplomacy is the key when dealing with managers – this goes for both July and August.

Money. This month, your finances are looking calm. You shouldn't expect any windfalls or major losses. Expect to receive the largest sums on July 4, 5, 21-22, and 31.

Love and family. No changes are on the horizon in your personal life. Couples who have been getting along will be resolving various household issues, of which there will be many. If your better half is going through a rough time, then nothing is stopping you from helping him or her, with words or deeds.

Those living in a rocky marriage will be able to improve their family situation a bit, and that help may come from an old friend.

Divorcing couples will be closing the door on a challenging past and trying to start over again somewhere new.

Health. In June, you may be feeling a lot of lethargy and fatigue. The reason is all the turbulence you are experiencing both at home and at work. Remember that your health comes first, and don't try to take yourself to the brink. Find some time to relax, everything will work out just fine.

Virgo

This month remember – a friend in court is better than a penny in purse. But there's another thing to keep in mind – trust but verify. If you are able to manage both, success is yours!

Work. In July, it is worth devoting more attention to expanding your social circle. First, because this is a very favorable time for you, and second, because you are in a period in which your greatest success will come from a group effort.

You might have an agreement with a partner with regard to financial investments in a shared business, but this has both advantages and many drawbacks. As far as advantages, you might be able to avoid material challenges, which will divide you and your partners, but at the same time, you will be dependent, which may hamper your freedom and influence in shared business. For both entrepreneurs and managers who might be in this situation, it is worth remembering that.

If that is your case, the stars recommend carefully studying any financial documents before signing them, in order to avoid falling into any traps.

Your ties with colleagues from faraway are developing nicely, and you might go on a successful trip.

For employees, you are on a positive streak, but in the near future, you may face a company reorganization or new leadership, which is unlikely to damage you. For now, though, you will be able to strengthen your relationship with both management and colleagues.

Money. In July, your wallet is looking good. You might see partners' making a financial investment in your business, credit, or bonuses and dividends.

Those who are not part of the business world can count on support from parents, a loved one, or a spouse.

You might have some rather pleasant expenses in July- vacation, leisure, or things for your children. In the business world, this is known as "hospitality expenses".

Love and family. Changes are underway in your personal life – maybe you have a new home, apartment, or summer home. That may be occupying the time of spouses with a harmonious marriage, thanks to money from a spouse or a loved one. In many cases, you may be moving to another city or abroad.

As far as couples, there are several possibilities. If you are attempting to dominate your partner and impose your own rules, that is unlikely to work out for you. Jupiter is firmly in the sector of the sky responsible for partnerships, and will not tolerate games like this. You can be assured of a strong rebuff. Respect is on the agenda, and this is the only way to build a strong union with your partner. This advice is equally valid for those who are married who are seeking to improve their relationship.

Health. All month long, you are full of energy and have no reason to fear falling ill.

Libra

This month, you can count on real progress toward reaching your goals. In the heavens, the roads are clear, with no traffics or accidents on the horizon.

Work. You are looking at an active, hardworking, and eventful month. Business partners with power and influence might play an important role in work-related events. That is, a team is coming together, and that will play a big role in your ability to significantly improve your position both this year and next.

However, working with others will involve making some concessions, and you will have to do the same. You may have disagreements on your shared business, but they should be resolved by August.

Your relationship with colleagues from other cities or abroad is developing nicely, and you might go on a successful trip where you hold constructive negotiations. It is worth carefully watching this area, as a bit later, in the fall, you might experience misunderstandings and have to revisit your current discussions. This may occur several times, and you need to be prepared for what might be coming.

Likewise, managers and entrepreneurs should keep a close eye on their subordinates, who may not be giving you what you need. In some cases, that may be due to laziness and incompetence, but in others, it may be a case of deception and sabotage. That is the weak link in your work, and it may cause endless problems later on.

Employees will periodically deal with intrigue from their colleagues and competition, but can count on managers supporting them. It is worth bringing up any issues like this.

Money. Your bank account is looking healthy in July. In addition to your usual income, you can count on support from business partners, dividends from the bank, and beneficial terms of credit. Those who are not part of the business world will receive help from parents, loved ones, and spouses.

Love and family. Your personal life is also looking rather eventful. A loved one is experiencing a lot of success at work, and he or she may support you in either words or deeds. You may experience some minor quarrels this month, maybe due to differing views on household matters or your children's education. You may have disagreements on construction, repairs, or rehabilitating an old home.

Your relationship with children is still demanding a lot of attention. Saturn, the planet of responsibility and discipline, is demanding you keep a closer eye on your children and support them if they need it.

Jupiter, which is firmly in the sector of the sky related to relationships, is lucky for single people. If you still haven't found anyone suitable, he or she is sure to appear- in some cases, it will last a long time, and in others, forever.

Any vacations you take will be successful, but it is better to plan them for the end of the months or in August. That is when you will have time for yourself and it is worth taking full advantage of it! As they say, you deserve it!

Health. In July, you are health, active, and up for adventure. You may even forget all about your health, which is always a good sign all is well.

Scorpio

Welcome to a hot summer full of hard work! While others are relaxing, you are able to climb mountains, moving in the right direction.

Work. July is a great time to build and strengthen relationships with friends, colleagues, and business partners. A new business you have ventured into recently is coming along nicely. Entrepreneurs and managers can seriously shake up any teams, and this may have even begun last month, though it will continue into July. You can expect new partners who you should view with cautious optimism. Here, you need to be able to separate the wheat from the chaff – remember – not all that glitters is gold. A new partner might come in handy in the future, though others may turn out to be rather useless – all bark and no bite.

Your relationships with colleagues from other cities or abroad are developing with varying success, and you might even face resistance that may become rather serious. Any situations in this area will improve closer to the end of July or in August, when you will be able to find a solution to the most pressing problems.

Employees will improve their position at work, but they will have to work hard in order to achieve that. Closer to the end of the month, or in August, you can expect a promotion with a significant raise and increase in your authority.

Money. This month, your finances are looking better, and that positive change will continue into August. You can expect to receive the largest sums on July 1, 2, 10-12, 18-20, and 28-30.

Your expenses this month are mostly personal in nature – your children, loved ones, and various matters related to your home.

Love and family. This is not the most promising time for your personal life – work comes first!

Couples may experience misunderstandings and arguments. In order to avoid that, the stars recommend being careful with your loved one and explaining why you are so busy lately. The situation will improve closer to the end of the month, when you will be able to go on a trip together, which will smooth things over in your relationship.

You are likely to run into a lover who lives in another city or abroad, or maybe meet someone interesting while traveling.

Women are especially lucky – they may meet a dashing hero, but the stars aren't saying yet where this story is headed. There is a possibility of this burning out fast, like a flame, leaving behind nothing but a vivid memory. If you are the type who likes risk and adventure, you can count on it.

Health. In July, you are energetic and have no reason to fear falling ill.

Sagittarius

July is a time for you to catch your breath between a turbulent, jam-packed June and what's going to be an active, dynamic August. Remember there's more to life than working, and act accordingly.

Work. In June, most Sagittarians would rather focus their energy on their families and personal matters than work-related responsibilities. Only the most incurable workaholics will be busy getting their business in order and dealing with administrative issues.

Entrepreneurs and managers are thinking about hiring new employees, as the stars are suggesting that your current staffing leaves a lot to be desired.

Employees who are still at work might have trouble dividing time between their personal and professional obligations. The stars recommend that you take a few days off and focus your energy where you really want to.

July is a good time to establish connections with colleagues and friends living in other cities or abroad. Perhaps one of them will remind you this month.

Money. July is not the best month for you, financially speaking. All month long, you will be spending money rather than making it. The astrologist predicts that many of your expenses in July will be either pleasant or practical, and related to your personal life, including family and your children's needs. However, you can count on the largest amounts coming in on July 4, 5, 13, 21, 22, and 31.

Love and family. Expect some real achievements in your personal life. Couples who get along will support their children, who are now on the path to prosperity and success. Some families may even be welcoming new members.

Your relationship with relatives is significantly better than it was, and a family member may come visit you.

When it comes to romance, you have had smooth sailing for a while, now. Your relationship is growing deeper and becoming warmer and more serious. If for some time it has seemed that you are on the same plane, right now, things are somewhat different, and this summer is likely to reveal the exact opposite.

Health. Some trouble lies ahead in July: your home and job are demanding your attention. Weekends out of the city, spending time in the woods or in a nearby park are a way to get away from the constant frenzy, but also good for the body and soul.

The stars also strongly urge you to be careful with your eating habits and avoid eating anything questionable. Generally speaking, a healthy diet will prevent a lot of problems, especially if you have issues with your weight or chronic digestive conditions.

Capricorn

In July, you will find yourself juggling several projects at once. Nothing is escaping your attention – and that's to your advantage!

Work. When confronted with a complex task, you are able to first assess its real scale. Then, you are able to come up with a plan, hope for success, and get to work. Right now, you are at the second stage of this, when you have to just grab the bull by the horns.

Entrepreneurs and managers might be expanding their business, and once again immersed in real estate transactions. In many cases, that will be taking place in another city or abroad. Trustworthy people will give you support right from the start, as will your faithful and consistent team.

You may experience some bobbles with partners, especially in the beginning and middle of the month. Closer to the end of July, things will be favorably resolved.

Employees who are not planning such heroics can expect to take part in some significant changes in their company. However disconcerting they might seem, and not only will your position not suffer, you may even thrive.

Money. Despite the many changes at work and at home, your financial situation is constant. Expect to receive the greatest sums on July 6, 7, 14, 15, 23, and 24.

Love and family. Many Capricorns are more focused on their personal life in July. Couples who get along will be dealing with various real estate transactions, both for themselves and for their children.

If you have been living in a tinderbox for a while now, you might finally divorce and go your separate ways. In many cases, this has been brewing for years, and a new affection may have been the straw that broke the camel's back. Uranus is the planet of the unexpected and surprises, and for five years, it has been in the love sector of your sky. All of that is very clear in 2022. All of this suggests that your new love is nothing like that of your past, and might completely change your life.

Health. In July, you are facing the fact that periods of joy may alternate with a sense of lethargy and fatigue. The strs recommend taking care of yourself – if you are tired, take a break, and remember to get enough sleep.

Aquarius

A crane in the sky is always more attractive than a sparrow in your hand. Though in order to reach the crane, you're going to have to build a high ladder and check each rung. In other words – roll up your sleeves and get to work!

Work. The doors to a better future have been opened. Those who want to expand their business to another city or abroad will be working with colleagues from afar, and this month things will be moving along, slowly but surely overcoming various obstacles, which are not as fundamental as they may seem at first glance. You may have to finish up some current issues and clarify some things. The situation will improve the last ten days of the month, and by August, you will see that you are on the right track.

Closer to the end of the month or in August you may take a trip, which will be very successful.

Those busy with thorny issues related to real estate will continue to resolve these longstanding problems. Things will gradually stabilize and finally come to an end.

Money. In July, your finances are looking very stable, and money will be coming in regularly, in slightly higher amounts. Entrepreneurs and managers may receive money from various real estate transactions, and those who are not part of the business world will resolve some issues related to that, and also receive a decent sum. Expect the largest amounts on July 8, 9, 16-18, 26, and 27.

Love and family. In your personal life, you will continue to deal with things that began in the recent past. Many Aquarians will be fully immersed with details from their day to day life. That might involve major home improvements, or acquiring or selling an apartment, home, or cottage. Household matters will take precedence, but that doesn't mean there won't be any romance!

Those who already have a long-term partner might work together on boring, household issues, and those who are still single might start talking to a very pleasant person.

Closer to the end of the month or in August, you might meet someone on a trip or among people who have come from faraway.

Your children will make you happy and your relationship with them will be unusually peaceful and harmonious.

Health. July is a great time to finally focus on your body and understand what you actually need. Maybe you will decide to get some testing done and begin eating a healthy diet. Luckily, it's summer and you will have plenty of opportunities.

Elderly people and those who have been weakened by disease should try to prevent any chronic issues. If you can, spend some time at a health resort.

Pisces

You are about to begin a fun summer month. You will be able to show off your enviable energy, confidence, and optimism. Everything is full speed ahead!

Work. Your personal and family life may turn out to be more important than work in July. That said, some Pisceans may not be able to imagine life without the stress of work, and the best thing they can do right now is strengthen their ties with people abroad or in other cities. You might be able to combine work with pleasure- and talk shop with friendly colleagues and contacts.

Entrepreneurs will be able to calmly resolve issues related to real estate, and fortunately find the money to do it.

Employees may take some time off and work on their own projects. You will return to work after the new moon on July 26, and by August you will again be quite busy.

Money. You cannot exactly call July a good time for your finances. It will, in fact, be rather ruinous: vacation time, entertainment, travel, shopping – none of that comes cheap. But on the other hand, what is money for? It only has value if you spend it and give it away. So, enjoy yourself and the memories you are making.

Those with families will spend a lot of time and money on their children's needs, but that is so important, it's almost sacred!

Love and family. July is a good time for romantic and family relationships. It is made for relaxing, fun, music, and dancing. Many Pisceans will spend some of July traveling, which they will thoroughly enjoy.

Couples who get along will get their home in order and be busy with their children's education. The stars will greenlight anything related to improving your home or even building a new one.

Health. In July, you are feeling strong and energetic, and able to resolve professional and personal tasks. Give yourself the gift of a week at the beach, and be sure to visit a spa. Right now is the best time for taking care of your body, spending time in nature, and doing some reasonable shopping. In short, enjoy life and don't overthink it!

August

New York Time		
Calendar Day	Lunar Day	Lunar Day Start Time
01/08/2022	5	9:37 AM
02/08/2022	6	10:40 AM
03/08/2022	7	11:44 AM
04/08/2022	8	12:49 PM
05/08/2022	9	1:58 PM
06/08/2022	10	3:07 PM
07/08/2022	11	4:16 PM
08/08/2022	12	5:22 PM
09/08/2022	13	6:20 PM
10/08/2022	14	7:10 PM
11/08/2022	15	7:52 PM
12/08/2022	16	8:28 PM
13/08/2022	17	9:00 PM
14/08/2022	18	9:29 PM
15/08/2022	19	9:57 PM
16/08/2022	20	10:26 PM
17/08/2022	21	10:56 PM
18/08/2022	22	11:30 PM
20/08/2022	23	12:08 AM
21/08/2022	24	12:50 AM
22/08/2022	25	1:38 AM
23/08/2022	26	2:30 AM
24/08/2022	27	3:27 AM
25/08/2022	28	4:26 AM
26/08/2022	29	5:27 AM
27/08/2022	1	4:16 AM
27/08/2022	2	6:28 AM
28/08/2022	3	7:30 AM
29/08/2022	4	8:33 AM
30/08/2022	5	9:37 AM
31/08/2022	6	10:42 AM

London Time		
Calendar Day	Lunar Day	Lunar Day Start Time
01/08/2022	5	9:23 AM
02/08/2022	6	10:34 AM
03/08/2022	7	11:46 AM
04/08/2022	8	1:00 PM
05/08/2022	9	2:17 PM
06/08/2022	10	3:35 PM
07/08/2022	11	4:51 PM
08/08/2022	12	6:00 PM
09/08/2022	13	6:58 PM
10/08/2022	14	7:43 PM
11/08/2022	15	8:17 PM
12/08/2022	16	8:45 PM
13/08/2022	17	9:07 PM
14/08/2022	18	9:28 PM
15/08/2022	19	9:47 PM
16/08/2022	20	10:07 PM
17/08/2022	21	10:29 PM
18/08/2022	22	10:54 PM
19/08/2022	23	11:25 PM
21/08/2022	24	12:02 AM
22/08/2022	25	12:46 AM
23/08/2022	26	1:39 AM
24/08/2022	27	2:39 AM
25/08/2022	28	3:45 AM
26/08/2022	29	4:53 AM
27/08/2022	30	6:02 AM
27/08/2022	1	9:16 AM
28/08/2022	2	7:13 AM
29/08/2022	3	8:24 AM
30/08/2022	4	9:36 AM
31/08/2022	5	10:50 AM

You can find the description of each lunar day in the chapter “A Guide to The Moon Cycle and Lunar Days”

Aries

This month, your motto is "All work and no play makes John a dull boy." You have certainly done the work, and now it is time to relax.

Work. The first half of August will be a bit slow at work, and most Aries will be taking some time off from their duties.

During the second half of the month, as you move closer to the end, you will slowly but surely come back to a full schedule. You will again have to deal with tasks related to expanding your business, construction, and real estate, but this is not the real source of concern.

The last ten days of August, you will be actively developing your ties with partners from other cities or abroad, but it is worth being careful and attentive here – not everything you agree on now will be carried out in the future. Quite the opposite is true – in the best-case scenario, things will be delayed for various reasons, and in the worst, you will have to give up a lot. So make sure to carefully read over any documents you are signing with colleagues from far away, including the clauses about force majeure.

Employees might be thinking about changing jobs, and that will happen at various times in 2022 or 2023. The last week of August and first week of September, you will be having negotiations about just that.

Money. Your financial situation is far from stable. However, in most cases, you can expect a lot of expenses, though most of them will be pleasant in nature. Vacations, travel, kids, and successful shopping sprees and visiting friends are expensive, and it adds up.

In any case, you won't end up in ruins, as recent achievements and future income mean that you will be able to cover everything. You will be able to shake it off, without having to deny yourself or your loved ones anything.

Expect the largest sums of money on August 1, 2, 9, 19, 17, 18, and 27-29. The largest expenses will be on August 5, 7, 11, 12, 27, and 28, while you can expect to make smaller expenditures almost every day.

Love and family. This month is one of the most dynamic and powerful months of the year when it comes to your romantic relationships. August may bring both major achievements and destruction, depending on your intentions.

Couples would be well advised to not cut corners and instead pamper their loved one, to avoid later accusations of stinginess and conflicts over money. This goes for those who are married and those who are not.

Parents should think about their children and show them moral and material support.

That said, it is certainly not a time to make bargains when it comes to personal affairs. Remember that and act accordingly.

Health. August is a great time to improve your health, take a trip to the beach, and have some fun with your friends. You will not have to grapple with any diseases, but any extremes are ill advised this month, especially August 4-6, 11, 12, 25, and 26.

Taurus

August is full of ups and downs for you. When it comes to resolving any practical issues, you are unparalleled, especially if you avoid any angry outbursts and keep a cool head at all times.

Work. When it comes to work, this is not the best time for you. The exception is those who work in construction or a field related to real estate. However, if that is the case, the stars still recommend being careful when it comes to relationships with management and the powers that be.

The explosive combination of aggressive Mars and unpredictable Uranus is in Taurus, so you can expect to be somewhat rash in both words and deeds.

All of these qualities will lead you to conflict and a worsening relationship with those around you, including the powers that be. Mid- and late August will be the most challenging time for you.

Money. You should be careful with your finances, not only in August, but in the months that follow, as well. You are looking down the road at a lot of expenses, in some cases related to work, but more likely due to your personal life.

In the near future, you can expect to be consumed with financial matters, and August is likely to be your last month in 2022 of relative financial prosperity.

Love and family. Your personal and family life might be your priority in August, but things are also rather turbulent, here. Many Taureans will be busy changing their place of residence, perhaps selling an old home or buying a new one, but that will not always be a peaceful, hassle-free process. It might involve conflict with your parents, relatives, or even your spouse.

The reason for such tension might be you, given your demanding nature, combined with your assertiveness, which may lead to misunderstandings within the entire family. If you are 100% sure of yourself, do what you feel you have to, but remember that a diplomatic approach never hurt anyone.

Alternatively, the stormy seas may be related to a family member's illness or difficult issues related to real estate.

Health. When it comes to your health, you have seen better days than in August. You are full of worries, which means you may not always feel confident or sure of yourself. If that happens, take a break and get some physical distance between you and your worries. This is definitely feasible, especially during the summer months.

Gemini

Walls have never been an obstacle for you – you are able to climb them or simply knock them down. Or even walk right through them. However you do it, the choice is yours.

Work. Things are still going well for you at work. You are actively developing your connections with colleagues in other cities and abroad, and may go on a trip or reach a successful agreement. You may manage to be successful in most of what you do, but also be on the receiving end of approval from both management and other influential individuals.

You might also enjoy support from friends, both old and new. During the first half of the beautiful summer month, you can expect everything to be coming up roses at work.

However, during the second half of August, remember that there's a fly in any ointment. This time, the fly may be conflicts with certain colleagues, including those who live in other cities or abroad. You might run into unexpected obstacles you will have to grapple with in August and into September. In some cases, this may involve documents, and in others, changes to legislation in other countries where you are trying to get work done.

Alternatively, you may run into unexpected legal issues, which will seriously complicate things and throw a wrench in a lot of your plans.

Either way, in August, you will need to study laws with a fine-toothed comb, as well as any instructions, regardless of where they are from. Nothing is insurmountable, no matter how difficult things will seem, and you will find the right path toward resolving any problems you come across.

Money. Financially, you are in for a successful month. Venus is in the financial sector of your sky for almost all of August, which means that there will be money. You can expect the largest sums on August 5, 6, 13, 14, 22, and 23.

You will have expenses this month, as well, mostly related to your day-to-day life, home, and family.

Love and family. Many Geminis will manage to combine their work and family affairs this month. During the second half of August, you will be busy with home improvements, and in more serious cases, move into a more comfortable home. These complicated matters will continue into the fall of 2022, and cause more trouble than you originally anticipated.

Your relationship with family members is calm and even, and you may find yourself resolving complicated household issues. Some unpleasant interactions with your relatives or in-laws may interfere with your peaceful pace of life. If it involves your in-laws, things will be even more difficult, and you will have to be flexible as you maneuver in an attempt to resolve the situation.

Unmarried couples can expect a similar situation to play out with an elderly relative.

The first half of August is the most favorable time for any travel, getting together with old friends, or meeting new acquaintances.

Health. All month long, you are healthy, energetic and very charming. The stars strongly urge you to be careful when traveling and behind the wheel, however. You have a high likelihood of accidents all month long, especially August 5, 11-13, and 25-27. This is the most conflicted periods of the month as well.

Cancer

The path to success is never smooth. Here, it is worth remembering the words of Winston Churchill - "Never, never, never give up!"

Work. It seems that you have grabbed the brass ring. Work is going great, your income is growing, and most importantly, you are feeling surer of yourself.

New projects have been keeping both entrepreneurs and all levels of managers busy, and in the near future, they will start to look very promising.

Employees can expect new responsibilities likely to lead somewhere good, and if this already happened in the recent past, you will be strengthening your position both professionally and financially. It might seem that everything is coming up roses, but... nothing is ever perfect. This time, the road to success blocked with debts and other obligations. That will become more complicated during the second half of August, when you will have to deal with the same problems over and over again. This may involve having to give something up.

Your relationship with colleagues in other cities or abroad is developing with varying success. Some things will work out for you, while others will remain pending. Most likely, you will have to work on this in both August and September.

Money. Your bank account is not exactly stable, this month. On one hand, you won't find yourself penniless, but your expenses are certainly going to be high. That may be related to paying off old debts, or possibly family-related problems, demands, or children.

Love and family. Your personal life is looking uneven and turbulent in August. That is especially the case for couples who, after a long period of calm, will once again start feeling a crisis. Remember that you can't take back something once it has been said, and try not to stick your foot in your mouth. This goes for your partner, as well. The most difficult time for this relationship will be the second half of August.

Parents are likely to experience problems involving their children. In the best-case scenario, that will involve expenses related to their vacations, education, and schooling, but in the worst-case scenario, it will involve arguments with adult children or financial sacrifices to solve their problems.

Your relationship with relatives is also less-than ideal, and their intentions may be significantly at odds with yours. There will not be an argument here, though, and you are likely to have to agree to disagree.

The stars predict that many issues this month will boil down to money. You will have to leverage every opportunity in order to provide for your loved ones. Don't worry, you'll manage it all!

Health. You are healthy and energetic this month, though the stars recommend that you avoid any traumatic situations, which are highly likely during the second half of the month. The most critical days are August 5, 6, 11, 12, and 25-27.

Leo

August is a good time for you. You are experiencing a burst of inspiration, along with hard work and energy levels that are sure to lead to incredible results. Buckle up!

Work. Many Leos will be very focused on work this month. Employees are likely to see a shakeup in their company, perhaps new leadership, and naturally, your team is going to feel concerned about those changes.

Alternatively, you are seeing new horizons open up in a different, more promising company, and that may be related to partners in other cities or abroad.

Entrepreneurs will have an excellent opportunity to expand their business, which will also happen with help from colleagues from far away.

At the same time, your relationship with certain partners is leaving a lot to be desired, and there is no reason to drag this burden into your brilliant future. This fall you will have a chance to resolve these problems, and cross out anything that has worn out its welcome.

The stars are giving the green light to those looking to change professions and do something new. Most likely any plans related to this will come to life in 2023.

Money. Your financial position is looking both strong and stable in August. Money will be coming in regularly, and you will see a lot more of it, too. Expect the largest amounts on August 1, 9, 10, 17, 17, and 27-29.

It is time to deal with your debt obligations; in some cases, this may be related to business expenses, and in others, to your personal life. This complicated process will become more active into the fall of 2022.

Love and family. Some major changes are underway in your personal life. Couples on the rocks are concerned about breaking up, and will have a key moment in August. Everything that has been bothering for a while may finally come to a head, and this is not just a temporary squabble – it may be a final separation. In any case, you can expect long discussions on dividing up property, your children's education and other moral and financial obligations.

Things for loving couples are very different – many will be deciding how their relationship will look in the future, as things cannot continue simply as they are. That means either a complete union or a painful breakup; there is no third way.

Health. In August, you are energetic and have no reason to fear falling ill. On the contrary, the stars are giving you the strength to resolve many problems right now, and suggest that you take advantage of this and use it efficiently and appropriately.

Virgo

What's that? You have to move and start over again? In many cases, that is indeed the case, but there are many, many different reasons for it.

Work. August is a very difficult time for you when it comes to work. Both entrepreneurs and managers are once again dealing with difficult relationships with partners from faraway, and this may be due to certain circumstances of force majeure.

You are likely to see new and unexpected legal problems rear their heads. The stars warn you that problems you encounter this month may worsen and continue throughout the fall of 2022, so get ready to defend yourself and try to find the best path toward a resolution. You need a compromise, and can't count on a complete victory, right now.

You can expect some support from friends, but coordinating everything and managing it all falls squarely on your shoulders.

The most successful Virgos will be thinking about expanding their business, acquiring real estate, and in some cases, that may take place in another city or abroad. If that is your case, then don't rush things and be careful with your documents and studying the laws in other countries.

Money. Financially, you are in for a turbulent month. For the most important events, you will find yourself having to use credit, negotiate with partners about financial support, and even their share of your shared business.

Those who are not part of the business world can count on help from loved ones. You might see profits from various real estate transactions.

Love and family. In many cases, the main events of August will concern your home and family. Many Virgos will be thinking about a new residence, and the reasons for that may vary. In some cases, you are dealing with a nasty divorce or separation that has dragged out for a long time. In others, you are acquiring new real estate, either abroad or simply outside of town.

You may be talking about a move, and in the case of new love or connecting with loved ones living in another city or abroad.

Health. This month, you are feeling sluggish, and should be especially careful if you are weakened or elderly. You are about to begin a period in which paying attention to yourself should be a standard part of life. Remember that it is easy to break the delicate balance between health and disease, and recovery can be difficult!

Young and healthy Virgos should avoid any situation related to danger and risk. During the second half of August, be careful when traveling or behind the wheel!

Libra

This month, the impossible becomes possible – you are able to do it all. And that goes for work, leisure, and your personal life.

Work. In August, many Libras find themselves at the epicenter of a whirlwind of activity, both pleasant and less-so.

The first half of the month is a good time to work on your contacts and meet new people, too. In order to seek new partners, you need support, and there's no better time to find it. Things change quickly, however, and by the second half of August, there are dark clouds looming on the horizon.

Your relationship with like-minded people, friends, or the powers that be is about to become much more complicated. You may experience some significant confrontation when it comes to ethical or financial issues. This situation will continue into the fall, so there is good reason to deal with the problems now, and not put them off until later. Do what you can and dig in for the long fight.

The last week of August will have you busy with a variety of organizational tasks, and this will continue into September.

Money. For many Libras, August is a ruinous month. You will be bleeding money in all directions – vacation, travel, kids, household and professional tasks – it will all require a huge amount of resources, more than you initially intended.

On the other hand, friends and powers that be will be insisting you pay them back what you owe, and this will also not come cheap. As a result, by the end of the month, many Libras will find themselves with empty pockets.

Love and family. August is a great time for vacations, outdoor parties, shopping, and traveling around the world. If you want to spend money, this is the time to do it. The best time for all of this is the first half of the month.

The second half of August will be more challenging, and you might face a litany of problems related to your children, which, naturally, require money to resolve.

For couples, the second half of August is also a test of endurance. You may face unexpected disagreements, possibly about differing viewpoints on various issues, or perhaps about money. For example, if you start to become stingy, you will not be able to avoid problems. So decide which is more important- love or money.

The last few days of the month, many Libras will be dealing with dull household matters, and this will continue into September.

Health. All month long, you are feeling energetic, charming, and attractive. Naturally, with those qualities, there's no time for falling ill!

Scorpio

August is a time to make a big leap forward. Roll up your sleeves and get to work! Rewards will quickly follow!

Work. Many Scorpios will have to devote their beautiful summer days to work, but that will all pay off.

Entrepreneurs and managers will be launching a new project with a lot of promise for the future. Most likely, that will be clear from the get-go. The stars still recommend carefully considering any financial perspectives, as there may still be risks involved. You will be going through some difficult times in the near future, and accurate financial calculations are a must.

Another thorn in your side this month will be your difficult relationship with a business partner. This may be due to large property or real estate.

Some serious problems are likely during the second half of August, but by September, things will look a lot smoother and be at least partially resolved.

Employees may be given new responsibilities, and if that already happened recently, you will strengthen your position. You might even count on a raise, so don't be afraid to speak to management and ask for one. You will be heard and understood.

Money. August is a great time for your wallet. Money will be coming in regularly, and you can expect slightly more of it, too. Expect the largest sums on August 7, 8, 15, 16, and 25-27.

Love and family. Your personal life may become somewhat complicated this month. Couples on the rocks might start divorce proceedings, and that will involve the appalling task of dividing up property, starting with your home.

Couples who get along might also be resolving various issues related to real estate, and together overcome obstacles from various opponents. The problems are a continuation of something from your past, so you are aware of them, and what you need to do. As you charge forward, you can say that by late August or September, things will be somewhat calmer. You might even find an intermediary from your social circle or support from an old friend.

Health. August is a time for working this year, and unfortunately, you are going to have to forget about a real vacation. Nothing is preventing you from spending your free time walking around in nature or in a nearby park, however. That will help keep your body and spirit healthy, allowing you to be in top form and take on everything work throws your way.

Sagittarius

All month long, you will be striving to reach new heights. This is a long, winding road, but it is a steep and toilsome way to the stars!

Work. This is a very busy time for you at work, and a very successful time, too. During the first ten days of the month, you may go on a trip, and you may be working on plans with colleagues from faraway. Everything should go as planned, though you may experience some unexpected disagreements along the way. They may look differently, depending on your field and future plans. In some cases, there may be issues with laws in another country, and in others, your own flaws will come out unexpectedly, right at a crucial moment.

Entrepreneurs and managers should be more careful when dealing with subordinates and meticulously check their work. Any errors might significantly set back your plans – keep that in mind and act accordingly.

The most difficult time for this is August 5-7 and 12 and 13. If you face any kind of obstacles, remember that in any case, you are moving ahead, so keep your eye on the prize and don't leave your chosen path.

Employees should be careful when dealing with colleagues and at any team-related events. In case of conflict, take no sides, and take pains to avoid any intrigue.

For all Sagittarians, it is important to avoid breaking any laws and to carefully prepare for any traveling, which is highly likely during various periods this month.

Money. Your finances are looking rather neutral this month, though the first few days of the month you can expect some gifts from Fate. Overall, however, you will not run into any major windfalls, though your expenses will remain modest. Expect the largest sums to come in on August 1, 2, 9, 10, 17-19, and 27-29.

Love and family. If your interests are focused on your family life, here you can expect several developments of various natures.

Things are moving along well for couples, whose relationship is growing and bringing them closer together. They might spend some time traveling together or on vacation, though it is worth carefully preparing for that, in order to avoid any unpleasant surprises.

In many families, you will continue to see positive changes related to children, though this will still require attention and money on your part. Of course, children are something sacred, and who, if not you?

Spouses who are dealing with a mountain of issues will run into a rocky period, and your relationship will feel pressure from the heavens. Mars, an active and aggressive planet will move into the sector of the sky related to long-term partners on August 20, and remain there for six months. Be prepared to tackle this event head on and consider any weak links in your relationship. That is the best you can do.

You might also face further trouble this month, in the form of unexpected problems involving your own family members. What that looks like may change depending on the person, and while you can't make any predictions, you can expect some turbulence. Most likely, this will involve old problems rearing their heads again, and looking more acute than they were.

Health. In August, you are energetic, though the stars urge you to be careful when traveling or driving. There is a danger of accidents, which is especially high on August 5-7, 12, 13, and 25-28. Be careful! These are days to watch out for!

Capricorn

Over the next month, you will be less busy at work, but are your loved ones about to heap something else on your shoulders? Remember, the willing horse carries the load – is this you?

Work. August is not a time for being too busy at work. Many Capricorns might prefer relaxing to work, right now, with the exception of those who work in construction or a field related to real estate. If that is your case, things are charging, full speed ahead. The most incurable workaholics who have a hard time conceiving of life without work, can busy themselves getting their office in order, dealing with administrative tasks and paperwork, and preparing for a more active period, which will begin in September.

Entrepreneurs who are planning on opening business to another city or even abroad will be busy this month with real estate decisions, as well as various administrative affairs related to that. You can expect a big leap forward, here.

Closer to the end of the month, many will be planning on traveling, and that will either be at the end of the month or in September.

Money. Your finances are difficult this month. You will be spending constantly, and in some cases, that will be related to work expenses, and in others, to your personal life. The biggest expenses will probably take place between August 5 and 14, so get ready for some material losses.

Love and family. Many Capricorns will be more focused on what is happening in their personal lives, this month. Parents should be attentive to their children, who may need both moral and financial support. This may be turn out to be much more serious than anticipated, and if that is your case, the stars recommend you parse out what is actually necessary, and what is just a want. Be very attentive with your smallest family members from August 5 to 15, when various accidents are highly likely.

August is also difficult for couples. You may find yourselves arguing regularly, over ethical, moral, and even financial matters, which will be far worse. Overall, if you want to make your loved one happy, go ahead and do it! Remember that no one bites the hand that feeds it, and generosity today will avoid a lot of problems now and in the future.

August is also a great time to once again resolve any issues related to real estate. In many cases, this will involve acquiring a new home in another city or abroad.

Health. You have been working a lot lately, and now you are coming back to earth. Give yourself the gift of a week or two at the beach. Get out, enjoy yourself and your surroundings. You need to relax.

Aquarius

In August, you will once again be dealing with issues that you had resolved long ago. You are handling it your own way – intelligently, creatively, and enthusiastically.

Work. Your main achievement this month will be expanding your circle of acquaintances. Most likely, that will take place while traveling or with people who have come from faraway. This is a very promising relationship during the first week of August.

In mid-August, from the 7th to 14th, you may face a series of problems that you have seen before. This time, however, they may be unexpectedly acute. This likely involves real estate, land, or other property. Even if you believe the situation is absolutely resolved, nothing will stop your opponents from bringing them up again.

There may be a silver lining, however, in that it will allow you to understand where you and your opponents stand. The new moon will be in Virgo on August 27, which will allow you to strengthen your position and once again fend off your opponents.

Money. Your financial situation is looking rather neutral in August. You do not have any major windfalls on the horizon, but your expenses will be modest, as always.

Love and family. If your personal life is much more important to you than work, here you can expect both advantages and drawbacks. The advantages include a better relationship with your relatives; possible travel, and reconnecting with family members who live in other cities or abroad.

The drawbacks might include constant difficulties related to real estate, which come up over and over again. Nothing is new here, though, and you are able to ward off any enemies' machinations. This concerns both stable marriages and divorcing couples.

Couples who are dating will face issues with one of their parents or an elderly family member. In order to avoid being completely bogged down with household and everyday squabbles, maybe take a trip. There will be an opportunity in August. This will allow you to relax and get a better look at things.

Health. Right now, you are in good shape and have no reason to fear falling ill. The exception to that is those who suffer from chronic diseases, who should go get a good massage and do some light stretching in the morning.

Pisces

In August, you are weighed down with a lot of tasks, and none of them are easy. The most important thing is to not get ahead of yourself, and keep a close eye on those around you.

Work. August is usually a time for relaxing, but you might be busy with various types of work. Entrepreneurs and managers will spend the first ten days of the month dealing with issues related to expanding their business, as well as finishing up earlier projects. Employees will have a great opportunity to strengthen their position, both socially and financially.

The dark side of August might be unexpected problems with business partners living in other cities or abroad. From the 7th to 15th, you can expect some force majeure events, and for a colleague to refuse to shoulder his or her responsibilities, which will lead to sudden, unexpected conflict. The most difficult situations will lead to a split, or at least that is how things will seem at first. But time heals all wounds, and by September, you will be in contact again.

Alternatively, old legal issues will rear their ugly heads, or you may unexpectedly face new ones. Be very careful as you stay on the right side of the law, and be sure to not violate any rules, laws, or instructions this month, as any punishments will be swift and hard.

Those who have already fallen on the wrong side of the law should be 100% ready for the next round of complications.

Money. Your bank account is looking healthy in August. August 1, 7, 8, 15, 16, 25, and 26 are particularly favorable days. You do not have many expenses, and those you do have are related to issues that will crop up mid-month. In some cases, they will be related to business, and in others, your personal life.

Love and family. The most important thing in your personal life is household tasks. These may occupy both spouses and unmarried couples with a solid relationship. Many Pisceans will have a new goal – a home, cottage, or simply updating where they live now. This is a cumbersome task that will occupy your entire fall and may even continue into 2023.

In many families, in mid-August, you will be dealing with a variety of problems involving relatives. That may include serious arguments, or unpleasant interactions that might concern a close relative.

Couples should watch their tongues and actions, as there are people who only want to interpret things as best suits their own needs. Gossip, unfortunately, is not off the table.

Health. In August, your energy levels are lagging, and you should be especially careful if you are elderly or weakened. Take some time this month to visit a health spa, as you will have an opportunity to do so.

From August 7 to 15, the stars recommend that all Pisces be very careful while traveling or driving. There is a high likelihood of accidents, injuries, and unexpected events. Be very careful with household appliances and avoid anything related to danger or risk.

September

New York Time		
Calendar Day	Lunar Day	Lunar Day Start Time
01/09/2022	7	11:49 AM
02/09/2022	8	12:57 PM
03/09/2022	9	2:05 PM
04/09/2022	10	3:10 PM
05/09/2022	11	4:10 PM
06/09/2022	12	5:01 PM
07/09/2022	13	5:45 PM
08/09/2022	14	6:23 PM
09/09/2022	15	6:56 PM
10/09/2022	16	7:26 PM
11/09/2022	17	7:55 PM
12/09/2022	18	8:24 PM
13/09/2022	19	8:54 PM
14/09/2022	20	9:27 PM
15/09/2022	21	10:04 PM
16/09/2022	22	10:45 PM
17/09/2022	23	11:31 PM
19/09/2022	24	12:22 AM
20/09/2022	25	1:17 AM
21/09/2022	26	2:15 AM
22/09/2022	27	3:15 AM
23/09/2022	28	4:17 AM
24/09/2022	29	5:19 AM
25/09/2022	30	6:22 AM
25/09/2022	1	5:54 PM
26/09/2022	2	7:27 AM
27/09/2022	3	8:33 AM
28/09/2022	4	9:40 AM
29/09/2022	5	10:49 AM
30/09/2022	6	11:58 AM

London Time		
Calendar Day	Lunar Day	Lunar Day Start Time
01/09/2022	6	12:06 PM
02/09/2022	7	1:23 PM
03/09/2022	8	2:38 PM
04/09/2022	9	3:48 PM
05/09/2022	10	4:48 PM
06/09/2022	11	5:37 PM
07/09/2022	12	6:14 PM
08/09/2022	13	6:44 PM
09/09/2022	14	7:08 PM
10/09/2022	15	7:30 PM
11/09/2022	16	7:50 PM
12/09/2022	17	8:10 PM
13/09/2022	18	8:31 PM
14/09/2022	19	8:55 PM
15/09/2022	20	9:24 PM
16/09/2022	21	9:58 PM
17/09/2022	22	10:40 PM
18/09/2022	23	11:30 PM
20/09/2022	24	12:28 AM
21/09/2022	25	1:31 AM
22/09/2022	26	2:38 AM
23/09/2022	27	3:47 AM
24/09/2022	28	4:58 AM
25/09/2022	29	6:10 AM
25/09/2022	1	10:54 PM
26/09/2022	2	7:23 AM
27/09/2022	3	8:38 AM
28/09/2022	4	9:54 AM
29/09/2022	5	11:12 AM
30/09/2022	6	12:29 PM

You can find the description of each lunar day in the chapter "A Guide to The Moon Cycle and Lunar Days"

Aries

A fun August has come to an end, and you are looking at some long days at work. As they say, though, business before pleasure!

Work. The best time for anything work-related is the first ten days of September. During this time, you will be able to deal with business, finances, and also define your relationship with certain colleagues. The stars recommend that entrepreneurs and managers keep a close eye on their teams, as some of your subordinates may not be doing their part to reach the goals of your growing business. Employees should be meticulous in their work in order to avoid any problems.

During the last 20 days of September, Mercury, the planet responsible for connections and contacts, will be in retrograde, which means that you can expect some serious delays. Try to avoid starting any new projects and just focus on those that have already begun. This is an ideal time for finding any shortcomings in your current projects and considering where you are headed.

Be especially careful when it comes to your connections with colleagues in other cities or abroad. Your relationship with them will quickly hit some turbulence, so if you are planning on any cooperation, consider any possible alternative, including those that may seem less than pleasant.

Money. In September, your bank account is looking healthy. After a financially ruinous August, many Aries will have a good opportunity to improve their financial situation. Expect the largest amounts to come in on September 5-7, 14, 15, and 23-25. Your expenses will be low, but also predictable and reasonable.

Love and family. During the first half of the month, your life will be peaceful and calm, whether you are married or just coupled up. Expect some petty squabbles during the second half of the month. If you do not address them, they may grow into major fights. One reason for this may be complicated relationships within your family and some ties with relatives.

The stars recommend that you avoid burning bridges and avoid saying things you can't take back or doing anything rash. Remember that everyone has their own opinions on life, and you need to respect that.

Health. In September, you are healthy and energetic, but the stars recommend that you cake care when driving or traveling. This is especially the case during the second half of September. During this time, try to take your time and be calm about things – there is a good reason why doctors say that nerves are behind every disease.

Taurus

Don't count on making any major achievements this month. At the same time, nothing is stopping you from finishing what you already started in the recent past, or thinking about what you are planning next.

Work. The stars recommend that you finish up any important business before September 10. After that, Mercury will be in retrograde, and this is a time when it is best to avoid any major decisions, and things are less likely to turn out in your favor. This will continue until October 2, and so it is best to focus on small, everyday tasks and lay the groundwork for your next steps.

Entrepreneurs will be continuing to expand their business and will be putting a lot of resources into various transactions related to real estate.

It would be best for employees to focus on their personal lives, where important changes are underway.

While Mercury is in retrograde, you can expect some minor misunderstandings, that may look differently depending on your life. Entrepreneurs might encounter challenges with their teams, or involving various audits or inspections from authorities.

Employees should be very careful with documents and keep an eye on their colleagues. You can expect gossip on your team, and if you participate, you will take the fall.

Money. The stars recommend that you keep an eye on your finances, in September as well as in the next several months this year. Aggressive Mars will be firmly in the sector of the sky responsible for money, and appears to have it in for you. In some cases, this may be related to work, and in others, to your personal life. Keep your spending in check and take steps to save. Right now, your motto is "Trust, yet verify".

Love and family. Many Taureans are spending most of their time with household tasks, this month. Home improvements are coming along nicely, and that may be taking the lion's share of your family's budget. You may also find yourself spending on your children's needs, which will be significant all month long.

Couples are going to begin a difficult period, in which their relationship will be put to the test in one way or another. It seems that the honeymoon is over, and things are about to get rough. You might learn that your partner has different values or other priorities in life. Alternatively, the path toward happiness together may be riddled with various material problems. In short, the love boat will collide with the cold, hard iceberg of real life. If you don't want it to sink, that's going to require some work from both of you. Keep that in mind and act accordingly!

Health. In September, many Taureans will have a great opportunity to travel, relax, and get away from it all. Give yourself the gift of a week or so at the beach, the spa, or something to cleanse your body and soul. If you aren't able to do that, then head to the countryside or a local park, and enjoy the last days of summer.

Gemini

In September, you will come to a fork in the road, and often the one that takes you to your goals is winding and difficult. Find a way out of these complicated mazes!

Work. At work, you will be able to consider September as an intermediate step that will take you closer to the goals you have set. You may have to take a step back and assess the situation and deal with various administrative issues and household matters, as well.

Your ruler, Mercury, will be in retrograde from September 10 to October 2, and as usual, that will entail a series of obstacles. Many Geminis will run into issues with friends or highly placed people you were counting on. You may also encounter opposition – perhaps you are planning on one thing, but those in charge have something else in mind. This is unlikely to be resolved in September, and may drag on for a while.

In every area of your life, mid-September is the most difficult time, while the first week of the month is the most favorable.

Money. You can describe your financial situation as neutral this month. You will not have any major windfalls, but your expenses will all be predictable and reasonable. The stars predict that much of them will be related to your personal life.

If necessary, many Geminis may count on help from parents, a spouse, or a loved one.

Love and family. Most Geminis are focused on their home and family in September. Though you are not experiencing stardom at work, this is a great time for any home improvement projects. Spouses with a harmonious marriage will tackle this with the help of love and wisdom.

In families experiencing conflict, things may become very tense. Mars is a tough, aggressive planet, and right now it is in your sky; most likely, that will be the case for the next six months, which means you may be lacking in tactfulness, diplomacy, and find yourself burning bridges over arguments. Remember that failing to hold your tongue or control your actions can cause very serious problems, so be careful and attentive. This is relevant advice for couples, whether or not they are married. If you simply no longer wish to save your relationship and have already made a decision, then feel free to ignore this advice.

Health. This month, you are healthy, energetic, and the stars strongly urge you to take advantage of this energy, but only for peaceful purposes. Right now, you are ready to move mountains!

Cancer

It seems that you have found an outlet for all of your talents! The stars have only one piece of advice – before you jump into something new, it is worth working with what you already have.

Work. It's time for some changes! You have new, productive relationships that will lead the start of some interesting projects, and that certainly means success and income.

However, there are some old problems lurking on the horizon, and the stars recommend that you tackle them as soon as possible.

Therefore, entrepreneurs and managers may be grappling with some difficult issues related to real estate, as well as various legal claims. You might be visited by inspection agencies, and it is worth taking this very seriously and preparing ahead of time.

Employees will take a step toward the future, and in some cases, that may involve a new job, while in others, a significant promotion right where they are. The best time for any of this is the first week of September.

From September 10 to October 2, Mercury, the planet of connections, ideas, and contacts, will be in retrograde. This is a bad time to start any new projects and promote your new ideas. You might find yourself missing the people you need, dealing with red-tape, and that you will have to keep coming back to deal with and reconsider small details.

This is why if you managed to make any progress in August or early September, hold onto your positions. If you intend on following through with your plans, remember that they will probably have to wait a bit.

Your relationship with colleagues from other cities or abroad will become more difficult for various reasons, and mid-September will be the most challenging time for this.

Money. Your financial situation is looking rather uneventful this month. You will not have any windfalls, but you will also not end up in ruins. Expect the largest sums to come in on September 3-5, 12, 13, and 21-23.

Love and family. Your personal life is not exactly smooth sailing, this month. A recent romance has unexpectedly started to stagnate. You might see some abrupt changes in mid-September, and you will start to realize you are on opposite sides of the barricades. It is hard to predict how things will play out in each individual case, but the stars suggest that some secrets that will seriously damage the relationship will come to light.

Do your reputation a favor and take pains to avoid any gossip! This is relevant both at home and at work!

Stable partnerships with families might be busy with various issues related to real estate or relatives' affairs.

In September, a relationship with a loved one will become much more difficult, and mid-month, you might find yourself dealing with a lot of grudges and hurt feelings. In some cases, this may be due to an inheritance or real estate. There may be other reasons, as well, but you are likely to find cause for concern, either way.

Health. Mars is a tough, aggressive planet, and it is in the part of the sky responsible for weakening positions on all fronts. Naturally, that includes health. In addition to feeling generally sluggish, you might face various issues when driving or on the road. The most challenging time for this is the last 20 days of the month, when the likelihood of accidents is very high. During this time, avoid any dangerous situations and take good care of yourself!

Leo

You have always known where you are headed, but right now, you might find yourself coming to a crossroads. As they say, "I want to go to heaven, but they won't allow any sins."

Work. A part of your professional life has come to a definitive end. That is not a bad thing – you are about to begin a fantastic new chapter in which you are starting over from scratch, but still able to achieve many things. Before you make that step into the future, however, you will have to deal with some matters from the distant past.

Entrepreneurs will have to dig in for the long battle ahead with a friend or a highly placed individual, and as usual, the problem is money or other material assets. In the most extreme cases, you may find yourself in court.

Alternatively, you will face major challenges from colleagues in other cities or abroad. This will also involve material plans, and may end in a lawsuit.

You may also run into problems involving official bodies – either in your own country or from another region or abroad. The last 20 days of the month will be the hardest, when everything will come to a head.

Money. Your situation at work is so complicated that it is only natural that you are likely to experience financial issues, as well. You will not find yourself completely penniless, but expect a lot of expenses this month.

In some cases, that may be due to difficulties at work, and in others, personal problems will be the culprit. Either way, the stars recommend that you keep an eye on your wallet, especially if you work in finance or banking.

What's more – if you really owe someone and claims from an opponent are founded, it is worth thinking about how to settle them as soon as you can.

Love and family. Your personal life is not going quite the way you had hoped. In many families, there are problems involving relatives, and in some cases, that may be due to close relatives' problems, or possibly a major fight.

Most couples are likely to face misunderstandings. Abrupt changes are underway, and this will probably take place in mid-September. They may be caused by external circumstances. Alternatively, you and your partner may suddenly discover that you have wildly different values, or worse – someone is claiming the other owes them money. It is a bad idea to mix love and money, but even if that is the case, the stars recommend not burning any bridges. Keep a cool head and don't make any definitive decisions just yet.

Health. Your biggest problem this month will be a difficult emotional situation, both at work and at home. The stress may mean that you will periodically feel disappointed, fatigued, and listless. Take care of yourself and try to move around, spend time in nature, and remember to get enough sleep.

Also be careful when traveling or driving! The last 20 days of the month are the most dangerous.

Virgo

September is a special month for you. You are beginning a period in which everything that was completed in previous years will literally be turned upside down. However, that does not mean that the life you are used to is better than what awaits.

Work. You have done a lot, and now you find yourself right at the heart of change. The past is coming to an end, and there are a lot of concerns about the future. You have a lot of work, including various administrative tasks, and many Virgos will have to grapple with material issues, as well.

Entrepreneurs and managers will potentially face a thorny situation involving a business partner. You may be dealing with mutual financial claims and various material misunderstandings. Resolving them is not something that you will manage to complete in one month, and these issues are likely to continue for another six months.

It is in your best interest to resolve these tasks as soon as you can, which means not taking advantage of things, but also remembering the people who have a professional relationship to your business. Alternatively, you may find that people who promised you support are in no rush to follow through with that. In the worst cases, they may refuse to take on any responsibilities at all.

Employees might see major changes in their leadership at work. This will be a long, difficult process, so here is no need to get upset, but rather keep calm and get through it. There is no point in looking for a new job right now, so be satisfied with what you have.

Money. Your money situation is looking up and down this month. On one hand, you will not find yourself penniless, but you will also face some hefty expenses. You may have to pay off some old debts, or deal with the needs of your home and family. Expect the largest sums to come in on September 4, 7, 8, 16, 17, 26, and 27.

Love and family. Your personal life is going through some tough times, and that may look differently for everyone. Couples who get along might be working on a move, improving the comfort of their home, or starting to consider real estate for opening their own business.

Couples with a less-than-ideal relationship and those who recently made the difficult decision to separate or divorce may be dealing with endless questions about who owes whom and who needs what. Naturally, this is not easy, and you might not be finished with these issues until the end of 2022.

Your ruler, Mercury, will be in retrograde from September 10 to October 2, and you know better than anyone that things have a tendency to stall during this time. What's more – this is a good time to step back and study the situation and make preparations for the future, but it's best to avoid any concrete plans right now. Don't rush things!

Health. You are not in the best of health right now. Be careful, especially if you are elderly, weakened, or suffer from chronic diseases. If that is you, think about how to take care of yourself, especially since you are about to begin a long period in which your body will constantly be put to the test.

Young and healthy Virgos should avoid any bad habits, eat a balanced diet, and get enough sleep.

Libra

September is one of the most difficult months of your year. Hold on and remember that you've got to break a few eggs to make an omelet!

Work. In September, many Libras may find themselves on the receiving end of a lot of spite and ill will. In some cases, that may mean disagreements with a business partner who promised one thing and then did quite another – or maybe nothing at all. Or maybe colleagues in other cities or abroad are behaving irresponsibly or maliciously. This conflict will become part of the background in your life in September and for the next several months.

Entrepreneurs and managers should keep a close eye on subordinates – one of them may still be playing their own game, which will lead to serious damages for your reputation and business. This may not be the first time, either, so watch your employees like a hawk.

What's more, a lot of things may have happened in secret without you noticing, and you will only learn about them in mid-September. Keep your finger on the pulse of things and look around for any weak points. This is relevant for entrepreneurs and employees alike, as competitors of all stripes may be sabotaging your work. Keep your eyes open and avoid gossip.

Money. Financially speaking, this month is not particularly promising, but that is no surprise given everything going on at work. Expect a lot of expenses and less income than usual, so avoid spending if you can and watch both your money and those around you.

Love and family. If your personal life is more important to you, get ready for some trouble here, too. Problems can appear out of thin air and still knock you off your feet.

Spouses with old grudges will be surprised to discover their partner is ready to take decisive action and unwilling to give in at all. Your attempts at smoothing things over will be seen as weakness and lead nowhere. If relatives get involved in your argument, things will get even worse.

Unmarried couples will also experience an unexpected deterioration in their relationship – especially if you find yourselves torn between two options. In September, some secrets will come to light, and you will not be able to sidestep a scandal! Remember that and take precautions. Remember that whatever happens in September will have longstanding and decisive consequences, so if you are planning any big changes at work or in your personal life, think things over again.

Health. Those who have managed to escape trouble at home or at work might find it in their health. In September, there is a high likelihood of old, chronic diseases flaring up again, and you might face some unexpected and new problems, as well. Be very careful when traveling or driving. The last 20 days of the month are the most dangerous.

Scorpio

After an incredibly successful and prosperous August, your feet are going to come crashing to the ground. If the pressure from the heavens feels like it's just too much, gather your strength as best you can and remember – one that's been caned is worth two that haven't.

Work. Things at work are getting unexpectedly difficult. Your relationship with friends or someone highly placed will become a challenge, possibly over money or other material values, with both parties having different ideas about shared rights and mutual obligations.

The stars recommend that employees take care when it comes to their responsibilities and avoid reacting to colleagues' vicious attacks and gossip. Nothing will make much sense, and it is impossible to avoid trouble if you join in. Entrepreneurs and managers should keep a close eye on their subordinates as there is trouble brewing on the team.

If you let things run their course, this situation may drag out for a long time and seriously hamper your work. From September 10 to October 2, Mercury, the planet responsible for connections and contacts, will be in retrograde, and in your case, that may lead to chaos and confusion at work as well as in your relationships with many people.

In order to minimize the damage, focus, dig in for the long haul, and try to anticipate any shortcomings in your work and projects. Only taking a cold, hard look at the situation will allow you to avoid problems this month and in those that follow.

Money. You are having some financial trouble, this month. You seem to be bleeding money, which is no surprise given your situation at work. Those whose lives revolve around family, love, and children might also experience problems. You will have a lot of expenses and hardly any income coming your way in September. Many will have to spend what they had previously earned.

Love and family. Your personal life is no picnic this month, either. Parents might face challenges involving their children, and in the best cases, you will be able to simply throw money at the problem, though in the worst case you will feel emotionally spent.

Couples might disappoint each other. You have been repressing some things that bothered you, and unexpectedly, they will suddenly rise to the surface. That will reveal a lot about your partner and answer the question – is this the person I need? Soon, you will know for sure. In the worst cases, your romance will simply burn to the ground... If you are not ready for that, then take a break and try to just wait it out.

Health. This is a challenging month and it may sap your energy and even cause serious health problems. Those who suffer from cardiovascular diseases or chronic drops in blood pressure will be feeling pressure from the heavens and need to be very careful in order to avoid things getting worse.

The last 20 days of September may lead to accidents and injuries, so be very careful when driving and take care to avoid any further risk. Watch your health and that of your family!

Sagittarius

In theory, September could be one of the best months of 2022 for you – everything you need is right there. But every rose has its thorn, and you might be dealing with a lot of thorns, right now.

Work. In September, you may find yourself very busy at work, and during the first 10 days of the month you will be very productive, too. From September 10 to October 2, however, Mercury, the planet responsible for connections and contacts, will be in retrograde, and you will realize that it is suddenly very difficult to move forward with anything (in the best of cases), if not impossible.

Many Sagittarians will be grappling with problems involving a friend or someone highly placed who once provided you with great support.

You will also feel a lot of tension with other people, and that may take on the form of unfriendly competition. Though you are in a strong position, be careful, as this situation is unlikely to end anytime soon. Competitors are not going to retreat, and they will begin making one demand after the next. It is worth taking this into consideration. In September, your negotiations with them will not go very far, and this is unlikely to be resolved for the next three to four months.

Money. Despite all the trouble at work, everything is looking good when it comes to your finances. You might receive a nice profit from some work you completed in the past, and you can expect the greatest sums to come in on September 5-7, 14, 15, and 25-27. You will have a lot of expenses, and they may be related to your work-related issues, or possibly your personal life.

Love and family. If, by the will of Fate, most of your excitement this month will happen in your personal life, peace and quiet is still only a dream.

In many families, you are experiencing disagreements with your children. The elder generation may be worried about various collisions between your personal and professional lives, while younger family members' behavior may leave much to be desired. Alternatively, your children's needs may require a huge amount of money and the entire family will feel the weight of that burden.

This will be a hard month for couples, as they will have to unexpectedly change their plans due to the emergence of new tasks and plans.

You will have to have a serious talk with a loved one in mid-September, and this may shed a lot of light on your relationship. This may allow both of you to better understand each other's nature. That is a good thing, as long as it allows you to move forward in understanding what is going on around you. Alternatively, your partner's position may be difficult for you to accept. If there is any love between you, you should be able to find some sort of compromise.

Married couples might also find themselves arguing. During the second half of the month, you might face unexpected complaints you may not have an answer for. Your arguing and conflict may continue through the rest of 2022, which will seriously weaken your family ties and force you to look at your relationship from a new perspective. Remember that and try to nip any fights in the bud, so they don't turn into an all-out forest fire.

Health. In September, you are feeling energetic, which means you are able to take on anything this month throws at you.

Capricorn

In September, you can expect a lot of imbalances on significant fronts. It may seem as if the world you know is falling into strange pieces, and it will take a

long time to pick them all up again.

Work. The first 10 days of September will be an incredibly productive and successful time. Things will be moving ahead, and you will be actively developing your contacts with people in other cities and abroad. However, during the last 20 days of the month, all of that will change. Mercury, the planet responsible for connections and contacts, will be in retrograde, and everything that was going so well will unexpectedly come to a screeching halt.

Entrepreneurs and managers might be disappointed in their subordinates, as one of them will start playing by his or her own rules. Don't take your eye off of this issue and be very careful as you observe the dynamic within your team. The stars suggest that this situation may continue in the future and will cause a lot of problems. It is even possible that employee negligence will harm useful relationships with associates, including with colleagues in other cities or abroad.

Any plans related to expanding your business or buying land or real estate will also slow down significantly.

Employees can expect major restructuring on their teams, and for some time, things may seem as though they are simply suspended. No matter which way you turn, it's a dead end. Sometimes, that's the way the cookie crumbles!

Money. At least for now, your difficulties at work will not be reflected in your finances, which will remain normal – no more and no less than usual. This makes it easy to be optimistic as you look toward the future and resolve problems as they arise. You are a tough one, and things are sure to work out for you in the end!

Love and family. Your personal life is unclear, right now. Couples who have been fighting might once again get into it over some real estate, but this month, it will not amount to anything. More harmonious families may face problems involving relatives who may be ill or going through tough times. You might have a serious argument on your hands, as well.

It is hard to say what is in store for unmarried couples, but the less-than favorable ambiance this month may suck them in, too. In the best cases, they will not see each other as much as they had hoped, and in the worst cases, they can expect to be seriously disappointed in one another and for things to seriously cool off. Whether that is temporary or chronic depends on each individual situation, as well as your future plans.

Health. The agitated, restless atmosphere this month may be reflected in your health, which doctors say depends not only on medicine, but on living a healthy lifestyle and taking care of your nervous system. Remember this, and keep in mind that there is a light at the end of the tunnel. All things shall pass! Remember those wise words of wise King Solomon, who was certainly right!

Aquarius

This month, you will understand that the path to the top is becoming more difficult and even the slightest movement forward requires incredible effort on your part. But that doesn't mean you should give up on your goals and do nothing! Take a break, take a step back and look around, and then get ready to continue charging ahead!

Work. The first 10 days of September are the best time of the month. During this time, you might take a trip, and be active when negotiating with colleagues in other cities or abroad. However, during the last 20 days of the month, you may notice that many projects that had been developing successfully in August and early September, have suddenly come to a halt. A series of obstacles now lie in your path, and this may look differently, depending on your field and your future plans.

Those planning on a move or collaborating with colleagues in other cities or abroad will run into difficulties. They may involve the laws of another country, or perhaps strange, erratic behavior from a colleague from faraway. Alternatively, you may see old legal troubles rear their heads again, or unexpected new ones may appear. In either case, remember that this month, and in the future, it is not worth breaking any laws. Be careful and follow any instructions you are given in order to avoid any problems that might haunt you until winter.

Money. Your financial situation is looking rather neutral this month. You will not receive any windfalls, but you will be able to avoid a lot of expenses. The astrologist predicts that most of the expenses you do have will be related to your personal life and family-related problems.

Love and family. Your personal life is looking uneven and turbulent in September. Families may face problems involving their children, and this may not come cheap. As you jump forward, you can say that any problems that come up this month may drag on, so it is worth giving your children's issues the attention they deserve.

Some difficult issues related to real estate may now be in their final stages of being resolved. Even if they appeared to have already been put away, there may still be some loose ends to tie up, and it may take more work than you anticipated.

In many families, there may be some tension involving relatives. You might find yourself in a huge argument with several of your loved ones. Alternatively, a relative might fall ill or suffer a very difficult period, and if that is the case, they will need some help, whether moral or financial.

September is a very difficult time for unmarried couples. A recent romance will suddenly cool down and you will fall back down to earth with a thud. The cause will be hard to predict, but there will probably be a reason for your dissatisfaction in one another. If the relationship means anything to you, then watch your tongue and control yourself as much as you can.

Health. In September, you are feeling less than energetic, so take care of yourself and remember that moderation is key. Be very careful when traveling and driving, as the last 20 days of the month will be the most dangerous time.

Pisces

September is a month of unexpected changes, so don't even try to follow the plans you have set for yourself. Try to look at the situation from a new angle – you might manage to find your way in Fate's intricate labyrinth.

Work. Money will be the biggest issue on your mind all month, because it is most likely seriously lacking. This will consume entrepreneurs and managers at every level. You might be expanding your business, or carrying out various real estate transactions, which will require a lot of resources. People you once counted on are nowhere to be found right now, and perhaps you have had an argument over financial issues.

Employees can expect changes, which might be something positive. However, even good intentions might end up hanging in the lurch simply due to a lack of funds.

The astrologist predicts that this situation will last, and you will need to think out of the box if you are going to find your way out of it. The stars recommend calculating everything ahead of time and paying close attention to your partners, leadership, and the powers that be. This will allow you to avoid any hassles, forces majeures, and unnecessary frenzy.

The last 20 days of the month will be the most difficult, when you will see problems crop up over and over.

Money. This month may be one of the most challenging for your finances. It may feel like you have a hole in your pocket, and that may be related to unresolved issues at work, or possibly due to family problems. Either way, every heart knows its own bitterness.

Be very careful if you work directly with money – as an accountant, broker, or banker, for example. There is a high chance of mistakes this month, and any risk may lead to serious losses. Remember this and act accordingly!

Love and family. You will be facing a dilemma in your personal life this month. You might be about to make some serious changes and build a future counting your spouse or partner supporting you in everything you do.

Alternatively, this may involve your family's home, building a house, summer home, or a new apartment. If that is the case, you will have to understand that not everything you were promised is going to become a reality. Were you counting on unreliable people? Or were there simply circumstances that had a less-than desirable effect on your relationships? Either way, remember that you will find a solution to this, but it will take patience. Do not demand more than what people can give you. Regardless of what you are facing, it is much better to take on problems as a team than alone.

Health. In September, you are feeling sluggish, but there is nothing serious going on, if you remember to stick to a schedule and take care to not put your body to the test. Elderly people and those who have been weakened by disease should especially take care of themselves and try to prevent any old chronic diseases from flaring up again.

October

New York Time		
Calendar Day	Lunar Day	Lunar Day Start Time
01/10/2022	7	1:04 PM
02/10/2022	8	2:04 PM
03/10/2022	9	2:57 PM
04/10/2022	10	3:43 PM
05/10/2022	11	4:21 PM
06/10/2022	12	4:55 PM
07/10/2022	13	5:25 PM
08/10/2022	14	5:54 PM
09/10/2022	15	6:23 PM
10/10/2022	16	6:52 PM
11/10/2022	17	7:24 PM
12/10/2022	18	7:59 PM
13/10/2022	19	8:39 PM
14/10/2022	20	9:23 PM
15/10/2022	21	10:12 PM
16/10/2022	22	11:06 PM
18/10/2022	23	12:03 AM
19/10/2022	24	1:02 AM
20/10/2022	25	2:03 AM
21/10/2022	26	3:04 AM
22/10/2022	27	4:06 AM
23/10/2022	28	5:10 AM
24/10/2022	29	6:16 AM
25/10/2022	1	6:48 AM
25/10/2022	2	7:25 AM
26/10/2022	3	8:35 AM
27/10/2022	4	9:46 AM
28/10/2022	5	10:55 AM
29/10/2022	6	11:59 AM
30/10/2022	7	12:55 PM
31/10/2022	8	1:42 PM

London Time		
Calendar Day	Lunar Day	Lunar Day Start Time
01/10/2022	7	1:41 PM
02/10/2022	8	2:44 PM
03/10/2022	9	3:35 PM
04/10/2022	10	4:15 PM
05/10/2022	11	4:46 PM
06/10/2022	12	5:11 PM
07/10/2022	13	5:33 PM
08/10/2022	14	5:53 PM
09/10/2022	15	6:12 PM
10/10/2022	16	6:33 PM
11/10/2022	17	6:55 PM
12/10/2022	18	7:22 PM
13/10/2022	19	7:54 PM
14/10/2022	20	8:34 PM
15/10/2022	21	9:21 PM
16/10/2022	22	10:16 PM
17/10/2022	23	11:17 PM
19/10/2022	24	12:22 AM
20/10/2022	25	1:30 AM
21/10/2022	26	2:39 AM
22/10/2022	27	3:50 AM
23/10/2022	28	5:03 AM
24/10/2022	29	6:18 AM
25/10/2022	30	7:35 AM
25/10/2022	1	11:48 AM
26/10/2022	2	8:54 AM
27/10/2022	3	10:14 AM
28/10/2022	4	11:30 AM
29/10/2022	5	12:38 PM
30/10/2022	6	12:33 PM
31/10/2022	7	1:16 PM

You can find the description of each lunar day in the chapter "A Guide to The Moon Cycle and Lunar Days"

Aries

Avoid rushing to the finish line in October, both at work and in your relationships. Keep calm and avoid any sudden moves. That's the most important thing right now!

Work. Your partnerships are the most important thing this month. For some time now, you have been very lucky that the expectations of those around you have largely coincided with what you want – and now the time has come to listen to your partners' views and a least make some partial concessions. If you do, your plans will move along much more quickly and smoothly, both for you and others involved.

The best time for anything work-related is the second ten days of October, when you may see some positive changes taking place.

The stars still recommend paying particularly close attention to your partners in other cities and abroad. If things in this area are going unusually smoothly during the second ten days of the month, closer to the end, things will change, and not for the better. You will begin a period in which for various reasons, previous agreements may suddenly hit a roadblock or simply not be carried out. If you can, find a way to secure your agreements with something significant, which will help you avoid any unpleasantness or at least mitigate it.

Money. This month, your finances are not looking their best. You might be spending constantly, and you can expect the largest expenses in mid-October. In any case, expect money to come in on October 2-4, 12, 21, and 22.

Love and family. The stars recommend that you give up some control over your loved ones. Control can look like excessive pressuring, gentle care and unobtrusive love, or something in between. This month, attempting to exert too much control over events in your personal life will only come back to haunt you.

You may still be busy with home improvements. Most likely, this involves a lot of small issues you will have to resolve. Alternatively, you will be working on finishing or purchasing furniture or other items for your home.

In many families, you will have to grapple with some issues involving relatives. For now, these are only warning signs of a future fight, but it is worth keeping an eye on things, since the situation can easily continue into the future.

Health. In October you are not threatened by any health problems, though you may notice a significant drop in energy levels from October 25-26, during the new moon. This time, the new moon is coinciding with an eclipse, so gather your strength and be sure to watch your diet and avoid abusing alcohol.

The eclipse can bring a lot of conflict with it, as well as the risk of injury and ruin, so be very patient and careful during this time.

Taurus

October is a great time to pause, take a step back, and fix any mistakes – and there's always something. You can always learn from mistakes, and not only those committed by other people!

Work. October is a good time to thoroughly analyze the situation and work on managing it. You might initially think that you are barely making any progress, but that is not the case. The world does not sit still, so make up for lost time and be decisive- you will soon be rewarded.

Entrepreneurs and managers should get things in order with their teams, in order to smooth over a situation that came up in September. Those with legal problems or other difficulties involving auditing authorities should also take steps to iron out any kinks.

Employees can strengthen their position within their team. In order to do that, though, you are going to have to put in some elbow grease.

For anything work-related, the best time is the second half of October, when things will be much calmer at work. Those who work with colleagues from other cities or abroad might continue to face obstacles, however. This will most likely be temporary, though they will not be resolved this month.

For various reasons, any trips panned for October may not come to fruition.

Money. Your bank account is looking much better this month than it did in the previous month. You are busy as a bee, and the results are starting to show. Near the end of the month, you will be back in the black.

Expect the largest sums to come in on October 5, 6, 13-15, 23, and 24. Of course you will have some expenses, but the astrologist predicts that they will be small and related to your job and current household needs.

Love and family. The astrologist predicts that your personal life will be on the back burner this month – work comes first. Couples may not see as much of each other as they might have liked, or things may start to cool off between them. Sometimes life throws these things at us, and we just have to get through it.

Alternatively, issues from last month are still making your life difficult and have dragged some skeletons out of either your or your partner's closet.

This is very pertinent to married couples who do not trust each other.

The solar eclipse on October 25 will bring several secrets to light, and no one will be spared.

Health. In October, many Taureans might not be feeling very well. Young and healthy people may be crushed by a mountain of work, while elderly people and those suffering from chronic disease might become seriously ill.

Remember that the most important thing is your health, and anything else will follow. If you feel unwell, visit a doctor.

Gemini

This month, you will find yourself being pulled between work and family or personal obligations. Maybe the latter will seem more important. In sum, your life is flourishing once again!

Work. October is chock full of meetings, discussions, and contacts. Some of them may be more useful than others. But you never know until you try, so try to separate the wheat from the chaff and remember that not all that glitters is gold.

The stars recommend that you avoid chasing any beautiful yet empty ideas. This advice is particularly relevant for the first ten days of October.

Your connections with colleagues in other cities and abroad are moving along nicely, but most likely this involves renewing past cooperation.

During the last 20 days of the month, those who work in creative fields – actors, artists, musicians – can expect particular success.

If you try, you might become a star of your social networks – this month your ingenuity and creativity will become the hallmarks of many Geminis.

Only the new moon on October 25 will force you to dive into your work, and require your utmost concentration, attention, and patience. After a creative period of relative freedom, you will become extremely busy and disciplined.

Money. In October, your financial situation may not be its best. You can expect a lot of expenses, and the stars predict that most of them will be related to your personal life and demands from your children and loved ones.

You might also have some unexpected surprises – gifts, help from parents, or a lucky alignment of various financial circumstances. You can count on money you earned at the end of the month, and the largest sums will come in on October 25-27.

Love and family. All month long, your romantic entanglements and family relationships may be occupying all of your time.

You can expect one of the most pleasant developments this month in your personal life – some time off, a romance developing, or even children being born.

Couples whose relationship was on the rocks in September may be able to kiss and make up. Here, a lot depends on you and your desire to meet your loved ones halfway. But if you do that, you will immediately get the reaction you were hoping for.

Spouses with a good relationship will spend a lot of time with their children, who will give you reasons to be happy.

Those busy improving their home might have to continue with some bothersome tasks during the first ten days of October. This time, it may not involve major construction, but tying up loose ends and details – furniture and interior décor.

Health. All month long, you are healthy, energetic, and very charming. Only the new moon and eclipse from October 25-27 can wear you out a bit, especially if you are weak or elderly.

Young and healthy Geminis should be careful when driving and avoid any dangerous situations. This is especially pertinent from October 1 to 6.

Cancer

This month is looking rather neutral for you, and you can expect a lot of routine tasks at work and no more. We all need periods like this, and it is a chance to think about how you can strengthen things on the home front.

Work. This is not the best time for anything work-related. Many Cancers will be taking some time off or spending time with their family. The exception to this is those who work in construction or whose business is somehow related to real estate, who can be assured of buyers' attention and financial success.

Entrepreneurs might also be busy strengthening their production base. You might be rehabbing facilities or overhauling your team or even studying and revising your business goals.

Employees are once again seeing some changes in their company. This time, those changes may be serious and long-term. If you want to make a clean break and run, remember that you are not likely to find a new job, at least not in the next two to three months.

If you are unable to change jobs during the summer months, try to hold onto your position and weather the changes.

Those with longstanding legal problems will be able to eventually resolve them, though that is likely to be a slow process that will not be completed in October.

Money. Your money situation will experience a lot of ups and downs in October. Much will depend on your field and problems from the past.

During the first ten days of October, Cancers will have pay back credit and other old debts. You might have a friend or former associate asking you to pay back something you owe.

Nonetheless, you can also expect some decent income from various real estate transactions, such as rent or a sale. You might also receive support from your parents or a loved one.

Love and family. Many Cancers will be focused on their home life and family in October. You may be busy with repairs or some major rehab projects on your home, which will turn out well. This will be the case for happy couples and those who have already divorced.

Those planning a move might also be busy with various day-to-day tasks related to this very tedious event.

The new moon and eclipse on October 26 will make you think about taking some time off and traveling, but that will have to wait until next month.

Health. In October, you are feeling a bit sluggish, so remember to follow a routine and don't forget the benefits of morning exercise, in order to greet the day in shape and avoid any lethargy, which is likely during this busy month.

Leo

You are looking at an active, positive month. The stars strongly urge you to not put things off for tomorrow that you can do today. Everything will work out in your favor!

Work. Your main task this month is resolving problems that appeared in the recent past. Difficult relationships with colleagues in other cities or abroad will be resolved favorably in October. You might have to turn to an intermediary in order to achieve that – they might be a friend or someone highly placed. This situation is also likely for those who are dealing with legal trouble or misunderstandings involving auditing agencies.

Your relationships with like-minded people, friends or someone highly placed will look much more difficult. Calm, flexibility, and consistency are your trump cards. Giving into your ego or trying to force things will not bring you to your goals, and will in fact only take you further from them. Be vigilant of your opponents' moods- and if you owe them something, give it to them – or at least commit to doing so. There's no avoiding mutual claims, but if you have a chance to settle up, you shouldn't let it pass you by.

The best time for anything work-related is the second ten days of the month. If you manage to reach an agreement during this time, try to back up any verbal agreements with something you can fall back on, like a signed contract.

Those planning on starting to do business in another city or abroad might be busy with various administrative tasks this month. That includes the finishing touches on projects and studying up on laws, as well as working with partners and defining your financial positions on both sides.

Employees should be careful with management, and in case of any issues, do not take things to the very top, but to the second in command.

Money. October is a neutral month for your finances. Your income will be modest, but your expenses will be reasonable and, according to the stars, mostly related to paying off old debts or household issues.

Love and family. Those who are focused on their personal lives this month will also find October to be a very beneficial month for their families. Any problems with relatives that popped up last month will be resolved, one way or another. Even if there is any residual resentment simmering, it is worth remembering that bad peace is better than a good war, which is very true.

Anyone planning a move might be busy with various issues related to real estate this month. You might be finishing up an interior and buying furniture and items for your décor.

Couples on the rocks and those divorcing might be dealing with thorny issues related to property, but this time they will be more peaceful about it. You might get some real support from an attorney or close relative.

Health. This month, you are active, healthy, energetic, and have no reason to fear falling ill. Any trips planned in October will be very successful, which is only fair in both your work and persona life.

Virgo

Your motto this month is "patience and hard work". You're used to that, so there is nothing new here!

Work. In October, you are working wonders with your ingenuity and entrepreneurship, in order to resolve some recent problems in your business. You will achieve a lot of what you set out to do! Difficult financial issues involving certain partners or opponents will be resolved favorably.

Entrepreneurs and managers will have to change a lot about their business, and this will continue into the future.

Employees' companies are undergoing changes. You might see new leadership, as well as reconsiderations of the direction business is going, though most Virgos will not have anything to worry about – for now. If you intend to look for a new job, this month you can negotiate some exit terms in your favor. You might receive some compensation that will give you some wiggle room to look for something better.

The eclipse and new moon on October 25 will make it possible for you to go on a trip or step up contacts with colleagues from afar. These changes will continue throughout October and also all of November.

Money. Your bank account is looking good in October. Money will be coming in regularly, and there will be significantly more of it, too. You might obtain profits or dividends from work you completed in the past, a bonus, or a raise. That will allow you to pay off some debts and resolve important tasks in business and in your personal life.

Love and family. Your personal life will continue to see problems that began in the past.

If you have ended a relationship or gotten divorced, your material issues will be satisfied. Right now, it is best to agree to the conditions offered to you, rather than dragging things on any further. But if you want more of something, then dig in and get ready for what may be a losing war...

Couples that get along will be able to resolve various issues related to their home together. If there is an idea related to opening a family business, the stars give you a very bright green light.

At the very end of the month, you can expect to take a trip or plan one.

Health. This month, the stars recommend that you do not wear yourself out at work, which will be a temptation for you. If you are tired, take a break, remember to take time to work and time to relax and have fun, as well. Don't hold back on that front.

Those who are weak or elderly should take very good care of themselves, as they are approaching a period in which they may see a resurgence of old, chronic diseases and unexpected new problems.

Libra

You can't move further until you've made peace with the past. The stars urge you to learn the lessons from your own mistakes, especially if you made them more than once. October is the best time to do it!

Work. Many Libras went through a dark period in September, and the clouds are beginning to clear. Difficult relationships with colleagues in other cities or abroad are slowly, but surely becoming predictable again. Of course, there are still some issues there, and it is worth paying attention to them, given that this has long been an area of turbulence in your professional life. There's no point in letting up just yet.

The stars recommend that you back up any agreements with colleagues in other cities or abroad with something tangible, like a signed contract. If things change, you can always back yourself up with this and remind your unreliable partners. If they'll go for it, of course.

Any trips planned for October will be very successful.

Managers and entrepreneurs should keep a close eye on their subordinates. They seem unreliable, incompetent, and possibly even dishonest at the worst possible time.

Employees should be careful with colleagues so long as things keep brewing on your team. In order to avoid any potential intrigue and gossip, you need to clearly identify who is a friend, who is an enemy, who is not a friend but not an enemy, etc.... and generally behave with more caution.

If you have any problems with someone from work, take it right to your management – there will be some opportunities to rectify things there.

Overall, October will be much better for you than September, and largely thanks to your own hard work.

Money. Your financial position is also looking up, especially as you get closer to the end of October. The largest sum will come in on October 25-28.

You have a lot of expenses, and the astrologist predicts this will be related to your personal and family life. You are improving your home, your children might have some more financial needs again, but the stars believe that closer to the end of the month, you will be back in the black.

Love and family. Your personal life is looking shaky and uneven right now. Parents are probably dealing with problems involving their children, who once again (!) are incurring huge expenses. You might have to pony up for your adult children's training and education, but if you don't do it, who will?

In the worst cases, you will have to resolve your children's problems, which will also require resources, effort, and nerves on your part.

Couples who get along will possibly spend a lot of money near the end of the month on home improvements. You may also be completing tasks like finishing a new home, buying furniture, or acquiring other items for your home décor.

Your relationship with your partner is far from ideal – you might have some major fights, and any reconciliation will be fragile. In order to build harmony in your relationships, you might take a trip together – you will definitely have an opportunity to do so.

Health. In October, you are feeling a lot more energetic than you were, and any illnesses from last month are sure to quickly pass.

Scorpio

Right now, it is the time to pause, take a deep breath, and look around. Your recent achievements are impressive, but you still have a lot of ground to cover. October is a great time to get ready for that.

Work. October is a good time to resolve various administrative issues. Entrepreneurs and managers might be dealing with some mutiny on their teams, and entrepreneurs may have to neutralize some workplace gossip.

Many Scorpios will have to resolve issues related to land or real estate that began in the past. This time, however, you are able to cover a lot of ground, though victory will still remain distant.

October is a difficult month, and that may be compounded by worsening relationships with colleagues in other cities or abroad. Partners from afar will show themselves to be unusually tenacious, and you may just have to give in a little. If that is unacceptable, then just wait it out – by November, things will be better, and you might be able to negotiate a decent compromise.

Money. Financially, October is a fairly calm month, but that is all. You will not have any windfalls, but you also will not experience any major losses. You might profit from various real estate transactions, or support from parents or loved ones.

You might also negotiate on credit or reach an agreement with partners on a financial investment in your business.

Love and family. Many Scorpios are more focused on their personal lives this month, as well as family matters. Couples who get along will be tackling issues related to home improvement both for themselves and their children.

Couples who are in the midst of a divorce might peacefully resolve difficult issues related to dividing up their property, especially their home.

Along with all this, October is a good time for relaxing, so take a week or two for yourself. Calm down, take a deep breath, and stop thinking that everything will come to a standstill without you.

Health. In October, you are feeling fairly sluggish. You might often feel fatigued and apathetic. The best medicine for that is taking some time off or at least getting a good night's sleep. A change of scenery is the best thing for you right now. A week under the palm trees or a weekend in nature will give you a new perspective, which is just what the doctor ordered right now!

Sagittarius

You are looking at an unusually successful month, in which you will literally be able to climb mountains. Your inherent optimism may sometimes simply shoot off the charts, and turn into risky adventurism. Be careful!

Work. October is a good time to hold onto your position and shake off some of the debris accumulated in the past. You will be adventurous, bold, and capable of drawing both friends and highly placed people to your business. You will also be able to easily resolve issues that require the goodwill of official authorities.

Entrepreneurs and managers will be able to continue work that had stalled in September. Your difficult relationship with a partner has been bothering you since last month, but things are looking up, though the future will reveal that things are still not stable. In October, however, you will have help from like-minded friends and someone highly placed, who will act as an intermediary and improve things significantly.

In this case, the astrologist suggests backing up any agreements with something tangible, like a signed contract. If your partners start to waver later on, then you will avoid a lot of headaches.

Employees are on a lucky streak at work, and management is taking notice of your efforts, as is someone highly placed.

Any business trips planned for October will go well, and make it possible to fix your relationship with a former colleague, as well as old friends.

Money. This month, your financial situation is looking good. You might find money you had forgotten about, or profits from your hard work in the past. Your expenses in October will be pleasant – shopping, going out with friends, and your loved ones' needs.

Love and family. October is a good time for your personal life, too. Your circle of friends is growing, and you are often visiting friends at gatherings, parties, events, and you are able to leave a favorable impression on anyone Fate places in your path. For single people, this is a great time to meet someone.

Spouses with a strong marriage will come back to some issues from the past as the month draws to a close. This will be related to fixing up a summer home, apartment, or a new home.

For those whose relationship leaves something to be desired, you may reach a truce, though it will be fragile and somewhat unreliable. But remember that bad peace is better than a good war, at least for some people ☺ Most likely, if there are any thorny material or moral issues, they will be resolved closer to mid-October.

Health. For most of October, you will be feeling energetic and have no reason to fear falling ill. However, during the new moon and eclipse, on October 25-27, you might feel a bit more sluggish. These are the most difficult days in October, so be sure to stay calm and avoid any risky situations.

Capricorn

In October, you will be patient, active, and consistent, which means you will get your way. Things are easy when you're a pro, and that is definitely your case this month.

Work. This is a great time for you at work. You're like a heavy tank, moving slowly but surely over one obstacle after the next, and by the end of the month, you will have significantly improved your position, both professionally and materially.

October is a great time for resolving issues requiring the god will of official agencies and highly placed people. Employees can improve their position as those in charge are sure to take notice of you.

A professional offer that skidded to a halt last month is now coming back to life. This is relevant for both employees and entrepreneurs.

The difficult side of October will probably be your relationship with colleagues in other cities or abroad. Though you faced problems in the past, they will in one way or another be resolved, though you will repeatedly have to deal with challenges again in the future.

Entrepreneurs and managers will keep their teams in line with an iron fist, but the improvements you are seeing this month all over will probably worsen a bit closer to the end of the month. Keep things under firm control, and keep an eye on people who should support you rather than harm you. This is very important in business.

Money. Your financial situation is looking great in October, and you might even call this one of the best months of 2022. Money will be coming in regularly, and you can expect the greatest sums to come in on October 5, 6, 13-15, and 23-25.

Love and family. This month, you will be so focused on work that your personal life might take a backseat. The exception is couples who work together – they will be able to harmoniously resolve professional tasks, and this will bring them close together.

Couples whose marriage is on the rocks will still be able to tackle difficult issues related to their home, but they will be unlikely to reach a peaceful compromise this month.

Your relationship with your children is still difficult – they still need something from the family's budget, and it might be expensive. Hopefully, this will only be a benefit, but the stars recommend separating needs from excess.

Those planning on moving or buying real estate in another city or abroad will come back to some administrative issues this month.

Health. You can expect some powerful energy in October. You will feel like you are in excellent health, and your vitality and achievements will inspire everyone around you, as well.

Aquarius

In October, you are slowly but surely scaling the mountain. In addition to progressing at work, you might also make a real leap, spiritually and when it comes to understanding yourself, the world, and others.

Work. This is a very successful month for you at work. You might be actively working with colleagues from other cities and abroad, or even go on a trip.

Difficult issues that have been bothering you recently will look much more manageable and like something you can resolve. This goes for problems involving your colleagues from afar as well as any legal issues.

Those with problems involving land or other real estate disputes might once again face a new round of demands from opponents, but you will be able to skillfully overcome this. This is a story that has been going on for some time now, and each time, you are able to find the right argument and support it with irrefutable facts. This will be the case this time, and everything will be resolved favorably closer to the end of the month, when things are clearer.

October is a great time for studying, learning new things, and a job. In some cases, this will take place in another city or abroad.

Money. Your finances are looking rather neutral this month. You will not have a lot of income, but your expenses will be reasonable, predictable, and mostly related to your family, children, and loved ones.

Things will be looking up in late October, when Jupiter, the planet of success, will return to the financial sector of your sky. If you do not receive money in late October, wait until November, when it is sure to show up.

Love and family. Things are also improving in your personal life. After some recent disagreements, couples will be able to find a path to each other's hearts. You might take a trip, which will bring you closer together if your relationship suffered in September.

Parents will strengthen their relationship with children, and visit them if they are currently studying or living in another city or abroad. Your children still need your support, both financially and morally. This situation is unlikely to change anytime soon, and it's true that children are like flowers, water them daily with love and watch them bloom.

Those dealing with challenges related to real estate will be able to grapple with these issues in mid-October. The situation is not hopeless – resolving it is taking some time, but with each step, you are closer to getting your way. Keep a cool head, act methodically, and you will see success.

Health. In October, you are noticeably more energetic, and you are also improving your confidence and mood. Even if you were recently ill, you will make a quick recovery.

Pisces

This month, the stars suggest you act methodically, systematically, without rushing things or creating unnecessary waves. Chop some wood and a tree will fall. Have patience, work hard, and you will achieve your goal.

Work. October is not the time for a quick fix at work. Rather, you should keep in mind that working behind the scenes is more effective than open hand-to-hand combat.

You might have to deal with some current administrative tasks, as well as various events related to real estate. This time, you should be careful and pay attention, as later on, you might have to reconsider everything you have done in October. Whenever possible, be sure to back everything up with something on paper. Signed and sealed contracts will pay off in dividends in the future.

Entrepreneurs and managers should get ready for inspections, which are highly likely in mid-October, as well as a resurfacing of old legal problems.

Those with ties to colleagues from other cities or abroad will also face difficulties. For various reasons, the situation will grow to be a thorn in your side, and that is likely to continue throughout October and November.

Money. Financially, October is not the greatest month, either. You will have less income, but more expenses. In some cases, that may be related to business, and in others, your personal life will be at fault. In the worst cases, you will receive help from loved ones – a spouse, parents, or an old friend. You might also get credit on very favorable terms, or support from a business partner.

Love and family. For many Pisceans, the most important action in October will take place in your personal life. Many of you will take some time off and busy yourself with your home and family. You might have major changes going on here – construction, serious repairs, or even buying a new home. Most likely, these troublesome tasks will drag on for a bit and require quite a bit of resources from you.

Your relationship with relatives will unexpectedly take a dark turn in October. This is not the first time, so there is nothing new you haven't seen before. The stars recommend that all Pisces be very careful and avoid entrusting secrets to anyone, as they may spill the beans at the worst possible moment. This is relevant for your personal life as well as at work.

Health. In October, you might feel less than confident and cheerful. In order to strike an inner balance and harmony, try to relax more often, focus on what you need, and remember that there's nothing like a good night's sleep. Be careful when driving or traveling, too! The first ten days of the month will be the riskiest!

November

New York Time		
Calendar Day	Lunar Day	Lunar Day Start Time
01/11/2022	9	2:23 PM
02/11/2022	10	2:57 PM
03/11/2022	11	3:27 PM
04/11/2022	12	3:56 PM
05/11/2022	13	4:24 PM
06/11/2022	14	3:52 PM
07/11/2022	15	4:22 PM
08/11/2022	16	4:56 PM
09/11/2022	17	5:33 PM
10/11/2022	18	6:16 PM
11/11/2022	19	7:04 PM
12/11/2022	20	7:56 PM
13/11/2022	21	8:52 PM
14/11/2022	22	9:50 PM
15/11/2022	23	10:49 PM
16/11/2022	24	11:49 PM
18/11/2022	25	12:50 AM
19/11/2022	26	1:52 AM
20/11/2022	27	2:56 AM
21/11/2022	28	4:03 AM
22/11/2022	29	5:13 AM
23/11/2022	30	6:25 AM
23/11/2022	1	5:57 PM
24/11/2022	2	7:37 AM
25/11/2022	3	8:45 AM
26/11/2022	4	9:47 AM
27/11/2022	5	10:39 AM
28/11/2022	6	11:23 AM
29/11/2022	7	12:00 PM
30/11/2022	8	12:31 PM

London Time		
Calendar Day	Lunar Day	Lunar Day Start Time
01/11/2022	8	1:50 PM
02/11/2022	9	2:16 PM
03/11/2022	10	2:38 PM
04/11/2022	11	2:58 PM
05/11/2022	12	3:17 PM
06/11/2022	13	3:36 PM
07/11/2022	14	3:58 PM
08/11/2022	15	4:22 PM
09/11/2022	16	4:52 PM
10/11/2022	17	5:28 PM
11/11/2022	18	6:12 PM
12/11/2022	19	7:05 PM
13/11/2022	20	8:03 PM
14/11/2022	21	9:07 PM
15/11/2022	22	10:13 PM
16/11/2022	23	11:21 PM
18/11/2022	24	12:30 AM
19/11/2022	25	1:41 AM
20/11/2022	26	2:53 AM
21/11/2022	27	4:09 AM
22/11/2022	28	5:27 AM
23/11/2022	29	6:48 AM
23/11/2022	1	10:57 PM
24/11/2022	2	8:08 AM
25/11/2022	3	9:23 AM
26/11/2022	4	10:25 AM
27/11/2022	5	11:15 AM
28/11/2022	6	11:52 AM
29/11/2022	7	12:21 PM
30/11/2022	8	12:45 PM

You can find the description of each lunar day in the chapter “A Guide to The Moon Cycle and Lunar Days”

Aries

This month, you will not be able to count on any quick fixes. However, you have the strength and patience to do whatever you think you need to do.

Work. This month, your ruler, Mars, is beginning to move into retrograde, and that will continue until January. This means that many issues will have to be reconsidered time and again, and some tasks may not turn out exactly as you had planned.

First of all, this will affect your relationship with colleagues in other cities or abroad. This is an area that has caused a lot of worry in the past, as on one hand, you have been dealing with less-than reliable people, and on the other, your relationship may have simply grown more complicated for objective reasons independently of both parties. Right now, any dealings with colleagues from afar will require special monitoring, attention, and intermediaries. You might see old friends or highly placed individuals fill in this role, and though their help will not come cheap, it will be well worth it.

You are expanding your business and things are going well. Entrepreneurs and managers will be fine-tuning things and in two to three months, they will be able to complete the project, or at least the lion's share of it.

Employees might find their companies struggling financially, and this may include various audits. This is also something to keep in mind for both entrepreneurs and managers.

Money. Financially speaking, November is a difficult month for you. You will be spending constantly, and in some cases that is due to your personal life, while in others, your work is the culprit. Either way, your expenses will be higher than you planned.

Love and family. Many Aries are immersed in personal matters throughout November. Those with a family are still working on improving their day-to-day lives, putting their heart and soul, along with a lot of resources into it.

Your relationship with relatives is significantly more difficult, and you can expect this situation to drag on for a while. Potentially, you can expect an argument, or alternatively, several close relatives will go through a lot of unpleasant events and you will have to help clean things up, in both November and December.

Couples' relationships are far from ideal, and prepare for a major fight near the end of the month. There may be various causes for this, and the stars recommend that you keep in mind that a chain is only as strong as its weakest link. Keep an eye out for where your weak links are, that will help you avoid any problems, whether you are married or not.

Health. Those who are able to deftly dodge any personal or professional difficulties may face health issues instead, this month. You are feeling sluggish, and that will be most noticeable near the full moon and eclipse on November 7-9. Try to take care of yourself and avoid any autumn colds, infections, and don't take any risks. All month long, be careful behind the wheel!

Taurus

In November, you need a detailed, well thought-out plan of action – that is the only way you will avoid mistakes and unpleasant encounters. Remember, God saves he who saves himself, and seek out any weak points at work and in your personal life.

Work. This is a very difficult time for you at work. Many Taureans will have to deal with competition, opposition from certain partners, and simply other peoples' opinions that might be contrary to your own.

You may also experience problems with government authorities and law enforcement. It is worth keeping your ears open with them, but you can be sure that nothing good will come from any of it.

Employees should be careful with management. Right now, this is not the time to go to your superiors with suggestions, much less with requests – you will only harm yourself. November is not a good time for you!

You may reconnect with people who have provided you with services in the past, whether they are friends or well-intentioned people in high places. You can count on them for support right now, but you should hash out any conditions for cooperation ahead of time, especially if it is in the form of financial assistance. Time will tell that your viewpoints may be drastically different.

The first half of November is the most difficult time for in all facets of your life. The second half might be a bit better and more comfortable. You will be able to smooth over some thorny issues and even the most stubborn opponents will be willing to compromise.

Money. This month, the stars strongly urge you to watch your wallet and avoid any impulsive spending decisions. Mars, the planet of aggression, is in the material sector of your sky, which may lead you to spend unwisely or suffer various losses.

Be very careful if you work in finance – as a broker, banker, accountant, etc. November and December are both risky months. You will not have any profits, but you can expect a lot of losses. Some money will come in on November 1, 2, 10, 28, and 29.

Love and family. Your personal life will be no bed of roses, either. This is most relevant for couples who have already gone through the bitter experience of trouble in the past. Slowly but surely, you may find yourselves coming to a breaking point, and the problem may lie with you and your insistence on doing things your way.

Uranus, the planet of freedom and revolution has been in your sign since May of 2018, and that may occasionally disrupt the harmony and calm of your family life.

Uranus and this year's eclipses mean that many Taureans are reconsidering their relationships and taking them to another level. If that has already happened, then nothing will stop you from thinking about the future. But it is worth studying the lessons from your past life.

Health. In November, you are not particularly energetic, and the 23-26 will be the most difficult time for you. Be attentive during these days and try to avoid overeating or excessive exercise. This is the new moon, a good time to take it easy and even let yourself be a bit lazy.

Gemini

This month, your motto is "with patience and effort, everything works out". Even if it is difficult, remember, the early bird gets the worm!

Work. Lately, your achievements have been impressive, but you are about to dive into some other tasks that are just as important, so get ready! This will take up most of November, and a lot of the time, you will find yourself focused on routine and administrative duties.

What's more, November will bring with it a series of difficult problems. One might become a difficult relationship with colleagues from other cities or countries. For various reasons, this situation is far from ideal, but you are doing everything you can on your end, and as a result, you will be able to cover a lot of ground.

The stars recommend seeking support among old friends and connections – here, you will find understanding and what you need.

You may also be facing an onslaught of unreliable or potentially deliberate disinformation, which you need to keep in mind when making important decisions. You may also see legal problems resurface (if they were an issue in the recent past).

Entrepreneurs and managers should be prepared for an audit, which is highly likely this month.

Employees might be dealing with workplace gossip, but your position is not in any danger. In case of any problems, you can count on management, and things will be resolved.

Many Geminis may find themselves shouldering additional responsibilities and unable to get rid of them. On the contrary, be grateful for the new work, as the stars can see how beneficial it will be for you. You might get a small promotion with a bit of a raise or more authority.

Money. This month, your bank account is looking great. You will regularly receive money, and a bit more of it, as well. You can expect the largest sums to come in on November 3, 4, 11, 12, 22, and 23.

Love and family. This month, your personal life leaves much to be desired. In the best-case scenario, you will simply will have no time for it, and you will put off any romantic dates for a better time. In the worst-case scenario, you and the object of your affection will end up disappointed and not ready to reconcile with one another. If you see that an argument is brewing, remember that bad peace is better than a good war, and act accordingly. But if, for various reasons, your relationship can't recover, these recommendations are in vain.

In many families, you will be facing a hard situation involving your relatives. That may be due to a serious argument, which you will attempt to smooth over with your usual deftness. Alternatively, you may have to help a loved one who has fallen ill or gone through tough times.

Be attentive in November, as there may be people who are secretly or openly wishing you ill. Take care of your reputation and watch your tongue, avoid any outbursts.

Health. This month, you are feeling sluggish, so take care of your body and avoid any autumn colds and infections, and lead a healthy lifestyle. Be careful when driving or traveling, too. It also wouldn't hurt to be extra careful handling machinery and equipment. There is a very high probability of accidents and injuries in November.

Cancer

In November, passions might be off the charts, and it would be a good idea to remember – haste makes waste.

Work. This month is better for relaxing and romantic intrigue than work, which is not exactly your forte in November, unless you work in the creative fields – as an actor, artist, writer, or musician, in which case you can expect new levels of popularity and a fascinating tour.

Entrepreneurs can expect improved relations with colleagues in other cities or abroad if their business is focused on partnerships abroad or in other cities. During the second half of November, you might take a successful trip.

The dark side of November will be the emergence of various obstacles that might not seem obvious at first, but in time they will cause you a lot of worries. You might see old legal problems resurface, and unexpected revelations of uncomfortable truths. If that sounds like you, be careful, as the situation may carry on for some time.

Money. November is not a good time for your wallet. You will seem to be bleeding money and, in some cases, that will be related to old debts or resolving problems at work.

Alternatively, most of your expenses will be due to children and loved ones. In either case, near the end of the month, your bank account will be in the red.

It is not worth lending money right now, even to the most reliable people, because you may find yourself without any money or friends in the end.

Love and family. In many cases, your personal life may be taking up more energy than work. Parents will have to deal with their children's affairs and work to improve their relationship with them. Moreover, this may require a lot of resources.

Couples might find themselves jumping out of the frying pan and into the fire. You and your partner should both be careful and tone things down, otherwise any extreme impulsivity, which is part of your nature, might lead to conflict. It might be over jealousy, so control yourself, and be aware of your surroundings, particularly around new people, even if they seem interesting.

If this is the case, remember that not all that glitters is gold, and act accordingly.

In November, many Cancers might take some time off to spend time with their family and household duties. If this is you, it is worth being careful and avoiding any risk, while also carefully preparing any documents.

Health. This month, you are healthy, energetic, and the stars strongly urge you to use your vigor for peaceful means.

Leo

November is a run-of-the-mill month for you. The most reasonable thing you can do is focus on tasks that you have simply not had time to finish, and which you keep putting off for later.

Work. November is not the best time to deal with difficult tasks such as handling management or official government bodies. Then again, it is not a bad time for administrative issues, such as organizing the office or working on expanding your business at a later date. This is going to take up both managers' and entrepreneurs' time.

Most employees will be focused on their homes and families.

Your relationship with certain partners may grow more complicated. This is not the first time, so you already know wherein lies the problem.

You may have to work with intermediaries in order to smooth over some problems – that may include old friends, or someone who is highly placed. Step by step, you will at least be able to neutralize things, even if you don't fully resolve them.

Money. Your finances may be up and down this month. You may need to shrink your budget and find ways to save.

You will not find yourself penniless, and you might get some small profits from various real estate transactions, as well as from unofficial sources.

Love and family. You will continue to see processes in your personal life that began in the past. Couples who get along might finish improving their homes, and periodically argue with each other.

Divorced couples may find themselves in conflict for the umpteenth time, and the reason will involve division of property or raising your children. Your ex might be resistant, and that means you will have to turn to a relative or friend, or possibly even adult children for help.

It is also possible that your ex will stick to their guns.

Alternatively, your partner may fall ill or deal with stress at work, which will be felt by the whole family.

Couples might face resistance from relatives, parents, and older family members. Hold on! Time heals all wounds.

Health. This month will turn your life upside down. Without a doubt, that will affect your health. You need to find the time to relax and quit thinking that everything will come to a halt without you. Take care of your body and avoid any autumn colds and infections.

The new moon on November 23 will strongly improve your situation, and by December, you can expect to be in tip-top shape.

Virgo

You are looking at a tense, turbulent month. Your task is to create some consistency in your relationships with both partners and foes. You can convince anyone of anything! The time has come to bring your best qualities to the forefront!

Work. November is a good month for you at work. You might be negotiating with people on whom your future projects depend. If that is the case, it is worth preparing some hard-hitting arguments and stocking up on some cold, hard facts. This may be with regard to financial investments in your business, which is a major factor for the future. The stars continue to recommend that you let your eloquence and persuasive qualities take a starring role, and soon you will get just what you want.

At the same time, there are major changes on the horizon at work, and there might even be a full restructuring.

You don't have enough resources – that is both people and money for long-term plans, and you need to change that. Don't delay! Come up with a specific plan and get to work!

Your connections to colleagues in other cities and abroad are moving along well, and you might take a successful trip in November.

Employees might see changes in their company, but the stars predict that things will remain where they are, and if you end up leaving, it will be your decision. At the end of the year, you might make a choice in that regard, and the stars will support you.

Money. November is neutral for your finances. You have modest income and reasonable expenses. Everything here is running smoothly and normally.

Love and family. You might find yourself strongly dependent on loved ones in your personal life. That may include relatives, and of course, your spouse. Your task is to find a common ground with those around you – it will be difficult, but it is certainly possible.

Couples who get along will be planning a move or setting up a new home, and these bothersome tasks might lead to arguments and disagreements.

Those whose relationship leaves much to be desired will have to resolve issues related to their home and a potential separation.

If this is your case, remember that the ball is in your partner's court, and you will simply have to concede. A relative may have a positive influence on things, but will be unlikely to resolve it all alone. However, the stars predict your family's advice will be useful.

Any trips planned for November will improve your relationship, so it is worth heading somewhere out of the ordinary with your family and getting away from the November doldrums.

Health. In November, your energy levels are high, and you have no reason to fear falling ill. However, during the first half of the month, you should be careful when traveling and driving. Study situations well, and if you are abroad, then try to avoid anything related to disagreements, risk, and danger. The worst time for this is the first ten days of the month.

Libra

In November, if you can't do everything, you can do the vast majority of what you dream up. A new chapter is about to begin in your life.

Work. This month, you will be incredibly busy at work. Right now, you in a state of not eating, drinking, or sleeping, and doing nothing but putting your nose to the grindstone.

In some areas, managers and entrepreneurs can boldly count on their subordinates, and in others, they will have to resolve things singlehandedly. The former includes current tasks and administrative matters. But it is worth keeping a firm grip on your relationship with colleagues from other cities or abroad, who may send things into yet another tailspin.

This is an area where you often run into difficulties, and you may already know exactly what you need to do. Right now, it is worth keeping an eye on resistance from your opponents, which will probably not end quickly, this time – you can expect a few months of negotiations and active confrontation and intrigue.

Entrepreneurs and managers should prepare for an audit, as it is highly likely by the end of this month.

Money. Money-wise, November is not bad. Many Libras will be flush with money, cash, and other material benefits.

Expect the largest sums on November 3, 4, 11-13, 22, and 23. However, as often happens, with income you also have expenses. Many will have to pay back debts, deal with family needs, and support a spouse or partner. As before, a significant chunk of your family budget is going toward your children's needs.

Love and family. Your personal life is looking both emotional and turbulent in November. You might not have time to be dealing with matters of the heart at all, and a loved one will bring various complaints and demands to you.

Alternatively, you may see a lot of resistance when it comes to money – what and how to spend your family budget. There is nothing wrong with you having differing ideas, but an argument is inevitable.

Things are more difficult for those who are dating – in the best-case scenario, they might not see each other as often as they would like, but in the worst-case, they may unexpectedly realize that they are very different in certain areas. If your relationship is important to you, then you will have to learn to compromise. If not, it's time for the train to leave the station.

Many Libras will deal with various problems involving relatives. Most likely, this involves your in-laws. Nothing here is new, but this time, things are more difficult and taking longer to resolve. That may be due to arguments, or possible challenges related to close family members.

Health. In November, you are feeling a bit sluggish, but you will avoid any major complications if you follow a schedule and do morning exercises.

Elderly people and those who are weakened by disease should take preventive measures against any chronic conditions and take care of themselves, avoiding any autumn colds and infections.

Scorpio

You are meeting your birth month ready for battle. And even if your path sometimes feels like a labyrinth, there is always a way out. Inner balance is the key to stability both at work and in your relationships this month.

Work. In November, you will have to bring a situation at work under firm control. This way, your relationships with colleagues from other cities and abroad will become more stable and predictable, and you may hold specific negotiations with them or go on a successful trip.

Those dealing with legal difficulties or problems involving auditing agencies might be able to count on significant improvements this time. In some cases, you may even put an end to this trouble!

However, your relationship with certain partners is tense. Most likely, there is an argument over property, possibly real estate. However, this month, your persistent opponents will receive a strong rebuff.

November is a good time for those in creative fields – they can improve their popularity and might go on a successful tour.

Money. Your bank account has seen better days than November. Your expenses will be higher than your income, and close to the end of the month, you might even find your accounts in the red. The astrologist predicts that much of your expenses will be related to your personal life and family and children's needs.

Things will improve somewhat after the new moon on November 23, and next month will be even better.

Love and family. Some passions worthy of Shakespeare are being played out in your personal life. Couples going through a rough patch will continue their battle and once again, their relationship and money are at stake, and possibly their children's fate.

Based on the position of the stars, you will not make any concessions, nor will your partner. The stars are on your side, and those around you will come to believe the same.

Couples who get along will work together to resolve important issues related to real estate, and once the fight is over, they can sit back and enjoy success.

Your children are going through serious changes, and that may look differently, but in any case, you will have to provide the younger generation with both moral and financial support.

This month is a good time for couples. You may see the return of an old flame, or maybe begin a whirlwind romance. You might alternate arguing with reconciling, but most likely, things will be nothing more than just another lovers' spat. At least, that is what we can hope.

Health. You are healthy energetic, and charming this month, which everyone Fate places in your path is noticing, too!

Sagittarius

Traditionally, November is a stressful month for you. That goes for this year, too, so stay on your toes, keep a cool head, and act carefully and with restraint.

Work. This is not exactly a good time for you at work. Entrepreneurs and managers at every level will face a whole host of problems.

Your relationships with colleagues in other cities and abroad have once again hit a wall. You may see breaches of previous agreements or new obstacles you will have to take into consideration.

Pay close attention to your associates – they may disappoint you. This is an area you have had to take a look at for some time, so it is worth coming up with a clear plan and shaking things up.

Many Sagittarians may come back to issues related to real estate. Those planning on expanding their business will have to add something or make changes. There is, however, hope that by New Year's, all of these administrative plans will be resolved, and in your favor.

Employees should keep an eye on colleagues. This month, you may run into some covert activities working against you, which will undermine your professional position and reputation.

Money. Financially, November might look differently. Some Sagittarians will receive payment from a previously completed job, while others will take on credit. You might profit from various real estate transactions, as well as receive financial support from a business partner.

Those who are not part of the business world can count on help from parents, a spouse, or loved ones. In sum, despite the stormy waters at work, you will not find yourself penniless.

Love and family. Many Sagittarians will be immersed in home improvements in November. You might be putting the finishing touches on your apartment, home, or summer home.

In more modest cases, you may be finishing major repairs. This may lead to spats between spouses, which is only natural when you are going through such bothersome, tedious tasks.

Your relationship with a relative will once again become difficult. You can expect serious conflicts in the first half of November, but this is nothing new – for the umpteenth time, you are seeing unresolved problems resurface. It may involve longstanding arguments, or support for a relative going through hard times.

For couples, November is a very difficult time. You might see information revealed that both parties would prefer to have kept secret. This will seriously damage your relationship, and in the most severe cases, it will lead to a separation. At the very least, you can expect a serious fight.

You know best what is important to you, and what you are willing to accept. What's more, you know what your deal breakers are.

Health. Take care of yourself, as November is sure to lead to the reemergence of old diseases, or possibly new ones. Be careful when traveling and behind the wheel. The first half of the month is especially critical, here. The 6th through 13th of November are the riskiest days of the month.

Capricorn

It isn't hard to change the little things in life, but a serious change requires you to be bold, responsible, and decisive. But no one compares to you when it comes to experience, skill, and strength – so go for it!

Work. This is a good time for you at work. Your relationship with colleagues from other cities or abroad is moving along rapidly, and you might have to come back to finish up some documents, network, or do what you have to in order to develop your business in another city or abroad. You might have to reconsider your staffing – you don't have the people you need, and you must find those who can take your business to new heights somewhere else.

Employees are likely to see a shakeup in their companies, but they are likely to be on the winning end of things.

Your friends or someone highly placed may have a big and clearly positive influence on major processes this month.

Money. Your finances this month are facing a lot of difficulties. All of the changes you are undertaking require a lot of investment, and you can only hope it will pay off in the future.

What's more, you will spend a lot on your children, their education, and upbringing. You will not find yourself penniless, this month, however. Money will be coming in from work, as well as from old sources that have stood the test of time.

Love and family. In your personal life, you might also see fateful scenarios being played out. If you are planning a move, you might take advantage of support from friends, as well as those who are highly placed in society.

Soon, many Capricorns will once again be coming back to serious issues related to real estate. In some cases, that will be a move to a new home, or potentially even a new country! Many will be planning on acquiring a home for their children, and these plans will begin to take shape in 2023.

Your relationship with a partner might become difficult, and the reasons will vary. However, if the person is important to you, just get through it. There is a light at the end of the tunnel, as long as you let things simply run their course and keep an eye on your own words and actions.

Any trips planned for November will be very successful. This is only fair, for both your personal and professional lives.

Health. In November, your energy levels are high, and you have no reason to fear any disease.

Aquarius

This month, Luck is knocking at your door. And this time, it is taking on a tangible, material shape. Jump on in! Time is on your side!

Work. Professionally speaking, November is one of the best months of the year for you. Entrepreneurs and managers can count on successfully resolving their problems, new projects, and profits from work previously completed.

Employees will have an incredible opportunity to move up the ladder at work, and if that recently took place already, you will have the chance to strengthen your position.

Thorny issues related to disputes over real estate will become less acute, and you may even find an acceptable, favorable resolution for both parties.

If you work in something related to construction, land, or real estate, keep your finger on the pulse of things – there is a high probability of people responsible for this enterprise stepping away from what had been planned.

Money. November is one of the best months of the year for you. For many Aquarians, it may even be your golden hour for money and other material benefits. Expect the largest sums to come in on November 3, 4, 11-13, 22, 23, and 30.

Of course, you have expenses, that is unavoidable, but most of them will be related to your family, children, and loved ones.

Love and family. Your personal life is looking much less positive than things at work.

Spouses might be arguing a lot, and once again, this is due to varying issues related to your home. Alternatively, you might have disagreements caused by parents or older relatives.

Issues related to your home might plague many Aquarians, but this is nothing new and you are used to it by now. You probably already know what to do, and how to put an end to this matter. The stars believe that things are coming to a favorable end.

Your relationship with a partner looks like bad fall weather – little sun and often filled with freezing drizzle. The stars recommend that you get through it, avoid dragging other people into your relationship, and rely on your intelligence, instead.

Health. In November, you are healthy, energetic, and full of strength. You naturally have no reason to fear any illness.

Pisces

November is full of ups and downs for you, though the stars' positive influence will clearly outweigh the bad. You will be on your own winding, bumpy path, crushing all the obstacles along the way.

Work. This is a very busy month for you. Jupiter, the planet of success, will be returning to your sign and opening up a shortcut to achieving your goals. You will see more contact with colleagues in other cities and abroad, possible constructive negotiations, and even a successful trip.

The second half of the month is most promising for this. During the first two weeks, you will run into various hold ups, obstacles, and hurdles to your plans. As a result, plan anything important during the second half of the month.

Those planning various real estate transactions might face problems and barriers. It is impossible to predict how they will look, but until January 2023, many Pisceans will have to repeatedly come back to these issues. You will have to reconsider some things, and completely redo others.

What's more, entrepreneurs and managers, as well as employees, will have a chance to show off their talent in full. The best time for this is the second half of November and December.

Money. November looks like a flywheel spinning out of control when it comes to your bank account. Everything you do this month will lead to handsome profits in the future months and 2023. There is good reason to put your nose to the grindstone – it will all pay off.

You will not find yourself penniless in November, but things in the future will look more successful.

Love and family. Things are looking turbulent at home for you. You might be dealing with repairs, a move, or other, similar events related to improving your home. As often happens, the results will not be immediate. You may have to redo things, reconsider previous decisions, and experience frustrations when things do not go as you might have hoped. The stars suggest keeping your nerves in check and remembering that any construction project causes a lot of stress. Be methodical and even, and success will be yours.

Couples should avoid getting involved in fights and trying to clarify their relationship, though there will be opportunities to take a trip together. The second half of November is the best time for this.

Health. This month, you are energetic, ambitious, and a bit of an adventurer. That is all a good thing, but keep your head on straight and your feet on the floor in early November – that is a very difficult time for you. Be careful when traveling, driving, and avoid risky situations.

December

New York Time		
Calendar Day	Lunar Day	Lunar Day Start Time
01/12/2022	9	1:00 PM
02/12/2022	10	1:27 PM
03/12/2022	11	1:55 PM
04/12/2022	12	2:24 PM
05/12/2022	13	2:56 PM
06/12/2022	14	3:31 PM
07/12/2022	15	4:11 PM
08/12/2022	16	4:57 PM
09/12/2022	17	5:48 PM
10/12/2022	18	6:42 PM
11/12/2022	19	7:40 PM
12/12/2022	20	8:39 PM
13/12/2022	21	9:38 PM
14/12/2022	22	10:37 PM
15/12/2022	23	11:37 PM
17/12/2022	24	12:39 AM
18/12/2022	25	1:42 AM
19/12/2022	26	2:49 AM
20/12/2022	27	3:58 AM
21/12/2022	28	5:10 AM
22/12/2022	29	6:22 AM
23/12/2022	1	5:17 AM
23/12/2022	2	7:28 AM
24/12/2022	3	8:27 AM
25/12/2022	4	9:17 AM
26/12/2022	5	9:58 AM
27/12/2022	6	10:32 AM
28/12/2022	7	11:03 AM
29/12/2022	8	11:31 AM
30/12/2022	9	11:59 AM
31/12/2022	10	12:28 PM

London Time		
Calendar Day	Lunar Day	Lunar Day Start Time
01/12/2022	9	1:05 PM
02/12/2022	10	1:24 PM
03/12/2022	11	1:42 PM
04/12/2022	12	2:03 PM
05/12/2022	13	2:25 PM
06/12/2022	14	2:53 PM
07/12/2022	15	3:26 PM
08/12/2022	16	4:07 PM
09/12/2022	17	4:56 PM
10/12/2022	18	5:53 PM
11/12/2022	19	6:55 PM
12/12/2022	20	8:00 PM
13/12/2022	21	9:07 PM
14/12/2022	22	10:15 PM
15/12/2022	23	11:23 PM
17/12/2022	24	12:32 AM
18/12/2022	25	1:44 AM
19/12/2022	26	2:59 AM
20/12/2022	27	4:18 AM
21/12/2022	28	5:38 AM
22/12/2022	29	6:56 AM
23/12/2022	30	8:07 AM
23/12/2022	1	10:17 AM
24/12/2022	2	9:04 AM
25/12/2022	3	9:49 AM
26/12/2022	4	10:22 AM
27/12/2022	5	10:49 AM
28/12/2022	6	11:11 AM
29/12/2022	7	11:30 AM
30/12/2022	8	11:49 AM
31/12/2022	9	12:09 PM

You can find the description of each lunar day in the chapter "A Guide to The Moon Cycle and Lunar Days"

Aries

This month is chock full of meetings, communications, and networking. Not all of them will be peaceful, but there is hope that this time, the truth is born in disputes.

Work. Your main task during the last month of 2022 is your relationship with colleagues in other cities or abroad. Here, once again, things might not go as planned, but you are used to this by now, and able to let it roll off your back.

This time, your problems might be related to objective obstacles as well as subjective causes. You might see a conflict of opinions, perhaps the emergence of questionable information, and this will significantly complicate your relationship.

Those who are unaffected by this might instead face audits and revelations that will deeply affect your position in society, as well as your reputation. At the same time, your business is developing, and you are even profiting, now. Closer to the end of the month, that will become very clear.

The second half of December should be a favorable time for most employees. You might see big changes where you are, or maybe a new job offer elsewhere. Even if you are still in the preliminary negotiations stage, don't worry – in 2023, everything you are preparing for now will become a reality.

Money. Financially, the best time for you is the last 10 days of the month. During this time, you might get a handsome profit from a sale or a job you previously completed, as well as awards and bonuses. Expect the largest sums to come in on December 5, 6, 13, 14, and 23-25.

Love and family. Your personal life might not take up as much energy as work this month. However, there will definitely be events requiring your participation and attention, this month. What's more, there are complicated relationships among your close circle of relatives. This may play out differently, regardless of what has happened in the recent past. In some cases, that may be arguments that involve your entire family, or possibly troubles faced by your relatives.

During the first two weeks of December, many Aries might face gossip in their social circles, involving people who will try to bring old skeletons out of your closet. Be careful, or your image and reputation might seriously suffer.

This very relevant advice whether you are married or not, especially if you have secrets you would rather your other half not know about.

Health. In December, you will avoid falling ill, but there is a high chance of injury and accidents. Be careful while driving and traveling, whether you are close to home or far away. If you can, try to schedule any trips for the second half of the month, during the first half, things are risky.

Taurus

You can't move any further until you reconsider the past. One good turn deserves another.

Work. December is not the best time for anything work-related. You might have serious disagreements with those around you, perhaps about money or something else material. In some cases, that may be related to your friends and like-minded people, and in others, a highly placed person or official body is to blame.

Most of the unpleasantness will take place during the first two weeks of the month, before the skies begin to clear.

Your ties to colleagues in other cities or abroad will become more active, and during the second half of the month, you may take a successful trip. Many Taureans will see partners from afar helping to smooth over several problems caused by a foe.

During the second half of the month, you will have a chance to renew some sorely needed connections and access useful information. This will help guide you and shed light on what tactics to employ.

Money. Financially speaking, you can safely call December ruinous. You will seem to be bleeding money, and in some cases that is work-related, while in others, your personal life is at fault. What's more, belligerent Mars is firmly in the financial sector of your sky, which means you should be careful. In addition to the usual expenses, you may face unplanned spending, as well as financial losses.

Pay attention and be careful with anything involving money and similar, material things. If you somehow work in finance or with money, be twice as careful. The first half of December is particularly unfavorable.

Love and family. Your personal life is complicated now for various reasons. Spouses who get along might be dealing with various household problems – perhaps you are buying a new home, or carrying out serious repairs on the one you already have.

Divorced couples might separate, and if this is your case, questions about housing are only natural.

December is not a good time for unmarried couples, either. During the first two weeks of the month, your relationship may look rather frosty, and there are various causes for this. The solution, as strange as it may seem, is to fully detach yourself from the situation and achieve a natural balance. Reconciliation is only possible near the end of December.

During the last few days of the final month of 2022, and in early January 2023, many Taureans might go on a trip. This will smooth your nerves after the year's tensions and significantly strengthen your relationship.

Health. December is a difficult time for your health, too. Right now, your energy potential is at its lowest, and you should keep that in mind if you already suffer from various chronic illnesses. If you face any issues, don't try to be your own doctor. You need a good specialist!

During the first two weeks of December, you might face some dangerous situations. Be careful when driving and avoid any risky adventures.

Gemini

The holidays are here, and it is a good time to start a new life with a clean slate. To do that, you have to deal with some business and relationships first, and December will give you an opportunity to do just that.

Work. In December, your life is unlikely to be a beacon of calm at work. Entrepreneurs and managers can expect conflict with partners or representatives of official bodies. The cause of the disagreements is likely to be differing views on how to develop your business or someone trying to divide things up. You are unlikely to reach a compromise this month, and things are likely to continue into 2023.

Your ties to colleagues from other cities or abroad are looking very solid, and you might turn to old partners or friends living far away for support.

Employees can expect serious competition to come their way. Perhaps a colleague is trying to undermine your achievements, and that will lead to serious conflict.

The stars recommend being very careful with management, as in December, your tendency to have a sharp tongue may cause some offense.

Money. Despite the many problems at work, for now, your bank account is in order. You can expect to receive your usual salary from your usual source – no more, no less. Expect to receive the largest amounts on December 1, 2, 9, 10, 20, and 27-29.

Love and family. The main focus of December will be your personal life, and it might look similar to things at work. Your spouse might have a differing perspective on many issues, and you will have a hard time reaching a compromise with them. Most likely, you will not even try to do that, however. You can expect to have to turn to a relative for help, here.

This is also the case for most unmarried couples. Serious disagreements are to be expected during the first two weeks of the month, and everyone's true nature will be revealed. The ball is in your court – if your loved one is important to you, you will be willing to compromise. If not, then any discussions are a waste of time. In any case, you can expect to either reconcile or break up closer to New Year's.

Health. In December, you are feeling a bit sluggish, and it is worth remembering to lead a healthy lifestyle, especially since nerves are at the root of all diseases. Your emotional state leaves a lot to be desired in December, so keep your feelings, opinions, and actions in check.

Cancer

The last month of the year might surprise you with its aggressiveness and unpredictability. It seems as though you are taking one step forward, two steps back. Of course, you will get through this, but that is for 2023.

Work. In December, Cancers who are part of the working world will have to deal with a whole host of problems. Entrepreneurs and managers will have to get their teams into order, as someone among your subordinates is trying to play by their own rules. What's more, you might face serious inspections and audits, or the reemergence of old legal problems.

Those planning on opening their business in another city or abroad will have to once again deal with various obstacles, which will be both objective and subjective in nature.

Most employees can expect turbulence. You might face conflict with colleagues, or seemingly endless office gossip. You can expect changes in your company, and at first this will be a source of worry, before you unexpectedly see new opportunities on the horizon.

Moving forward, you can say that everything that happens this month will be resolved favorably during the first few months of 2023.

Money. Financially speaking, December might look differently. Chaos is the word of the day when it comes to your job, and that will probably be reflected in your bank account, which seems to be shrinking. However, you will receive some money on December 3, 4, 11, 12, 21-23, 29, and 30.

Love and family. Your personal life might be on the back burner in December – work and its problems are taking up most of your head space.

Those planning on moving will have to deal with various obstacles, which you are unlikely to overcome in December.

This is a hard time for couples – for various reasons, your relationship is now more difficult. We all have skeletons in our closets, but this month, it might be your turn. Keep your head on straight and remember that silence is golden.

Health. Those who are able to happily skip the personal and professional difficulties of December might instead face health problems. You might see old diseases resurface, or unexpected new ones.

December is not only a time full of conflict, but you need to also be very careful when driving and avoid traveling too far from home – injuries are highly likely. The most difficult time is during the first half of the month.

Leo

In December, you will see a gulf appear between your wishes and what you are able to actually accomplish. You need a clear, concise plan if you are going to avoid exacerbating this imbalance any further.

Work. December is not the best time for anything work-related. You might experience serious disagreements with friends or people who provided you with various services in the past. This may be about repaying debts, and perhaps both parties will have a different view of this awkward issue. On the other hand, you might just not have enough resources to give your opponents their due right now. In time, things will fall into place, but that will probably not be until 2023.

In December, you will have to look for money, and you may speak to an intermediary about that. Alternatively, you might need a lot of resources in order to expand your business, and for various real estate transactions.

Employees will be able to resolve challenging financial matters with guidance from management. You may have to find a new job, and 2023 is sure to bring that opportunity with it.

You are beginning a new cycle in your life – you are leaving behind all of the bad in your life and only the good will remain, which will certainly be a help as you move forward.

Money. December is a rather difficult month, financially speaking, and you might even consider it ruinous. In some cases, you may have major expenses related to work, while in others, your personal life will be to blame. In order to avoid financial collapse, you need plan your expenses and eliminate anything you can.

Love and family. Many Leos will be more focused on their home and family this month. You might be finishing up major repairs, or buying furniture and other items for your décor. These bothersome tasks may be for you, or possibly for your children. The stars recommend that you keep an eye on the smaller members of your family, as not everything is going as you hoped and planned, right now.

December is also a hard time for couples. Sometimes, the chasm between our desires and duty is vast, and overcoming this hurdle is more difficult than you would have hoped. Remember that in order to make your wishes come true, as long as you want it hard enough. That is to say that a lot of things depend on you and you alone, right now.

Divorced couples might discuss what to do with their children this month, as well as various financial issues. This is unlikely to be peaceful, but divorce is divorce, and conflict is usually unavoidable.

Health. This month, you are up to your neck in activity, and in order to restore some energy balance, you should at least take a weekend off, for both physical strength and to clear your mind.

Virgo

Events in December will have a longstanding effect on your life and activities. Hold onto what works, and quietly let go what doesn't. You are looking at a major transition to another life, and that will bring with it a lot of new and interesting things.

Work. You are continuing to see changes at work, and not all of them are exactly peaceful You might have problems involving partners, and some of them may have various complaints and demands, when it comes to both money and business. Disagreements about real estate are highly likely. You may resolve some of these issues in December, but the astrologist predicts that most of them will not be over until 2023.

Employees will continue to see changes, too, and that may continue into the first half of 2023, so if something is not working for you, you can think about another place for your talents. However, it is worth keeping in mind that any job searches will be lengthy, so don't make any sudden moves, and if you can, stay where you are, a least for now.

Money. December is not a great time for your finances. You will have major expenses all month long, with the largest toward the end of December. Of course, you will have some money coming in, but it will be modest, to say the least.

Love and family. Many Leos will be more focused on home and family this month. In most cases you can expect something revolutionary, when things finally come to a head.

Couples who have lost feelings for one another might be vicious as they divide up their real estate and argue over their children's upbringing. If that is your case, you can expect things to end only after spending a large amount of money.

December is even hard for couples who otherwise get along – they may experience disagreements over home improvements, or other household matters. If you can, try to put off any major decisions until 2023. December will be a very hard time for you, and you simply will not be able to make the right decision.

This advice is also relevant for most couples. The first half of December has the greatest risk of conflict, before things improve somewhat.

Health. Naturally, the turbulence around you this month will be reflected in your health. You need to remember you are no made of steel. Remember that sooner or later, all this conflict will affect your body, so try to find at least a little bit of calm during a trying month.

Libra

You tend to play by the rules and expect the same out of others. However, it is wise to remember that if you want peace, you need to prepare for war.

Work. Your relationship with partners from other cities or abroad will be your greatest task this month. Here, everything will once again be difficult, and this time, you may be pushed to your limits. You are unlikely to find a peaceful resolution to things, as there is too much conflict lately on both sides. During the first half of December, you might even think about totally cutting ties.

Your relationship with subordinates will also be a problem this month. This is a difficult issue that has come up in the past, but nonetheless you are unable to count on certain team members.

Don't discount the possibility that your decisions will not be carried out, or carried out in such a way that does not live up to your expectations. If that is your case, managers at every level should stick to their guns and watch everything happening on their team like a hawk.

In December, you might be inspected or audited, so be ready to defend yourself on all fronts. You are a tough cookie, you'll get through it!

Money. December is a rather neutral time for your finances. Your troubles at work will not be reflected in your bank account, at least for now. Expect to receive the largest sums on December 1, 2, 9-11, 20, 21, 27, and 28.

Love and family. In your personal life, you can expect problems with those around you. In many cases, you will see the emergence or continuation of problems with close relatives. In some cases, there may be an argument, and nearly every family member will be dragged into it. Alternatively, a relative might fall ill or go through a difficult time and that will be reflected in the entire family ambiance.

This month, many Virgos will see things brought to light you would have preferred to keep quiet. That may affect your relationship with loved ones and cause serious fights, too. In all relationships, the first half of December is the hardest time, before the skies begin to clear.

Health. In December, you are cheerful, energetic, and incredibly active. The stars still recommend that you take care when driving and traveling.

During the first half of the month, the stars urge you to avoid traveling, whether near or far from home, as this will bring you nothing but trouble. Wait until a more favorable time, such as the second half of December.

Scorpio

During the last month of 2022, you are grappling with a series of problems. There are difficulties at home, as well as in the workplace. Every heart knows its own bitterness.

Work. Your main task this month will be household and material endeavors. You will have to come back to some issues related to real estate, such as old debts – both moral and financial in nature. Arguments over this may leave an unpleasant taste in your mouth during the first half of the month, and this will also be the period with the greatest number of conflicts. During the second half of the month, things will be significantly better. You can count on support from well-wishers around you, as well as from older relatives.

Your relationships with colleagues in other cities or abroad are moving along nicely, and closer to the end of the month, you might take a trip or at least begin planning one.

Money. When it comes to money, this month is full of missteps. Various financial circumstances might fall on your shoulders and become an unbearable burden. In some cases, you may have to pay back old debts and resolve various issues at work, while in others, you may have to deal with difficulties in your personal life. Either way, remember that this is not a time for risk, as you might find yourself empty-handed in the end.

Take care of your property and avoid nastiness over money – don't give anyone money as a loan, and don't ask anyone for anything, either – instead of support, you may encounter a harsh, rude rejection. The only exception is relatives – here you can count on at least something.

Love and family. Many Scorpios are focused on their family life, this month.

Feuding couples will once again go to battle this month, over their children's future and their own, as well. This may go hand in hand with mutual accusations and demands of a totally different nature.

Emotional outbursts and serious arguments are on the menu for couples. The stars recommend not making any rash decisions, or thinking about your own ambitions, but also about today. If you break up, will you come to regret that?

Couples who get along may spend a lot of resources on their children, their education, and development. Alternatively, children may cause various problems which will drive their parents to the brink. If that is your case, your family budget may suffer the consequences.

If you can't deal with all of these problems on your own, turn to your relatives – this is the only source of moral and financial support this month.

Health. This month, the elderly and those who are weakened might be vulnerable to the reemergence of old diseases, or the unexpected appearance of new ones. If that is your case, the stars recommend taking preventive measures.

Young and healthy Scorpios should avoid anything risky – this is especially true during the first half of the month.

Sagittarius

In December, you will be bold, persistent, and a bit of an adventurer. In an eternal battle, we only dream of peace!

Work. In December, many Sagittarians will have to come back to issues from the recent past. Most likely, this involves land, real estate, or other major property, and both you and your partners will have differing views on how it should be used and who owns it.

Regardless of what happens in your case, it is impossible to predict how things will turn out, but one thing is clear – the underlying cause of this problem is in the past, and everyone has one. This situation will continue until late December, when you might be able to find an acceptable solution for both parties.

Your connections to colleagues in other cities or abroad are moving along nicely. Old friends might act as intermediaries in case of any difficulties with stubborn opponents.

Money. Despite the ups and downs this month at work, overall, your finances will be unscathed. You will have regular income, and that is especially noticeable closer to the end of December. Expect the largest sums to come in on December 5, 6, 13-15, and 23-25.

Love and family. In many cases, you are focused on your personal life more than work this month. You might have conflicts on your hands, no matter how well your family gets along, and the cause is most likely various issues related to your home.

Couples who are on the rocks might be closer than ever to divorce in December, and that situation is likely to become extremely tense. A close relative might be the link who brings warring spouses together.

In some families, you may deal with problems related to your parents. That may involve a serious argument, or possibly an illness or other problems that may afflict the elder members of your family.

Generally speaking, life is not exactly calm right now, and things start to look a little more peaceful toward the end of the month.

Health. All month long, you will feel cheerful and confident. That means you are able to resolve a lot of problems this month, and take a bold look toward the future and 2023.

Capricorn

Don't expect any groundbreaking achievements this month. Most likely, you will be picking up the pieces leftover from the past, and laying the groundwork for a better life.

Work. You are on an unusually negative streak at work. Your connections to colleagues in other cities or abroad are significantly more difficult, and there is certainly a reason behind it. Maybe the law is standing in the way of your full cooperation, and it will take time to parse things out. Alternatively, you might be facing some unfortunate coincidences that are getting in the way of any constructive progress.

Entrepreneurs and managers should get ready for an audit or inspection, which is likely in December. It is worth keeping a close eye on employees, who might be feeling mutinous this month.

Employees should be prepared for disagreements with fellow team members, as well as gossip. If that is your case, be careful and do not trust any information. Rely on your own intuition and common sense, instead. These guidelines will keep you on the straight and narrow.

Money. The stormy waters at work might be felt in your finances, which will suddenly be suffering this month. At least, you can count on money coming in on December 7-8, 16, 17, and 25-27.

Love and family. If circumstances have brought you to be busier with your personal life, then you can expect a whole host of problems this month.

If you are planning on a move, you might experience some hiccups, and that will put the brakes on your plans, though it won't cancel them. Closer to the end of the month, you can expect some improvements, and in the first half of 2023, you will have found a solution.

In some families, you may be dealing with disagreements with relatives, and that may lead to a serious argument. Everyone's passions will calm down, and you will have resolved things near the end of the month. You might find it a difficult pill to swallow, but remember that bad peace is better than a good war.

You may also face problems involving unwanted information this month. Something you would have liked to have kept secret may be revealed, so be careful and don't give anyone anything to talk about.

It is worth noting that you are about to begin a new chapter in your life – things will be calmer, more comfortable, and more focused. The first few flickers of that change will be felt in the last ten days of December – if you find yourself having to redo things during the first half of the month, remember that everything will fall into place.

Health. Those who were happily able to skirt any professional or personal difficulties this month may instead feel them in their health. You are feeling sluggish in December, and are likely to suffer from various ailments. What's more, the stars recommend being very careful when traveling and driving.

Aquarius

Your trump card is your ability to react quickly and think out of the box. In December, you will do just that, as this is going to be a very difficult month.

Work. Expect the first half of December to be marred by conflicts and disagreements. This may be due to various material obligations and the warring parties may have differing positions on such a delicate issue. Perhaps they were once friends or at least like-minded individuals, or alternatively, you are dealing with a hostile government body representative. This may be over land, real estate, or other major assets. If during the first half of the month, you are unable to reach an agreement, during the second half, you will be on track to reach your goals. Very soon, you may finally be rid of this exhausting and now ancient problem.

Money. Given your challenges at work, money trouble is all but inevitable. You will be spending constantly and not only on professional issues, but also on your loved ones' and children's needs. As a result, near the end of the month, your bank account will be in the red.

Love and family. If you are more focused on your family life this month, get ready for some Shakespearean drama.

Things look most difficult for unmarried couples – you might be arguing, and your friends and loved ones may get involved, too. Your integrity is being seriously put to the test – it will be clear what is truly important to you, and what you are able to actually give up. What's more, your deal breakers will also become obvious.

Families may experience trouble involving children – perhaps the younger generation will be feeling rather mutinous, or alternatively, your children may be going through difficult times and you will have to help with a kind word and some money.

Difficult issues related to real estate will be resolved, slowly but surely. You will be making some very positive steps in that direction during the second half of December.

Health. In December, many Aquarians will feel like they have been broken down entirely. Work, dealing with professional and personal problems, anxieties- this means that close to the end of the month, you might feel as though you are teetering on the brink.

Take a few days to get away from home, and the endless hustle and bustle. You need a real break for the holidays, more than anyone, so see if you can take some extra days off.

Pisces

December will be a stressful time for you. You made your bed and now you have to lie in it, there are no guilty parties here. But don't just sit there and cry over spilled milk. Pull yourself up by your bootstraps and get to work doing what you have to do.

Work. You will face a mountain of tasks this month, and you can expect some great achievements at work. Entrepreneurs and managers will continue projects they recently started, and things look promising for the future. You might be expanding your business, and that involves a lot of administrative details. If you are dealing with real estate, construction, repairs, then you need to keep your ears to the ground, as not everything is going to go according to plan. Conflicts are likely during the first two weeks of December, but you will be able to overcome resistance from your opponents and stick to your guns.

During the second half of the month, you will be communicating more frequently with old friends and highly placed people in society. That will help promote your new projects, as well as with problem solving. What's more, new partners from other cities or abroad are on the horizon; you may be engaged in active negotiations, or perhaps go on a trip.

Employees are on a positive streak at work, though the stars recommend paying attention to the way you address management and the powers that be. Keep your head down in December – that will save you from misunderstandings and conflicts, which are highly likely during the first two weeks of the month.

Money. Expect good things to happen for you financially this month. You will have regular income, and somewhat more of it, too. Best of all – this is a positive trend that will continue into 2023.

Love and family. Your personal life might look very differently, and everything depends on your relationships and intentions for the future. Couples who get along might be busy with home improvements, while also overcoming various obstacles on this long and winding road.

Those who have decided to divorce may experience conflict over property, mostly your home. This painful situation might not be resolved until 2023. You will not be on the losing end here, and instead will get what you came for.

Health. In December, you are healthy, full of vigor, and the stars recommend you use this exclusively for peaceful purposes.

A Guide to The Moon Cycle and Lunar Days

Since Ancient times, people have noticed that the moon has a strong influence on nature. Our Earth and everything living on it is a single living being, which is why the phases of the moon have such an effect on our health and mental state, and therefore, our lives. Remember Shakespeare and his description of Othello's jealousy in his famous tragedy:

"It is the very error of the moon, She comes more nearer Earth than she was wont And makes men mad."

If our inner rhythm is in harmony with that of the cosmos, we are able to achieve much more. People were aware of this a thousand years ago. The lunar calendar is ancient. We can find it among the ancient Sumerians (4000-3000 BC), the inhabitants of Mesopotamia, Native Americans, Hindus, and ancient Slavs. There is evidence that the Siberian Yakuts had a lunar calendar, as did the Malaysians.

Primitive tribes saw the moon as a source of fertility. Long before Christianity, the waxing moon was seen as favorable for planting new crops and starting a new business, for success and making money, while the waning moon was a sign that business would end.

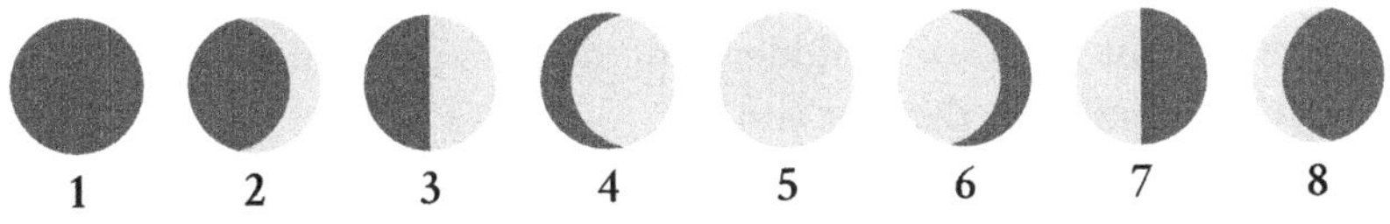

What are the phases of the moon?

- Phase 1 – new moon
- Phase 2 – waxing crescent moon
- Phase 3 – first quarter moon
- Phase 4 – waxing gibbous moon
- Phase 5 – full moon
- Phase 6 – waning gibbous moon
- Phase 7 – third quarter moon
- Phase 8 – waning crescent moon

To simplify things, we can divide the month into two phases:
Waxing crescent moon - before the full moon
Waning crescent moon - after the full moon

New Moon

We cannot see the new moon, as it is hidden. People might complain about feeling weak, mental imbalance, and fatigue. During this time, we want to avoid taking on too much or overdoing things. Generally, people are not very responsive and react poorly to requests, which is why it is best to look out for yourself, while not keeping your plate too full.

The new moon is a bad time for advertising – it will go unnoticed. It is not worth preparing any presentations, parties, or loud gatherings. People are feeling constrained, not very social, and sluggish.

This is also a less than ideal time for surgery, as your recovery will be slow, and the likelihood of medical error is high.

It is also difficult to get an accurate diagnosis during the new moon – diseases might seem to be hidden, and doctors might not see the real underlying cause of what ails you.

The new moon is also a bad time for dates, and sexual encounters may be dissatisfying and leave you feeling disappointed. Ancient astrologers did not advise planning a wedding night during the new moon.

Waxing Crescent Moon

It is easy to identify a waxing crescent moon. If you draw an imaginary line between the two "horns", you should see the letter P. The waxing moon is then divided into one and two quarters.

During the first quarter moon, we need to focus on planning – setting goals and thinking of how we will set about achieving them. However, it is still a good idea to hold back a bit and not overdo things. Energy levels are still low, though they are growing along with the moon. It is still a good idea to avoid any medical procedures during this time.

The second quarter is a time for bold, decisive action. Things will come easy, and there is a greater chance of a lucky break. This is a good time for weddings, especially if the moon will be in Libra, Cancer, or Taurus. Nevertheless, it is a good idea to put off any advertising activities and public speaking until closer to the full moon, if you can.

Full Moon

During the full moon, the Earth is located between the sun and the moon. During this time, the moon is round and fully illuminated. This takes place during days 14-16 of the lunar cycle.

During the full moon, many people feel more vigorous than usual. They are emotional, sociable, and actively seeking more contact, so this may be a good time for any celebrations.

However, be careful not to drink too much – you can relax to the point that you lose control, and the consequences of that can be very unpleasant. If you are able to stick to moderation, there is no better time for a party!

The full moon is also the best time for advertising, as not only will your campaign be widely seen, people will be apt to remember it.

The full moon is also a favorable time for dates, and during this time, people are at their most open, romantic, and willing to tell each other something important that might take their relationship to the next level of trust and understanding.

Moreover, during the full moon, people feel a surge of energy, which may lead to hyperactivity, restlessness, and insomnia.

It will be harder to keep your emotions in check. You might face conflicts with friends, disasters, and accidents. During the full moon, any surgeries are **not a good idea**, as the risk of complications and bleeding is on the rise. Plastic surgery is also a bad idea, as swelling and bruises might be much worse than in another lunar phase. At the same time, the full moon is a good time to get an accurate diagnosis.

During this time, try to limit your calories and liquid intake (especially if you deal with bloating and excess weight), as your body is absorbing both calories and liquids faster during the full moon, and it can be very difficult to get rid of the weight later on.

Waning Crescent Moon

The full moon is over, and a new phase is beginning – the waning moon. This is a quieter time, when all of the jobs you started earlier are being partly or entirely completed (it all depends on the speed and scale).

Surgery will turn out much better if it is performed during the waning moon. Your recovery will be faster, and the likelihood of complications is much lower. If you have any plans to lose weight, the waning moon is the best time to do that. This is also a good time for quitting bad habits, such as smoking or cursing.

The waning moon can also be divided into the third and fourth quarters.

Third quarter - this is a favorable period, and you are able to resolve a lot of problems without conflict. People are calming down and ready to listen and take in information, while still being active. However, this is not the best time to begin any major projects, especially if you are unsure if you will be able to complete them by the start of the new lunar month.

The third quarter is a good time to get married, especially if the moon is in Cancer, Taurus, or Libra.

Fourth quarter – This is the most passive period of the lunar cycle. You are not as strong as usual. Your energy is lagging. You will be tired until reaching a new beginning. The best thing you can do as the lunar cycle comes to an end is to get things in order, and avoid anything that might get in your way at work or in personal relationships. Examine your successes and failures.

Now, let's discuss the lunar days in greater detail. For centuries, people around the world have described the influence of lunar days, and modern astrologers only add to this work, as they compare old texts to modern life.

The 1st lunar day

The first lunar day is extremely important for the rest of the lunar month. This is a much-needed day to carefully plan your activities and lay the groundwork for the rest of the lunar month. Remember that the first lunar day is not a good day for major activities, but rather for sitting down and planning things.

Avoid conflicts on this day, unless you want them to overshadow the rest of the month. Try to see the positive side of things and imagine that the lunar month will bring you good things both at work and in love. The more vividly you can imagine this, the sooner your desires will come to fruition. Perhaps it would be a good idea to jot down plans that will bring you closer to achieving your dreams. This is the best time for both manifesting and making wishes!

This is also a favorable day when it comes to seeking a new job or starting an academic program.

It is fine to go out on a date on the first lunar day, but limit any sexual contact, as your energy levels are low, and you are likely to end up disappointed.

Getting married on the first lunar day is not recommended.

Avoid getting a haircut – there are many indications that cutting your hair on the first lunar day will have a negative effect on your health and life expectancy.

Under no circumstances should you undergo any major cosmetic procedures, including plastic surgery. Energy levels are low, your skin is dull and almost stagnant. The results will not live up to your expectations, and in the worst-case scenario, you will end up looking worse than before. It is common for cosmetic procedures performed on this day to be disappointing or even useless. Even the best surgeons are less capable.

Your good dreams on the first lunar day foretell happiness and joy. Bad ones usually do not come true.

The 2nd lunar day

This is considered a lucky day, and is symbolized by a cornucopia. It is not an exaggeration to say that the second lunar day is a favorable time for both work and love. It is a time for action, and a great period to work on yourself, look for a new job, start something new, or complete any financial transaction, whether a sale or purchase. This is also a great time for creative and scientific insights, and a good time for any meeting – whether political or romantic.

Any romantic dates or sexual encounters during the second lunar day are unlikely to disappoint. This is also a good day for weddings or taking a trip with someone special.

During the second lunar day, the moon is beginning its waxing phase, which is a good time for anything you might to do nourish and restore your skin. This is a great time for any cosmetic procedures aimed at preservation, though it is best to put off any plastic surgery until the waning moon. If that is not possible, then the second lunar day is acceptable, if not ideal, and you will not run into any complications.

Folklore tells us that this is not a good day for a haircut, as that may lead to arguments with a loved one.

This is the best time for exercise – your body is in good shape, and you are able to handle new exercise regimens. If the moon happens to be in Scorpio, though, be careful.

This is a good day for anything positive, but avoid any conflicts, discussions about the status of your relationship, or litigation.

Dreams of the second lunar day are usually not prophetic.

The 3rd lunar day

On this day, we are usually able to make out a thin sliver of the lunar crescent. It is a longstanding tradition to show money during the new month – it is believed that as the moon grows, so will your savings.

However, astrological systems around the world consider this an unlucky, unfavorable day. It is not a good idea to travel, begin any new business, or give into your bad mood.

You might run into many a lot of problems at work on this day, which will cause you a lot of anxiety. However, it is a good day to take a step back and identify and set about fixing any flaws and shortcomings. Remember that everything tends to look worse on this day than it actually is.

It is not the time to ask management for anything – you are likely to walk away disappointed, and end up unfairly reprimanded rather than receiving a promotion or raise. Instead, focus on areas of work that need to be smoothed over or studied further. It will be clear what problems you are facing, and you will easily be able to find a remedy.

Do not rush to criticize your loved ones – things may not be as they appear. "Measure twice and cut once" is your motto on this day.

This is not a good day to get married, as the couple is likely to have a turbulent, short-lived marriage.

You can schedule a cosmetic procedure for this day, but only if it is relatively minor. Plastic surgery should wait.

Do exercises as usual, without overdoing it or adding any new routines.

Dreams on this day do not mean anything.

The 4th lunar day

These are relatively neutral days, in that they are unlikely to bring anything bad, but they also will not bring you any windfalls. The fourth lunar day is symbolized by a tree of paradise, the tree of knowledge, and the choice between good and evil. Things ultimately depend on us and our final decisions.

This is a great day for anything money-related – signing contracts, agreements, or even taking on credit. There are also a lot of contradictions on this day – on one hand, we are likely to receive money, which is a good thing, but on the other, we will have to give some of it away, which is never particularly fun or pleasant. There is good reason to consider all of your opportunities and possibilities before acting.

It is not a good day to get married, as the wedding will not be as fun as you had hoped. However, the fourth lunar day is, in fact, a good day for sex and conceiving a healthy child.

Be careful on this day if you happen to engage in any physical exercise, as it is not a good idea to overeat or abuse alcohol. Take care of yourself.

Any illnesses which began on this day may be extremely dangerous, if they are not dealt with immediately.

Cosmetic procedures are not contraindicated, as long as they are to preserve your appearance. Plastic surgery can be performed if you truly feel it is necessary.

However, avoid getting a haircut, as it is unlikely to grow back healthily, and will become brittle and dull. However, if the moon is in Leo, you can disregard this advice.

Dreams may turn out to be real.

The 5th lunar day

Traditionally, the fifth lunar day is one of the worst of the lunar month. It is symbolized by a unicorn. Unicorns need to be tamed, but only a virgin is capable of doing so. Many people will feel drained on this day, or frustrated with themselves, those around them, and life in general.

Try to avoid arguments- any conflicts are likely to drag out for a long time, and then you may be overcome with guilt. This advice is relevant for both work and love.

Sexual encounters may be pleasant, but this is not a good day to plan a wedding, as it is likely to lead to a marriage full of unpleasant incidents.

Do not start any new businesses, or ask those around you for favors- you may be misunderstood and rejected.

It is fine to engage in physical exercise, but if you overdo it on this day, you may injure yourself.

Your energy levels are low. Cosmetic procedures may not be effective, and avoid any plastic surgeries.

It is good if you dream something connected with the road, trips or with movement in general. A bad dream might be a sign of a health problem which should be addressed.

The 6th lunar day

The symbol of the sixth lunar day is a cloud and a crane. This is a philosophical combination that suggests that it is not worth rushing things on these days. This is a very positive, lucky day for both work and love. Creative work will be especially successful, as will any attempts at opening a new business in your field.

The sixth lunar day is a good time for resolving any financial matters. There is one limitation, however – do not give anyone a loan, as they may not pay it back. But you can certainly sponsor and support those who are more vulnerable than you.

This day is a good time to go on a trip, whether close to home or far away.

This is also a good day for dates, weddings, and marriage proposals. Remember that energy is more romantic than sexual, so it is better to give the gift of roses and a bottle of champagne than hot, passionate sex.

It is a good idea to get some exercise, but do not overdo things, though you will probably not want to, either.

Cosmetic procedures will be successful, and you can even have plastic surgery performed, so long as the moon is not in Scorpio.

It is still a good idea to avoid getting your hair cut, as you might "cut off" something good in addition to your hair.

It is better to not discuss dreams as they are usually true. Your dreams of this day can remind you of something that needs to be completed as soon as possible.

The 7th lunar day

This is also a favorable lunar day, and it is symbolized by a fighting cock, which is an Avestan deity. Avoid any aggression on this day, and instead work on yourself, spend time at home or in nature. Avoid discussing the status of your relationship with anyone, arguing, or wishing bad things on anyone. Everything will come back to haunt you, remember, silence is golden.

Business negotiations and contracts will be successful. You can find support, sponsors, and people ready to help you in both words and deeds.

Lighten up with your colleagues and subordinates. Pay attention not only to their shortcomings, but also to their skills. This is a good day for reconciliation and creating both political and romantic unions.

The seventh lunar day is good for traveling, no matter how near or far from home.

It is also a favorable time for love and marriage.

Exercise moderately, and any plastic surgeries will go very smoothly, as long as the moon is not in Scorpio.

Dreams of this day may become a reality.

The 8th lunar day

The symbol for this day is a Phoenix, which symbolizes eternal rebirth and renewal, because this day is a great time for changes in all areas of your life. Your energy is likely to be high, and you want to do something new and unusual. This is a good time to look for a new job or begin studying something. Any out-of-the-box thinking is welcome, along with shaking things up a bit in order to improve your life.

However, avoid any financial transactions, as you may incur losses.

Avoid aggression. You can share your opinion by presenting well-founded arguments and facts, instead.

The phoenix rises from the ashes, so this is a good time to be careful with electrical appliances and fire in general. The risk of housefires is high.

Avoid any major financial transactions on the eighth day, as you may end up facing a series of complications. You can pay people their salaries, as this is unlikely to be a large sum.

This is a good day for weddings, but only if you and your future spouse are restless, creative souls and hope to achieve personal development through your marriage.

Any cosmetic procedures and plastic surgeries will go well today, as they are related to rebirth and renewal. Surgeons may find that they are true artists on this day!

You can try to change your hairstyle and get a fashionable haircut on this day.

You can trust your dreams seen on this day.

The 9th lunar day

The ninth lunar day is not particularly auspicious, and is even referred to as "Satan's" day. You may be overcome with doubt, suspicions, even depression and conflicts.

Your self-esteem will suffer, so don't overdo things physically, and avoid overeating or abusing alcohol.

This is a negative day for any business deals, travel, or financial transactions.

This is a particularly bad day for any events, so keep your head down at work and avoid any new initiatives.

It is better to avoid getting married on "Satan's" day, as the marriage will not last very long. Avoid sex, as well, but you can take care of your partner, listen them, and support them however they need.

Any cosmetic procedures will not have a lasting effect, and avoid any plastic surgery. A haircut will not turn out as you hoped.

Dreams of this day are usually prophetic.

The 10th lunar day

This is one of the luckiest days of the lunar month. It is symbolized by a spring, mushroom, or phallus. This is a time for starting a new business, learning new things, and creating.

The 10th lunar day is particularly lucky for business. Networking and financial transactions will be a success and bring hope. This is an ideal time for changing jobs, shifting your business tactics, and other renewals.

This is a perfect time for people in creative fields and those working in science, who may come up with incredible ideas that will bring many successful returns.

This is a very successful day for building a family and proposing marriage. This is a good time for celebrations and communication, so plan parties, meet with friends, and plan a romantic date.

One of the symbols for this day is a phallus, so sexual encounters are likely to be particularly satisfying.

The 10th lunar day is the best time to begin repairs, buying furniture, and items for home improvement.

You can exercise vigorously, and cosmetic procedures and plastic surgery will be very effective.

Dreams of this day will not come true.

The 11th lunar day

This is one of the best lunar days, and seen as the pinnacle of the lunar cycle. People are likely to be energetic, enthusiastic, and ready to move forward toward their goals.

The 11th lunar day is very successful for any financial transactions or business deals and meetings.

You might actively make yourself known, approach management to discuss a promotion, or look for a new job. This is an auspicious time for advertising campaigns, performances, and holding meetings.

Any trips planned will be a great success, whether near or far from home.

Romantic relationships are improving, sex is harmonious, and very desired.

Weddings held on this day will be fun, and the marriage will be a source of joy and happiness.

Exercise is a great idea, and you might even beat your own personal record.

This is an ideal time for any cosmetic procedures, but any more serious plastic surgeries might lead to a lot of bruising and swelling.

A haircut will turn out as you had hoped, and you can experiment a bit with your appearance.

You can ignore dreams of this day – usually they do not mean anything.

The 12th lunar day

This day is symbolized by the Grail and a heart. As we move closer to the full moon, our emotions are at their most open. During this time, if you ask someone for something, your request will be heeded. This is a day of faith, goodness, and divine revelations.

For business and financial transactions, this is not the most promising day. However, if you help others on this day, your good deeds are sure to come back to you.

This is a day for reconciliation, so do not try to explain your relationships, as no one is at fault, and it is better to focus on yourself, anyway.

Avoid weddings and sex on this day, but if you want to do what your partner asks, there is no better time.

Many may feel less than confident and cheerful during this day, so take it easy when working out. Avoid overeating, stay hydrated, and avoid alcohol.

The 12th lunar day is not the best for getting married or having sex, but the stars would welcome affection and a kind word.

Avoid getting a haircut, or any plastic surgeries. This is a neutral day for minor cosmetic procedures.

Nearly all dreams will come true.

The 13th lunar day

This day is symbolized by Samsara, the wheel of fate, which is very erratic and capable of moving in any direction. This is why the 13th lunar day is full of contradictions. In Indian traditions, this day is compared to a snake eating its own tail. This is a day for paying off old debts and returning to unfinished business.

Avoid beginning any new business on this day. It is preferable to finish old tasks and proofread your work. Information you receive on this day may not be reliable and must be verified.

It is worth resolving financial problems very carefully, and avoid arguments and conflict.

Do not change jobs on this day or go to a new place for the first time. Do not sit at home alone, though, go see old friends, parents, or older family members.

Minor cosmetic procedures are welcome on this day, but avoid any plastic surgery, as you may experience major swelling and bruising. Avoid any haircuts, too.

As a rule, all dreams will come true.

The 14th lunar day

It's a full moon! The 14th lunar day is one of the happiest, and it is symbolized by the trumpet. Pay attention – you may run into new, much-needed information. Networking will be successful, and you can confidently sign agreements, meet with people, and attend fun gatherings or other leisure activities. This is one of the best days for advertising, performances, and concerts, and those working in creative professions should keep this in mind, as should those who work in politics. Do not sit in place on this day – you need to get out and see others, make new connections, and try to be visible.

This is one of the best days for communication with and making requests from management, as your initiatives will be noticed and welcome. You might talk about a promotion, raise, or something similarly related to professional growth.

Couples will see their relationship is moving along well on this day, and it is also a good day for getting married.

Any sex on this day will be vigorous and memorable for a long time. The full moon is the best time for conceiving a child.

Any cosmetic procedures will be effective, but avoid any major changes to your appearance, as there is a high likelihood of bleeding and bruising. A haircut will turn out well.

Your dreams of this day will be more or less doubtful.

The 15th lunar day

It's a full moon! This day is symbolized by a serpent of fire. This is the energy peak of the entire lunar cycle, and a lot will depend on where you are focusing your energy.

You might face a lot of temptations on this day, for example, you might tell someone else's secret or your own to others, and come to regret it for a long time. The stars suggest exercising restraint in both your words and actions, as the 15th day of the lunar cycle is a day of deception and weaknesses.

This is a very active time, and many people might take unnecessary risks. This is not the best day for signing any agreements or contracts. For any performances, concerts, or advertising, however, this is one of the best days of the month.

You can get married on the 15th day, but only if you know each other well and have carefully considered your partnership, without any hasty decisions. This is also a favorable day for a second marriage.

Your romantic relationship is looking wonderful – you are on cloud 9, writing poetry, and deeply convinced of how right your partner is for you – and they feel the same way. It is important that this does not suddenly lead to an abrupt disappointment.

Avoid getting any haircuts on the 15th day of the month, as you may end up with a headache.

Conservative cosmetic procedures and creams will be very effective, but avoid any injections or plastic surgery today. Bleeding, swelling, and bruising are all but guaranteed.

Dreams on the 15th day nearly always come true.

The 16th lunar day

This day is symbolized by a dove. The full moon is over, and the moon is now in its waning phase. Usually, after the turbulent days of the full moon, people feel a bit under the weather. They are not cheerful, and want to avoid excess worry and give themselves a chance to breathe.

Don't ignore your body's wishes, take it easy with physical activities, and take some time for yourself. You might spend time in nature, in the forest, or at a country home.

The 16th day of the lunar month is a time for moderation in all areas – your behavior, eating, and even in your clothes. If you overate during the full moon period, now is the time to diet a bit or at least avoid fatty foods and meat.

This is not a promising day for resolving any financial matters. Keep your documents in order and get ready for any future meetings, instead. If you help a loved one, your good deed will come back 100 times over.

Avoid getting married today, as well as sex.

Cosmetic procedures are likely to be a success, especially if they are related to cleansing your skin, but it is best to avoid any plastic surgery or injections. Your body is not ready to accept them. A haircut will turn out as you hoped.

Any dreams are likely to come true, but that also depends on a correct interpretation.

The 17th lunar day

This day is represented by a vine and bell. It is a happy day and both successful and fun-filled. It is also a good time for negotiations, concluding small business deals, shaking up staffing, and creativity. However, you should keep in mind that the 17th day is only favorable for minor business, and you should avoid starting any major events.

Avoid any major financial transactions on this day. Do not give anyone money as a loan or borrow anything yourself, either.

Any travel, whether for business or pleasure, is likely to be a success.

The 17th day is a great time to get married, and an ideal day for dates. Any sexual encounters will bring you happiness and joy.

Avoid getting your hair cut on this day, but cosmetic procedures and plastic surgery will be a success. Women will look better than usual.

Your dreams are likely to come true in three days.

The 18th lunar day

This day is represented by a mirror. It is a difficult, and generally unpromising day, too. Just as the mirror reflects our imperfections back to us, we need to remember that moderation and modesty are key.

The 18th day is not a favorable time for any business meetings or financial transactions. You can, however work on jobs you already began. It is, however, a positive day for those who work in research or the creative fields.

Your motto of the day is to keep a cool head when it comes to your opportunities and the opportunities of those around you. This is relevant for both work and romantic relationships. It is not a good time to criticize others – any conflicts or arguments may lead to lasting consequences, which you do not need.

Avoid getting married on this day, as well as sexual encounters, which are likely to be disappointing. It is a good time to take a trip together, which will only be good for your relationship.

Avoid getting your hair cut, though this is a relatively neutral day for a haircut, which might turn out well, and though it will not exceed your expectations, it will also not leave you upset. Avoid any plastic surgeries.

Dreams on this day will come true.

The 19th lunar day

This is a very difficult day and it is represented by a spider. The energy is complicated, if not outright dangerous. Don't panic or get depressed, though – this is a test of your strength, and if you are able to hold onto all you have achieved. This is relevant for both work and love. On the 19th day, you should avoid taking any trips.

The energy of the 19th lunar day is very unfavorable for beginning any major projects, and business in general. Work on what you started earlier, get your affairs in order, think over your ideas and emotions, and check to make sure that everything you have done hitherto is living up to your expectations. Do not carry out any financial transactions or take out any loans – do not loan anyone else money, either. Do not ask your managers for anything as they are unlikely to listen to what you have to say, and make judgments instead.

This is a day when you might face outright deception, so do not take any risks and ignore rumors. Do not work on anything related to real estate or legal matters.

This is a very hard time for people with an unbalanced psyche, as they may experience sudden exacerbations or even suicidal ideations.

This is a very unlucky day to get married. Sexual encounters might be disappointing and significantly worsen your relationship.

Avoid any haircuts or cosmetic procedures or surgeries.

Your dreams of this day will come true.

The 20th lunar day

This is also a difficult day, though less so than the 19th. It is represented by an eagle. This is a good time to work on your own development and spiritual growth, by speaking to a psychologist or astrologer.

Avoid pride, anger, arrogance, and envy.

The 20th lunar day is a good time for people who are active and decisive. They will be able to easily overcome any obstacles, flying over them just like an eagle. If you have to overcome your own fears, you will be able to do so – don't limit yourself, and you will see that there is nothing to be afraid of. It is a good day for any financial transactions, signing contracts, and reaching agreements, as well as networking.

The 20th lunar day is a favorable time for those who work in the creative fields, as they will be able to dream up the idea that will open up a whole host of new possibilities. Avoid conflicts – they may ruin your relationship with a lot of people, and it will not be easy to come back from that.

This is a lucky day for getting married, but only if you have been with your partner for several years, now. Sexual encounters will not be particularly joyful, but they also will not cause you any problems.

Avoid getting your hair cut, but you can certainly get it styled. The 20th lunar day is a good day for those who are looking to lose weight. You will be able to do so quickly, and it will be easy for you to follow a diet.

Cosmetic procedures will be a success, as will any plastic surgeries.

Pay attention to dreams of this day as they are likely to come true.

The 21st lunar day

This is one of the most successful days of the lunar month, and it is symbolized by a herd of horses – imagine energy, strength, speed, and bravery. Everything you think up will happen quickly, and you will be able to easily overcome obstacles. A mare is not only brave but also an honest animal, so you will only experience this luck if you remember that honesty is always the best policy.

This is also a favorable day for business. Reaching new agreements and signing contracts, or dealing with foreign partners – it is all likely to be a success. Any financial issues will be resolved successfully.

Those in the creative world will be able to show off their talent and be recognized for their work. Anyone involved in the performing arts can expect success, luck, and recognition. A galloping herd of horses moves quickly, so you might transition to a new job, move to a new apartment, or go on a business trip or travel with your better half.

The 21st lunar day is one of the best to get married or have a sexual encounter.

This is a great time for athletes, hunters, and anyone who likes adventurous activities.

But for criminals and thieves, this is not a lucky or happy day – they will quickly be brought to justice.

Any haircuts or cosmetic procedures are likely to be a huge success and bring both beauty and happiness. You will recover quickly after any surgeries, perhaps without any swelling or bruising at all.

Dreams tend to not be reliable.

The 22nd lunar day

This day will be strange and contradictory. It is symbolized by the elephant Ganesha. According to Indian mythology, Ganesha is the patron saint of hidden knowledge. so this is a favorable day for anyone who is trying to learn more about the world and ready to find the truth, though this is often seen as a hopeless endeavor. This is a day for philosophers and wisemen and women. However, it is an inauspicious day for business, and unlikely to lead to resolving financial issues, signing contracts, agreements, or beginning new projects. You can expect trouble at work.

For creative people, and new employees, this is a successful day.

This is a good day for apologies and reconciliation.

Avoid getting married, though you can feel free to engage in sexual encounters.

For haircuts and cosmetic procedures, this is a fantastic day. Surgeries will also turn out, as long as the moon is not in Scorpio.

Dreams will come true.

The 23rd lunar day

This is a challenging day represented by a crocodile, which is a very aggressive animal. This is a day of strong energy, but it is also adventurous and tough. Your main task is to focus your energy in the right direction. There may be accidents, arguments, conflicts, fights, and violence, which is why it is important to strive for balance and calm.

Keep a close eye on your surroundings – there may be traitors or people who do not wish you well, so be careful.

However, this is still a favorable day for business – many problems will be resolved successfully. You are able to sign contracts and receive credit successfully, as long as you remain active and decisive in what you do.

This is not a day for changing jobs or working on real estate transactions or legal proceedings. This is not a favorable day for traveling, no matter how near or far you plan on going.

This is not a promising day to get married – things may end in conflict, if not an all-out brawl.

Sexual relations are not off the table, as long as the couple trusts one another.

Haircuts or cosmetic procedures will not turn out as you had hoped, so avoid them.

Dreams during this lunar day usually mean something opposite of what awaits you, so you can disregard them.

The 24th lunar day

This is a neutral, calm day that is symbolized by a bear. It is favorable for forgiveness and reconciliation.

This is also a good day for learning new things, reading, self-development, and taking time to relax in nature.

This is a great day for any type of financial activity, conferences, academic meetings, and faraway travel.

The 24th lunar day is a good time for love and getting married, as any marriage will be strong and lasting.

Cosmetic procedures and plastic surgery will be a success, and you can expect a speedy recovery.

Avoid getting a haircut on this day, however, as your hair will likely thin and grow back slowly.

Dreams of this lunar day are usually connected with your personal life.

The 25th lunar day

This is still another quiet day, symbolized by a turtle.

Just like a turtle, this is not a day to rush, and it is best to sit down and take stock of your life. This is a good time for resolving any personal problems, as the moon's energy makes it possible for you to calm down and find the right path.

This is also not a bad day for business. It is believed that any business you begin on this day is sure to be a success. This is especially the case for trade and any monetary activities.

The 25th lunar day is not a good day to get married, especially if the couple is very young.

This is a neutral day for sexual encounters, as the moon is waning, energy is low, so the decision is yours.

Avoid any cosmetic procedures, except those for cleansing your skin. This is not a favorable day for haircuts or plastic surgery – unless the moon is in Libra or Leo.

You can have a prophetic dream on this day.

The 26th lunar day

The 26th lunar day is full of contradictions and complicated. It is represented by a toad.

It is not time to start or take on something new, as nothing good will come of it. Avoid any major purchases, as you will later come to see that your money was wasted. The best thing you can do on this day is stay at home and watch a good movie or read a good book.

Avoid traveling on this day, as it may not turn out well.

The 26th lunar day is a negative day for any business negotiations and starting new businesses. Do not complete any business deals or financial transactions. Your colleagues may be arguing, and your managers may be dissatisfied. But if you have decided to leave your job, there is no better time to do so.

This is not a good day to get married, as both partners' expectations may fall flat, and they will soon be disappointed.

The waning moon carries a negative charge, so avoid any haircuts and surgeries, though you can get cosmetic procedures if they are relatively minor.

Your dreams will come true.

The 27th lunar day

The 27th lunar day is one of the best days of the month, and it is represented by a ship. You can boldly start any new business, which is sure to be promising. This is a great day for students, teachers, and learning new things. Any information that comes to you on this day may be extremely valuable and useful to you.

The 27th day is good for communication and travel, whether near or far from home, and no matter whether it is for work or pleasure.

This is also a good day for any professional activities or financial transactions. If there are people around you who need help, you must support them, as your good deeds will come back 100-fold.

Romantic dates will go well, though any weddings should be quiet and subdued. This is a particularly good day for older couples or second marriages.

The waning moon means that hair will grow back very slowly, but in general, you can expect a haircut to turn out well. This is a great day for plastic surgery or cosmetic procedures, as the results will be pleasing, and you will have a speedy recovery, without any bruising or swelling, most of the time.

However, beware if the moon is in Scorpio on this day – that is not a good omen for any plastic surgery.

Do not pay any attention to dreams on this day.

The 28th lunar day

This is another favorable day in the waning moon cycle, and it is represented by a lotus. This is a day of wisdom and spiritual awakening. If possible, spend part of the day in nature. It is important to take stock of the last month and decide what you need to do during its two remaining days.

This is a good time for any career development, changing jobs, conducting business, decision-making, and signing agreements, as well as going on a trip. You might conclude any business deal, hold negotiations, work with money and securities.

This is also a good day for any repairs or improvements around your home or apartment.

Anyweddingstodayshouldbesubduedandmodest,andrestrictedtofamily members only. A loud, raucous wedding might not turn out very well.

Your hair will grow slowly, but any haircuts will turn out very elegant and stylish. Cosmetic procedures and surgeries are not contraindicated. You will recover quickly with little bruising and swelling.

Do not take any dreams too seriously.

The 29th lunar day

This is one of the most difficult days of the lunar month, and it is considered a Satanic day, unlucky for everyone and everything. It is symbolized by an octopus.

This is a dark day, and many will feel melancholy, depression, and a desire to simply be left alone. This is a day full of conflict and injuries, so be careful everywhere and with everyone. If you can, avoid any travel, and be particularly careful when handling any sharp objects. Do not engage in any business negotiations, sign any contracts, or take part in any networking.

Astrologers believe that anything you start on this day will completely fall apart. For once and for all, get rid of things that are impeding you from living your life. This is a good time to avoid people who you do find unpleasant.

This is also a time for fasting and limitations for everyone. Do not hold any celebrations, weddings, or have sexual relations – these events may not turn out as you hoped, and instead bring you nothing but suffering and strife.

Avoid getting a haircut, as well, as it will not make you look more beautiful and your hair will come back lifeless and dull. Cosmetic procedures can go ahead, but avoid any surgeries.

Dreams are likely to be true.

The 30th lunar day

There is not always a 30th lunar day, as some lunar months have only 29 days. This day is represented by a swan. The 30th lunar day is usually very short, and sometimes, it lasts less than an hour. This is a time for forgiveness and calm.

You might take stock of the last month, while also avoiding anything you do not need around you. Pay back loans, make donations, reconcile with those who recently offended you, and stop speaking to people who cause you suffering.

This is a good time for tying up loose ends, and many astrologers believe that it is also a good day to start new business.

However, avoid celebrations or weddings on this day. Spouses will either not live long, or they will quickly grow apart.

Do not get a haircut on this day, though cosmetic procedures are possible, as long as you avoid any surgeries.

Dreams promise happiness and should come true.

A Guide to Zodiac Compatibility

Often, when we meet a person, we get a feeling that they are good and we take an instant liking to them. Another person, however, gives us immediate feelings of distrust, fear and hostility. Is there an astrological reason why people say that 'the first impression is the most accurate'? How can we detect those who will bring us nothing but trouble and unhappiness?

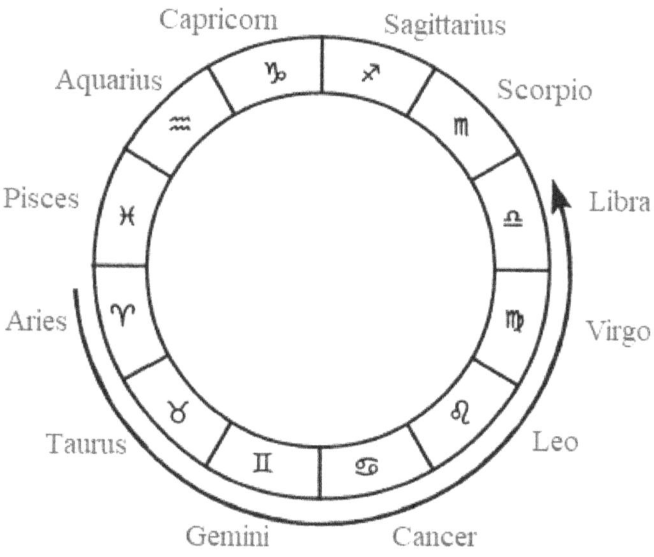

Without going too deeply into astrological subtleties unfamiliar to some readers, it is possible to determine the traits according to which friendship, love or business relationships will develop.

Let's begin with problematic relationships - our most difficult are with our **8th sign**. For example, for Aries the 8th sign is Scorpio, for Taurus it is Sagittarius and so on. Finding your 8th sign is easy; assume your own sign to be first (see above Figure) and then move eight signs counter clockwise around the Zodiac circle. This is also how the other signs (fourth, ninth and so on) that we mention are to be found.

Ancient astrologers variously referred to the 8th sign as the symbol of death, of destruction, of fated love or unfathomable attraction. In astrological terms, this pair is called 'master and slave' or 'boa constrictor and rabbit', with the role of 'master' or 'boa constrictor' being played by our 8th sign.

This relationship is especially difficult for politicians and business people.

We can take the example of a recent political confrontation in the USA. Hilary Clinton is a Scorpio while Donald Trump is a Gemini - her 8th sign. Even though many were certain that Clinton would be elected President, she lost.

To take another example, Hitler was a Taurus and his opponents – Stalin and Churchill - were both of his 8th sign, Sagittarius. The result of their confrontation is well known. Interestingly, the Russian Marshals who dealt crushing military blows to Hitler and so helped end the Third Reich - Konstantin Rokossovsky and Georgy Zhukov - were also Sagittarian, Hitler's 8th sign.

In another historical illustration, Lenin was also a Taurus. Stalin was of Lenin's 8th sign and was ultimately responsible for the downfall and possibly death of his one-time comrade-in-arms.

Business ties with those of our 8th sign are hazardous as they ultimately lead to stress and loss; both financial and moral. So, do not tangle with your 8th sign and never fight with it - your chances of winning are remote!

Such relationships are very interesting in terms of love and romance, however. We are magnetically attracted to our 8th sign and even though it may be very intense physically, it is very difficult for family life;

'Feeling bad when together, feeling worse when apart'.

As an example, let us take the famous lovers - George Sand who was Cancer and Alfred de Musset who was Sagittarius. Cancer is the 8th sign for Sagittarius, and the story of their crazy two-year love affair was the subject of much attention throughout France. Critics and writers were divided into 'Mussulist' and 'Sandist' camps; they debated fiercely about who was to blame for the sad ending to their love story - him or her. It's hard to imagine the energy needed to captivate the public for so long, but that energy was destructive for the couple. Passion raged in their hearts, but neither of them was able to comprehend their situation.

Georges Sand wrote to Musset, "*I •on't love you anymore, an• I will always a•ore you. I •on't want you anymore, an• I can't •o without you. It seems that nothing but a heavenly lightning strike can heal me by •estroying me. Goo•-bye! Stay or go, but •on't say that I am not suffering. This is the only thing that can make me suffer even more, my love, my life, my bloo•! Go away, but kill me, leaving.*" Musset replied only in brief, but its power surpassed Sand's tirade, "*When you embrace• me, I felt something that is still bothering me, making it impossible for me to approach another woman.*" These two people loved each other passionately and for two years lived together in a powder keg of passion, hatred and treachery.

When someone enters into a romantic liaison with their 8th sign, there will be no peace; indeed, these relationships are very attractive to those who enjoy the edgy, the borderline and, in the Dostoevsky style, the melodramatic. The first to lose interest in the relationship is, as a rule, the 8th sign.

If, by turn of fate, our child is born under our 8th sign, they will be very different from us and, in some ways, not live up to our expectations. It may be best to let them choose their own path.

In business and political relationships, the combination with our **12th sign** is also a complicated one.

We can take two political examples. Angela Merkel is a Cancer while Donald Trump is a Gemini - her 12th sign. This is why their relations are strained and complicated and we can even perhaps assume that the American president will achieve his political goals at her expense. Boris Yeltsin (Aquarius) was the 12th sign to Mikhail Gorbachev (Pisces) and it was Yeltsin who managed to dethrone the champion of Perestroika.

Even ancient astrologers noticed that our relationships with our 12th signs can never develop evenly; it is one of the most curious and problematic combinations. They are our hidden enemies and they seem to be digging a hole for us; they ingratiate themselves with us, discover our innermost secrets. As a result, we become bewildered and make mistakes when we deal with them. Among the Roman emperors murdered by members of their entourage, there was an interesting pattern - all the murderers were the 12th sign of the murdered.

We can also see this pernicious effect in Russian history: the German princess Alexandra (Gemini) married the last Russian Tsar Nicholas II (Taurus) - he was her 12th sign and brought her a tragic death. The wicked genius Grigory Rasputin (Cancer) made friends with Tsarina Alexandra, who was his 12th sign, and was murdered as a result of their odd friendship. The weakness of Nicholas II was exposed, and his authority reduced after the death of the economic and social reformer Pyotr Stolypin, who was his 12th sign. Thus, we see a chain of people whose downfall was brought about by their 12th sign.

So, it makes sense to be cautious of your 12th sign, especially if you have business ties. Usually, these people know much more about us than we want them to and they will often reveal our secrets for personal gain if it suits them. However, the outset of these relationships is, as a rule, quite normal - sometimes the two people will be friends, but sooner or later one will betray the other one or divulge a secret; inadvertently or not.

In terms of romantic relationships, our 12th sign is gentle, they take care of us and are tender towards us. They know our weaknesses well but accept them with understanding. It is they who guide us, although sometimes almost imperceptibly. Sexual attraction is usually strong.

For example, Meghan Markle is a Leo, the 12th sign for Prince Harry, who is a Virgo. Despite Queen Elizabeth II being lukewarm about the match, Harry's love was so strong that they did marry.

If a child is our 12th sign, it later becomes clear that they know all our secrets, even those that they are not supposed to know. It is very difficult to control them as they do everything in their own way.

Relations with our **7th sign** are also interesting. They are like our opposite; they have something to learn from us while we, in turn, have something to learn from them. This combination, in business and personal relationships, can be very positive and stimulating provided that both partners are quite intelligent and have high moral standards but if not, constant misunderstandings and challenges follow. Marriage or co-operation with the 7th sign can only exist as the union of two fully-fledged individuals and in this case love, significant business achievements and social success are possible.

However, the combination can be not only interesting, but also quite complicated.

An example is Angelina Jolie, a Gemini, and Brad Pitt, a Sagittarius. This is a typical bond with a 7th sign - it's lively and interesting, but rather stressful. Although such a couple may quarrel and even part from time to time, never do they lose interest in each other.

This may be why this combination is more stable in middle-age when there is an understanding of the true nature of marriage and partnership. In global, political terms, this suggests a state of eternal tension - a cold war - for example between Yeltsin (Aquarius) and Bill Clinton (Leo).

Relations with our **9th sign** are very good; they are our teacher and advisor - one who reveals things we are unaware of and our relationships with them very often involve travel or re-location. The combination can lead to spiritual growth and can be beneficial in terms of business.

Although, for example, Trump and Putin are political opponents, they can come to an understanding and even feel a certain sympathy for each other because Putin is a Libra while Trump is a Gemini, his 9th sign.

This union is also quite harmonious for conjugal and romantic relationships.

We treat our **3rd sign** somewhat condescendingly. They are like our younger siblings; we teach them and expect them to listen attentively. Our younger brothers and sisters are more often than not born under this sign. In terms of personal and sexual relationships, the union is not very inspiring and can end quickly, although this is not always the case. In terms of business, it is fairly average as it often connects partners from different cities or countries.

We treat our **5th sign** as a child and we must take care of them accordingly. The combination is not very good for business, however, since our 5th sign triumphs over us in terms of connections and finances, and thereby gives us very little in return save for love or sympathy. However, they are very good for family and romantic relationships, especially if the 5th sign is female. If a child is born as a 5th sign to their parents, their relationship will be a mutually smooth, loving and understanding one that lasts a lifetime.

Our **10th sign** is a born leader. Depending on the spiritual level of those involved, both pleasant and tense relations are possible; the relationship is often mutually beneficial in the good times but mutually disruptive in the bad times. In family relations, our 10th sign always tries to lead and will do so according to their intelligence and upbringing.

Our **4th sign** protects our home and can act as a sponsor to strengthen our financial or moral positions. Their advice should be heeded in all cases as it can be very effective, albeit very unobtrusive. If a woman takes this role, the relationship can be long and romantic, since all the spouse's wishes are usually met one way or another. Sometimes, such couples achieve great social success; for instance, Hilary Clinton, a Scorpio is the 4th sign to Bill Clinton, a Leo. On the other hand, if the husband is the 4th sign for his wife, he tends to be henpecked. There is often a strong sexual attraction. Our 4th sign can improve our living conditions and care for us in a parental way. If a child is our 4th sign, they are close to us and support us affectionately.

Relations with our **11th sign** are often either friendly or patronizing; we treat them reverently, while they treat us with friendly condescension. Sometimes, these relationships develop in an 'older brother' or 'high-ranking friend' sense; indeed, older brothers and sisters are often our 11th sign. In terms of personal and sexual relationships, our 11th sign is always inclined to enslave us. This tendency is most clearly manifested in such alliances as Capricorn and Pisces or Leo and Libra. A child who is the 11th sign to their parents will achieve greater success than their parents, but this will only make the parents proud.

Our **2nd sign** should bring us financial or other benefits; we receive a lot from them in both our business and our family life. In married couples, the 2nd sign usually looks after the financial situation for the benefit of the family. Sexual attraction is strong.

Our **6th sign** is our 'slave'; we always benefit from working with them and it's very difficult for them to escape our influence. In the event of hostility, especially if they have provoked the conflict, they receive a powerful retaliatory strike. In personal relations, we can almost destroy them by making them dance to our tune. For example, if a husband doesn't allow his wife to work or there are other adverse family circumstances, she gradually becomes lost as an individual despite being surrounded by care. This is the best-case scenario; worse outcomes are possible. Our 6th sign has a strong sexual attraction to us because we are the fatal 8th sign for them; we cool down quickly, however, and often make all kinds of demands. If the relationship with our 6th sign is a long one, there is a danger that routine, boredom and stagnation will ultimately destroy the relationship. A child born under our 6th sign needs particularly careful handling as they can feel fear or embarrassment when communicating with us. Their health often needs increased attention and we should also remember that they are very different from us emotionally.

Finally, we turn to relations with **our own sign**. Scorpio with Scorpio and Cancer with Cancer get along well, but in most other cases, however, our own sign is of little interest to us as it has a similar energy. Sometimes, this relationship can develop as a rivalry, either in business or in love.

There is another interesting detail - we are often attracted to one particular sign. For example, a man's wife and mistress often have the same sign. If there is confrontation between the two, the stronger character displaces the weaker one. As an example, Prince Charles is a Scorpio, while both Princess Diana and Camilla Parker Bowles were born under the sign of Cancer. Camilla was the more assertive and became dominant.

Of course, in order to draw any definitive conclusions, we need an individually prepared horoscope, but the above always, one way or another, manifests itself.

Love Description of Zodiac Signs

We know that human sexual behavior has been studied at length. Entire libraries have been written about it, with the aim of helping us understand ourselves and our partners. But is that even possible? It may not be; no matter how smart we are, when it comes to love and sex, there is always an infinite amount to learn. But we have to strive for perfection, and astrology, with its millennia of research, twelve astrological types, and twelve zodiac signs, may hold the key. Below, you will find a brief and accurate description of each zodiac sign's characteristics in love, for both men and women.

Men

ARIES

Aries men are not particularly deep or wise, but they make up for it in sincerity and loyalty. They are active, even aggressive lovers, but a hopeless romantic may be lurking just below the surface. Aries are often monogamous and chivalrous men, for whom there is only one woman (of course, in her absence, they can sleep around with no remorse). If the object of your affection is an Aries, be sure to give him a lot of sex, and remember that for an Aries, when it comes to sex, anything goes. Aries cannot stand women who are negative or disheveled. They need someone energetic, lively, and to feel exciting feelings of romance.

The best partner for an Aries is Cancer, Sagittarius, or Leo. Aquarius can also be a good match, but the relationship will be rather friendly in nature. Partnering with a Scorpio or Taurus will be difficult, but they can be stimulating lovers for an Aries. Virgos are good business contacts, but a poor match as lovers or spouses.

TAURUS

A typical Taurean man is warm, friendly, gentle, and passionate, even if he doesn't always show it. He is utterly captivated by the beauty of the female body, and can find inspiration in any woman. A Taurus has such excess physical and sexual prowess, that to him, sex is a way to relax and calm down. He is the most passionate and emotional lover of the Zodiac, but he expects his partner to take the initiative, and if she doesn't, he will easily find someone else. Taureans rarely divorce, and are true to the end – if not sexually, at least spiritually. They are secretive, keep their cards close, and may have secret lovers. If a Taurus does not feel a deep emotional connection with someone, he won't be shy to ask her friends for their number. He prefers a voluptuous figure over an athletic or skinny woman.

The best partners for a Taurus are Cancer, Virgo, Pisces, or Scorpio. Sagittarius can show a Taurus real delights in both body and spirit, but they are unlikely to make it down the aisle. They can have an interesting relationship with an Aquarius – these signs are very different, but sometimes can spend their lives together. They might initially feel attracted to an Aries, before rejecting her.

GEMINI

The typical Gemini man is easygoing and polite. He is calm, collected, and analytical. For a Gemini, passion is closely linked to intellect, to the point that they will try to find an explanation for their actions before carrying them out. But passion cannot be explained, which scares a Gemini, and they begin jumping from one extreme to the other. This is why you will find more bigamists among Geminis than any other sign of the Zodiac. Sometimes, Gemini men even have two families, or divorce and marry several times throughout the course of their lives. This may be because they simply can't let new and interesting experiences pass them by. A Gemini's wife or lover needs to be smart, quick, and always looking ahead. If she isn't, he will find a new object for his affection.

Aquarians, Libras, and Aries make good partners for a Gemini. A Sagittarius can be fascinating for him, but they will not marry before he reaches middle age, as both partners will be fickle while they are younger. A Gemini and Scorpio are likely to be a difficult match, and the Gemini will try to wriggle out of the Scorpio's tight embrace. A Taurus will be an exciting sex partner, but their partnership won't be for long, and the Taurus is often at fault.

CANCER

Cancers tend to be deep, emotional individuals, who are both sensitive and highly sexual. Their charm is almost mystical, and they know how to use it. Cancers may be the most promiscuous sign of the Zodiac, and open to absolutely anything in bed. Younger Cancers look for women who are more mature, as they are skilled lovers. As they age, they look for someone young enough to be their own daughter, and delight in taking on the role of a teacher. Cancers are devoted to building a family and an inviting home, but once they achieve that goal, they are likely to have a wandering eye. They will not seek moral justification, as they sincerely believe it is simply something everyone does. Their charm works in such a way that women are deeply convinced they are the most important love in a Cancer's life, and that circumstances are the only thing preventing them from being together. Remember that a Cancer man is a master manipulator, and will not be yours unless he is sure you have throngs of admirers. He loves feminine curves, and is turned on by exquisite fragrances. Cancers don't end things with old lovers, and often go back for a visit after a breakup. Another type of Cancer is rarer – a faithful friend, and up for anything in order to provide for his wife and children. He is patriotic and a responsible worker.

Scorpios, Pisces, and other Cancers are a good match. A Taurus can make for a lasting relationship, as both signs place great value on family and are able to get along with one another. A Sagittarius will result in fights and blowouts from the very beginning, followed by conflicts and breakups. The Sagittarius will suffer the most. Marriage to an Aries isn't off the table, but it won't last very long.

LEO

A typical Leo is handsome, proud, and vain, with a need to be the center of attention at all times. They often pretend to be virtuous, until they are able to actually master it. They crave flattery, and prefer women who comply and cater to them. Leos demand unconditional obedience, and constant approval. When a Leo is in love, he is fairly sexual, and capable of being devoted and faithful. Cheap love affairs are not his thing, and Leos are highly aware of how expensive it is to divorce. They make excellent fathers. A Leo's partner needs to look polished and well-dressed, and he will not tolerate either frumpiness or nerds.

Aries, Sagittarius, and Gemini make for good matches. Leos are often very beguiling to Libras; this is the most infamous astrological "master-slave" pairing. Leos are also inexplicably drawn to Pisces – this is the only sign capable of taming them. A Leo and Virgo will face a host of problems sooner or later, and they might be material in nature. The Virgo will attempt to conquer him, and if she does, a breakup is inevitable.

VIRGO

Virgo is a highly intellectual sign, who likes to take a step back and spend his time studying the big picture. But love inherently does not lend itself to analysis, and this can leave Virgos feeling perplexed. While Virgo is taking his time, studying the object of his affection, someone else will swoop in and take her away, leaving him bitterly disappointed. Perhaps for that reason, Virgos tend to marry late, but once they are married, they remain true, and hardly ever initiate divorce. In bed, they are modest and reserved, as they see sex as some sort of quirk of nature, designed solely for procreation. Most Virgos have a gifted sense of taste, hearing, and smell. They cannot tolerate pungent odors and can be squeamish; they believe their partners should always take pains to be very clean. Virgos usually hate over-the-top expressions of love, and are immune to sex as a mean s of control. Many Virgos are stingy and more appropriate as husbands than lovers. Male Virgos tend to be monogamous, though if they are unhappy or disappointed with their partner, they may begin to look for comfort elsewhere and often give in to drunkenness.

Taurus, Capricorn, and Scorpio make the best partners for a Virgo. They may feel inexplicable attraction for Aquarians. They will form friendships with Aries, but rarely will this couple make it down the aisle. With Leos, be careful – this sign is best as a lover, not a spouse.

LIBRA

Libra is a very complex, wishy-washy sign. They are constantly seeking perfection, which often leaves them in discord with the reality around them. Libra men are elegant and refined, and expect no less from their partner. Many Libras treat their partners like a beautiful work of art, and have trouble holding onto the object of their affection. They view love itself as a very abstract concept, and can get tired of the physical aspect of their relationship. They are much more drawn to intrigue and the chase- dreams, candlelit evenings, and other symbols of romance. A high percentage of Libra men are gay, and they view sex with other men as the more elite option. Even when Libras are unhappy in their marriages, they never divorce willingly. Their wives might leave them, however, or they might be taken away by a more decisive partner.

Aquarius and Gemini make the best matches for Libras. Libra can also easily control an independent Sagittarius, and can easily fall under the influence of a powerful and determined Leo, before putting all his strength and effort into breaking free. Relationships with Scorpios are difficult; they may become lovers, but will rarely marry.

SCORPIO

Though it is common to perceive Scorpios as incredibly sexual, they are, in fact, very unassuming, and never brag about their exploits. They will, however, be faithful and devoted to the right woman. The Scorpio man is taciturn, and you can't expect any tender words from him, but he will defend those he loves to the very end. Despite his outward control, Scorpio is very emotional; he needs and craves love, and is willing to fight for it. Scorpios are incredible lovers, and rather than leaving them tired, sex leaves them feeling energized. They are always sexy, even if they aren't particularly handsome. They are unconcerned with the ceremony of wooing you, and more focused on the act of love itself.

Expressive Cancers and gentle, amenable Pisces make the best partners. A Scorpio might also fall under the spell of a Virgo, who is adept at taking the lead. Sparks might fly between two Scorpios, or with a Taurus, who is perfect for a Scorpio in bed. Relationships with Libras, Sagittarians, and Aries are difficult.

SAGITTARIUS

Sagittarian men are lucky, curious, and gregarious. Younger Sagittarians are romantic, passionate, and burning with desire to experience every type of love. Sagittarius is a very idealistic sign, and in that search for perfection, they tend to flit from one partner to another, eventually forgetting what they were even looking for in the first place. A negative Sagittarius might have two or three relationships going on at once, assigning each partner a different day of the week. On the other hand, a positive Sagittarius will channel his powerful sexual energy into creativity, and take his career to new heights. Generally speaking, after multiple relationships and divorces, the Sagittarian man will conclude that his ideal marriage is one where his partner is willing to look the other way.

Aries and Leo make the best matches for a Sagittarius. He might fall under the spell of a Cancer, but would not be happy being married to her. Gemini can be very intriguing, but will only make for a happy marriage after middle age, when both partners are older and wiser. Younger Sagittarians often marry Aquarian women, but things quickly fall apart. Scorpios can make for an interesting relationship, but if the Sagittarius fails to comply, divorce is inevitable.

CAPRICORN

Practical, reserved Capricorn is one of the least sexual signs of the Zodiac. He views sex as an idle way to pass the time, and something he can live without, until he wants to start a family. He tends to marry late, and almost never divorces. Young Capricorns are prone to suppressing their sexual desires, and only discover them later in life, when they have already achieved everything a real man needs – a career and money. We'll be frank – Capricorn is not the best lover, but he can compensate by being caring, attentive, and showering you with valuable gifts. Ever cautious, Capricorn loves to schedule his sexual relationships, and this is something partners will just have to accept. Women should understand that Capricorn needs some help relaxing – perhaps with alcohol. They prefer inconspicuous, unassuming women, and run away from a fashion plate.

The best partners for a Capricorn are Virgo, Taurus, or Scorpio. Cancers might catch his attention, and if they marry, it is likely to be for life. Capricorn is able to easily dominate Pisces, and Pisces-Capricorn is a well-known "slave and master" combination. Relationships with Leos tend to be erratic, and they are unlikely to wed. Aries might make for a cozy family at first, but things will cool off quickly, and often, the marriage only lasts as long as Capricorn is unwilling to make a change in his life.

AQUARIUS

Aquarian men are mercurial, and often come off as peculiar, unusual, or aloof, and detached. Aquarians are turned on by anything novel or strange, and they are constantly looking for new and interesting people. They are stimulated by having a variety of sexual partners, but they consider this to simply be normal life, rather than sexually immoral. Aquarians are unique – they are more abstract than realistic, and can be cold and incomprehensible, even in close relationships. Once an Aquarius gets married, he will try to remain within the realm of decency, but often fails. An Aquarian's partners need uncommon patience, as nothing they do can restrain him. Occasionally, one might encounter another kind of Aquarius – a responsible, hard worker, and exemplary family man.

The best matches for an Aquarius are female fellow Aquarians, Libras, and Sagittarians. When Aquarius seeks out yet another affair, he is not choosy, and will be happy with anyone.

PISCES

Pisces is the most eccentric sign of the Zodiac. This is reflected in his romantic tendencies and sex life. Pisces men become very dependent on those with whom they have a close relationship. Paradoxically, they are simultaneously crafty and childlike when it comes to playing games, and they are easily deceived. As a double bodied sign, Pisces rarely marry just once, as they are very sexual, easily fall in love, and are constantly seeking their ideal. Pisces are very warm people, who love to take care of others and are inclined toward "slave-master" relationships, in which they are the submissive partner. But after catering to so many lovers, Pisces will remain elusive. They are impossible to figure out ahead of time – today, they might be declaring their love for you, but tomorrow, they may disappear – possibly forever! To a Pisces, love is a fantasy, illusion, and dream, and they might spend their whole lives in pursuit of it. Pisces who are unhappy in love are vulnerable to alcoholism or drug addiction.

Cancer and Scorpio make the best partners for a Pisces. He is also easily dominated by Capricorn and Libra, but in turn will conquer even a queen-like Leo. Often, they are fascinated by Geminis – if they marry, it will last a long time, but likely not forever. Relationships with Aries and Sagittarians are erratic, though initially, things can seem almost perfect.

Women

ARIES

Aries women are leaders. They are decisive, bold, and very protective. An Aries can take initiative and is not afraid to make the first move. Her ideal man is strong, and someone she can admire. But remember, at the slightest whiff of weakness, she will knock him off his pedestal. She does not like dull, whiny men, and thinks that there is always a way out of any situation. If she loves someone, she will be faithful. Aries women are too honest to try leading a double life. They are possessive, jealous, and not only will they not forgive those who are unfaithful, their revenge may be brutal; they know no limits. If you can handle an Aries, don't try to put her in a cage; it is best to give her a long leash. Periodically give her some space – then she will seek you out herself. She is sexual, and believe that anything goes in bed.

Her best partners are a Sagittarius or Leo. A Libra can make a good match after middle age, once both partners have grown wiser and settled down a bit. Gemini and Aquarius are only good partners during the initial phase, when everything is still new, but soon enough, they will lose interest in each other. Scorpios are good matches in bed, but only suitable as lovers.

TAURUS

Taurean women possess qualities that men often dream about, but rarely find in the flesh – they are soft, charming, practical, and reliable – they are very caring and will support their partner in every way. A Taurus is highly sexual, affectionate, and can show a man how to take pleasure to new heights. She is also strong and intense. If she is in love, she will be faithful. But when love fades away, she might find someone else on the side, though she will still fight to save her marriage, particularly if her husband earns good money. A Taurus will not tolerate a man who is disheveled or disorganized, and anyone dating her needs to always be on his toes. She will expect gifts, and likes being taken to expensive restaurants, concerts, and other events. If you argue, try to make the first peace offering, because a Taurus finds it very hard to do so – she might withdraw and ruminate for a long time. Never air your dirty laundry; solve all your problems one-on-one.

Scorpio, Virgo, Capricorn, and Cancer make the best matches. A relationship with an Aries or Sagittarius would be difficult. There is little attraction between a Taurus and a Leo, and initially Libras can make for a good partner in bed, but things will quickly cool off and fall apart. A Taurus and Aquarius make an interesting match – despite the difference in signs, their relationships are often lasting, and almost lifelong.

GEMINI

Gemini women are social butterflies, outgoing, and they easily make friends, and then break off the friendship, if people do not hold their interest. A Gemini falls in love hard, is very creative, and often fantasizes about the object of her affection. She is uninterested in sex without any attachment, loves to flirt, and, for the most part, is not particularly affectionate. She dreams of a partner who is her friend, lover, and a romantic, all at once. A Gemini has no use for a man who brings nothing to the table intellectually. That is a tall order, so Geminis often divorce and marry several times. Others simply marry later in life. Once you have begun a life together, do not try to keep her inside – she needs to travel, explore, socialize, attend events and go to the theater. She cannot tolerate possessive men, so avoid giving her the third degree, and remember that despite her flirtatious and social nature, she is, in fact, faithful – as long as you keep her interested and she is in love. Astrologists believe that Geminis do not know what they need until age 29 or 30, so it is best to hold off on marriage until then.

Leo and Libra make the best matches. A relationship with a Cancer is likely, though complex, and depends solely on the Cancer's affection. A Gemini and Sagittarius can have an interesting, dynamic relationship, but these are two restless signs, which might only manage to get together after ages 40-45, once they have had enough thrills out of life and learned to be patient. Relationships with a Capricorn are very difficult, and almost never happen. The honeymoon stage can be wonderful with a Scorpio, but each partner will eventually go their own way, before ending things. A Gemini and Pisces union can also be very interesting – they are drawn to each other, and can have a wonderful relationship, but after a while, the cracks start to show and things will fall apart. An Aquarius is also not a bad match, but they will have little sexual chemistry.

CANCER

Cancers can be divided into two opposing groups. The first includes a sweet and gentle creature who is willing to dedicate her life to her husband and children. She is endlessly devoted to her husband, especially if he makes a decent living and remains faithful. She views all men as potential husbands, which means it is dangerous to strike up a relationship with her if your intentions are not serious; she can be anxious and clingy, sensitive and prone to crying. It is better to break things to her gently, rather than directly spitting out the cold, hard truth. She wants a man who can be a provider, though she often earns well herself. She puts money away for a rainy day, and knows how to be thrifty, for the sake of others around her, rather than only for herself. She is an excellent cook and capable of building an inviting home for her loved ones. She is enthusiastic in bed, a wonderful wife, and a caring mother.

The second type of Cancer is neurotic, and capable of creating a living hell for those around her. She believes that the world is her enemy, and manages to constantly find new intrigue and machinations.

Another Cancer, Virgo, Taurus, Scorpio, and Pisces make the best matches. A Cancer can often fall in love with a Gemini, but eventually, things will grow complicated, as she will be exhausted by a Gemini's constant mood swings and cheating. A Cancer and Sagittarius will initially have passionate sex, but things will quickly cool off. A relationship with a Capricorn is a real possibility, but only later in life, as while they are young, they are likely to fight and argue constantly. Cancer can also have a relationship with an Aries, but this will not be easy.

LEO

Leos are usually beautiful or charming, and outwardly sexual. And yet, appearances can be deceiving – they are not actually that interested in sex. Leo women want to be the center of attention and men running after them boosts their self-esteem, but they are more interested in their career, creating something new, and success than sex. They often have high-powered careers and are proud of their own achievements. Their partners need to be strong; if a Leo feels a man is weak, she can carry him herself for a while- before leaving him. It is difficult for her to find a partner for life, as chivalrous knights are a dying breed, and she is not willing to compromise. If you are interested in a Leo, take the initiative, admire her, and remember that even a queen is still a woman. Timid men or tightwads need not apply. Leos like to help others, but they don't need a walking disaster in their life. If they are married and in love, they are usually faithful, and petty gossip isn't their thing. Leo women make excellent mothers, and are ready to give their lives to their children. Their negative traits include vanity and a willingness to lie, in order to make themselves look better.

Sagittarius, Aries, and Libra make the best matches. Leos can also have an interesting relationship with a Virgo, though both partners will weaken each other. Life with a Taurus will lead to endless arguments – both signs are very stubborn, and unwilling to give in. Leos and Pisces are another difficult pair, as she will have to learn to be submissive if she wants to keep him around. A relationship with a Capricorn will work if there is a common denominator, but they will have little sexual chemistry. Life with a Scorpio will be turbulent to say the least, and they will usually break up later in life.

VIRGO

Virgo women are practical, clever, and often duplicitous. Marrying one isn't for everyone. She is a neat freak to the point of annoying those around her. She is also an excellent cook, and strives to ensure her children receive the very best by teaching them everything, and preparing them for a bright future. She is also thrifty – she won't throw money around, and, in fact, won't even give it to her husband. She has no time for rude, macho strongmen, and is suspicious of spendthrifts. She will not be offended if you take her to a cozy and modest café rather than an elegant restaurant. Virgos are masters of intrigue, and manage to outperform every other sign of the Zodiac in this regard. Virgos love to criticize everyone and everything; to listen to them, the entire world is simply a disaster and wrong, and only she is the exception to this rule. Virgos are not believed to be particularly sexual, but there are different variations when it comes to this. Rarely, one finds an open-minded Virgo willing to try anything, and who does it all on a grand scale – but she is rather the exception to this general rule.

The best matches for a Virgo are Cancer, Taurus, and Capricorn. She also can get along well with a Scorpio, but will find conflict with Sagittarius. A Pisces will strike her interest, but they will rarely make it down the aisle. She is often attracted to an Aquarius, but they would drive each other up the wall were they to actually marry. An Aries forces Virgo to see another side of life, but here, she will have to learn to conform and adapt.

LIBRA

Female Libras tend to be beautiful, glamorous, or very charming. They are practical, tactical, rational, though they are adept at hiding these qualities behind their romantic and elegant appearance. Libras are drawn to marriage, and are good at imagining the kind of partner they need. They seek out strong, well-off men and are often more interested in someone's social status and bank account than feelings. The object of their affection needs to be dashing, and have a good reputation in society. Libras love expensive things, jewelry, and finery. If they are feeling down, a beautiful gift will instantly cheer them up. They will not tolerate scandal or conflict, and will spend all their energy trying to keep the peace, or at least the appearance thereof. They do not like to air their dirty laundry, and will only divorce in extreme circumstances. They are always convinced they are right and react to any objections as though they have been insulted. Most Libras are not particularly sexual, except those with Venus or the Moon in Scorpio.

Leos, Geminis, and Aquarians make good matches. Libra women are highly attracted to Aries men - this is a real case of opposites attract. They can get along with a Sagittarius, though he will find that Libras are too proper and calm. Capricorn, Pisces, and Cancer are all difficult matches. Things will begin tumultuously with a Taurus, before each partner goes his or her own way.

SCORPIO

Scorpio women may appear outwardly restrained, but there is much more bubbling below the surface. They are ambitious with high self-esteem, but often wear a mask of unpretentiousness. They are the true power behind the scenes, the one who holds the family together, but never talk about it. Scorpios are strong-willed, resilient, and natural survivors. Often, Scorpios are brutally honest, and expect the same out of those around them. They do not like having to conform, and attempt to get others to adapt to them, as they honestly believe everyone will be better off that way. They are incredibly intuitive, and not easily deceived. They have an excellent memory, and can quickly figure out which of your buttons to push. They are passionate in bed, and their temperament will not diminish with age. When she is sexually frustrated, a Scorpio will throw all of her energy into her career or her loved ones. She is proud, categorical, and "if you don't do it right, don't do it at all" is her motto. Scorpio cannot be fooled, and she will not forgive any cheating. Will she cheat herself? Yes! But it will not break up her family, and she will attempt to keep it a secret. Scorpios are usually attractive to men, even if they are not particularly beautiful. They keep a low profile, though they always figure out their partner, and give them some invisible sign. There is also another, selfish type of Scorpio, who will use others for as long as they need them, before unceremoniously casting them aside.

Taurus is a good match; they will have excellent sexual chemistry and understand each other. Scorpio and Gemini are drawn to each other, but are unlikely to stay together long enough to actually get married. Cancer can be a good partner as well, but Cancers are possessive, while Scorpios do not like others meddling in their affairs, though they can later resolve their arguments in bed. Scorpio and Leo are often found together, but their relationship can also be very complicated. Leos are animated and chipper, while Scorpios, who are much deeper and more stubborn, see Leos as not particularly serious or reliable. One good example of this is Bill (a Leo) and Hillary (a Scorpio) Clinton. Virgo can also make a good partner, but when Scorpio seemingly lacks emotions, he will look for them elsewhere. Relationships with Lira are strange and very rare. Scorpio sees Libra as too insecure, and Libra does not appreciate Scorpio's rigidity. Two Scorpios together make an excellent marriage! Sagittarius and Scorpio are unlikely to get together, as she will think he is shallow and rude. If they do manage to get married, Scorpio's drive and persistence is the only thing that will make the marriage last. Capricorn is also not a bad match, and while Scorpio finds Aquarius attractive, they will rarely get married, as they are simply speaking different languages! Things are alright with a Pisces, as both signs are emotional, and Pisces can let Scorpio take the lead when necessary.

SAGITTARIUS

Sagittarius women are usually charming, bubbly, energetic, and have the gift of gab. They are kind, sincere, and love people. They are also straightforward, fair, and very ambitious, occasionally to the point of irritating those around them. But telling them something is easier than not telling them, and they often manage to win over their enemies. Sagittarius tends to have excellent intuition, and she loves to both learn and teach others. She is a natural leader, and loves taking charge at work and at home. Many Sagittarian women have itchy feet, and prefer all kinds of travel to sitting at home. They are not particularly good housewives – to be frank, cooking and cleaning is simply not for them. Their loved ones must learn to adapt to them, but Sagittarians themselves hate any pressure. They are not easy for men to handle, as Sagittarians want to be in charge. Sagittarius falls in love easily, is very sexual and temperamental, and may marry multiple times. Despite outward appearances, Sagittarius is a very lonely sign. Even after she is married with children, she may continue living as if she were alone; you might say she marches to the beat of her own drum. Younger

Sagittarians can be reckless, but as they mature, they can be drawn to religion, philosophy, and the occult.

Aries and Leo make the best matches, as Sagittarius is able to bend to Leo's ways, or at least pretend to. Sagittarians often end up with Aquarians, but their marriages do not tend to be for the long haul. They are attracted to Geminis, but are unlikely to marry one until middle age, when both signs have settled down. Sagittarius and Cancer have incredible sexual chemistry, but an actual relationship between them would be tumultuous and difficult. Capricorn can make a good partner- as long as they are able to respect each other's quirks. Sagittarius rarely ends up with a Virgo, and while she may often meet Pisces, things are unlikely to go very far.

CAPRICORN

Capricorn women are conscientious, reliable, organized, and hard-working. Many believe that life means nothing but work, and live accordingly. They are practical, and not particularly drawn to parties or loud groups of people. But if someone useful will be there, they are sure to make an appearance. Capricorn women are stingy, but not as much as their male counterparts. They are critical of others, but think highly of themselves. Generally, they take a difficult path in life, but thanks to their dedication, perseverance, and willingness to push their own limits, they are able to forge their own path, and by 45 or 50, they can provide themselves with anything they could want. Capricorn women have the peculiarity of looking older than their peers when they are young, and younger than everyone else once they have matured. They are not particularly sexual, and tend to be faithful partners. They rarely divorce, and even will fight until the end, even for a failed marriage. Many Capricorns have a pessimistic outlook of life, and have a tendency to be depressed. They are rarely at the center of any social circle, but are excellent organizers. They have a very rigid view of life and love, and are not interested in a fling, as marriage is the end goal. As a wife, Capricorn is simultaneously difficult and reliable. She is difficult because of her strict nature and difficulty adapting. But she will also take on all the household duties, and her husband can relax, knowing his children are in good hands.

Taurus, Pisces, and Scorpio make good matches. Aries is difficult, once things cool off after the initial honeymoon. When a Capricorn meets another Capricorn, they will be each other's first and last love. Sagittarius isn't a bad match, but they don't always pass the test of time. Aquarius and Capricorn are a difficult match, and rarely found together. Things are too dull with a Virgo, and while Leo can be exciting at first, things will fall apart when he begins showing off. Libra and Aquarius are both difficult partners for Capricorn, and she is rarely found with either of them.

AQUARIUS

A female Aquarius is very different from her male counterparts. She is calm and keeps a cool head, but she is also affectionate and open. She values loyalty above all else, and is unlikely to recover from any infidelity, though she will only divorce if this becomes a chronic trend, and she has truly been stabbed in the back. She is not interested in her partner's money, but rather, his professional success. She is unobtrusive and trusting, and will refrain from listening in on her partner's phone conversations or hacking into his email. With rare exceptions, Aquarian women make terrible housewives. But they are excellent partners in life – they are faithful, never boring, and will not reject a man, even in the most difficult circumstances. Most Aquarians are highly intuitive, and can easily tell the truth from a lie. They themselves only lie in extreme situations, which call for a "white lie" in order to avoid hurting someone's feelings.

Aquarius gets along well with Aries, Gemini, and Libra. She can also have a good relationship with a Sagittarius. Taurus often makes a successful match, though they are emotionally very different; the same goes for Virgo. Aquarius and Scorpio, Capricorn, or Cancer is a difficult match. Pisces can make a good partner as well, as both signs complement each other. Any relationship with a Leo will be tumultuous, but lasting, as Leo is selfish, and Aquarius will therefore have to be very forgiving.

PISCES

Pisces women are very adaptable, musically inclined, and erotic. They possess an innate earthly wisdom, and a good business sense. Pisces often reinvent themselves; they can be emotional, soft, and obstinate, as well as sentimental, at times. Their behavioral changes can be explained by frequent ups and downs. Pisces is charming, caring, and her outward malleability is very attractive to men. She is capable of loving selflessly, as long as the man has something to love. Even if he doesn't, she will try and take care of him until the very end. Pisces' greatest fear is poverty. They are intuitive, vulnerable, and always try to avoid conflict. They love to embellish the truth, and sometimes alcohol helps with this. Rarely, one finds extremely unbalanced, neurotic and dishonest Pisces, who are capable of turning their loved ones' lives into a living Hell!

Taurus, Capricorn, Cancer, and Scorpio make the best matches. She will be greatly attracted to a Virgo, but a lasting relationship is only likely if both partners are highly spiritual. Any union with a Libra is likely to be difficult and full of conflict. Pisces finds Gemini attractive, and they may have a very lively relationship – for a while. Occasionally, Pisces ends up with a Sagittarius, but she will have to fade into the background and entirely submit to him. If she ends up with an Aquarius, expect strong emotional outbursts, and a marriage that revolves around the need to raise their children.

Tatiana Borsch

Made in the USA
Middletown, DE
15 January 2022

58753880R00179